elephants are dainty birds

A language and literature experience

The elephant is a dainty bird:
It whistles like a cow;
It builds its nest in a rhubarb tree
And flits from bough to bough.

elephants are dainty birds

A language and literature experience

sadler / hayllar / powell

Stanley Thornes (Publishers) Ltd.

This edition © Stanley Thornes (Publishers) Ltd.,
EDUCA House, Liddington Estate, Leckhampton Road,
Cheltenham, GL53 0DN, England.

First published 1978 by
Jacaranda Wiley Ltd.
65 Park Road, Milton,
Queensland, Australia.
This edition not for sale in
Australia, New Zealand and the Pacific,
U.S.A., Canada and Philippines.

© Jacaranda Wiley Ltd. 1978

This edition first published 1980

ISBN 0 85950 454 9

Typesetting by Savage & Co. Pty. Ltd., Brisbane
Printed in Hong Kong

Contents

Preface

For many years, the little word "from" at the end of an extract has frustrated students and teachers alike by signalling,

> "No matter how deeply involved you've become in this story (or play) there's just no way you're going to be able to finish it short of visiting a library."

Now *Elephants Are Dainty Birds* will change all that. In this book we've brought together the most gripping stories, plays and poems we could find, and tested them in classrooms against the two criteria of obvious literary merit and entertainment. Then, rejecting any thought of hacking them about and destroying unity in a futile search for "suitable extracts", we've published them complete. Consequently, in *Elephants Are Dainty Birds* we've been able to present and develop such basic literary concepts as plot, characterisation and setting within the scope of *finished* pieces of literature.

Side by side with the stories, poems and plays, we've introduced students to the language and visual material of the mass media as used by the TV studio, the film producer, the book reviewer, ad people, the popular cartoonist and others.

The concepts and exercises of the language work that forms the other most important part of the book are involved with and illustrated from the literature and media content. This close association of the creative with the formal side of language has the aim of presenting English as a living, working proposition in the hands of speakers and writers of all kinds and in all kinds of situations.

The formal language concepts presented are accompanied by exercises that we have tried to make relevant to students' interests. Wherever a formal exercise can be made more interesting and entertaining (without interfering with its force) by using a games approach, we've done it. On the other hand, where pure formality obviously has more practical value, we haven't hesitated to go for this approach instead.

Finally, we've taken every opportunity to encourage students to use the ideas and techniques presented in creative writing exercises of their own.

R. Sadler, T. Hayllar and C. Powell
October 1978

Acknowledgments

The authors and publisher gratefully acknowledge the kind permission of the following copyright holders to reproduce the material in this book.

"Duel in the Dark" by Gilbert Wright, from *Argosy*, vol. 30, No. 6, June 1969, by permission of John Farquharson Ltd, London; "National Hero" by Len Fox, © Len Fox 1957, by permission of the author; "Mercedes Benz" by Janis Joplin, Michael McClure and Bobby Neuwirth, © 1970 Strong Arm Music (U.S.A.), all rights for Australia and New Zealand controlled by April Music Pty Ltd, Sydney; "The Harry Hastings Method" by Warner Law, originally appeared in *Playboy* magazine, copyright © 1971 by Warner Law, reprinted by permission of H. N. Swanson Inc., Los Angeles; "A Winter Scene" by Reed Whittemore, reprinted with permission of Macmillan Publishing Co. Inc., from *The Self-made Man and Other Poems* by Reed Whittemore, © Reed Whittemore 1958; "Unholy Marriage" by David Holbrook, from *Imaginings* by David Holbrook, Putnam 1961, by permission of the author; "My Father's Hands" by Calvin Worthington, from the *News Sunday Magazine*, 30 November 1975, copyright 1975 New York News Inc., reprinted by permission; "My Father" by Ted Hughes, reprinted by permission of Faber and Faber Ltd from *Meet My Folks* by Ted Hughes; "The Surgeon's Choice" by permission of Grace Gibson Radio Productions Pty Ltd; "Water Skier" by Thomas W. Shapcott, by permission of the author from *Time on Fire*, 1961; "The Mullet Run" by Robert Adamson, first published in *Cross the Border* by Robert Adamson, Prism Books, Sydney, 1977, by permission of the author; "The Crabs" by Richmond Lattimore, from *Sestina for a Far-off Summer* by Richmond Lattimore, by permission of the author; "My Love Is Like a Red, Red Rose" by Frank Muir from *The My Word! Stories* by Frank Muir and Denis Norden, by permission of Frank Muir and Eyre Methuen Ltd; "Gutter Press" by Paul Dehn from *Fern in the Rock* by Paul Dehn, copyright © 1965 by Paul Dehn, Hamish Hamilton Ltd, London; "The Possum" by Ray Mathew, reprinted from *South of the Equator* by permission of Angus and Robertson Publishers, copyright © Ray Mathew 1961; "Why Did They Knock Down the Trees, Daddy?" by Colin Thiele, by permission of Rigby Ltd; "The Man Who Sold Rope to the Gnoles" by Idris Seabright, copyright © 1951 by Mercury Press Inc., reprinted by permission of McIntosh and Otis Inc., New York; "Woman of the Future" by Cathy Warry, first published in the *Australian Women's Weekly*, 24 December 1975, by permission of the author; "Splendid Girls" by John Normanton, © London Magazine Editions, reprinted by permission; "First Frost" by Andrei Vosnesensky translated by Stanley Kunitz from *Antiworlds and the Fifth Ace* by Andrei Vosnesensky, 1968, by permission of the Oxford University Press; "The Tell-tale Heart" by permission of Grace Gibson Radio Productions Pty Ltd; "The Salmon Rule" by F. J. Teskey, reprinted from *Themes to Explore — the Urge to Mate* by F. J. Teskey and T. J. Parker by kind permission of Blackie and Son Ltd, Glasgow and London, and F. J. Tesky; "Foxes Among the Lambs" by Ernest G. Moll, reprinted from *Poems 1940–1955* by E. G. Moll, by permission of Angus and Robertson Publishers, copyright © 1957 by E. G. Moll; "Hawkins's Pigs" by Brian James, copyright © Brian James 1946, reprinted from *Cookabundy Bridge and Other Stories* by permission of Angus and Robertson Publishers; "In the New Landscape" by Bruce Dawe by permission of Longman Cheshire Pty Ltd and Bruce Dawe; "Small Town" by B. A. Breen from *Behind My Eyes* by B. A. Breen, reprinted by permission of Melbourne University Press and Mr B. A. Breen; "Testimonials" by Bruce Dawe by permission of Longman Cheshire Pty Ltd and Bruce Dawe; "Orbit" by Audrey Longbottom, first published in the *Sydney Morning Herald*, 1976, reproduced by permission of the author; "The Calamander Chest" by Joseph Payne Brennan, reprinted by permission of Arkham House Publishers Inc., Sauk City, Wisconsin, U.S.A.; "The Microscope" by Maxine Kumin, copyright © 1963 by the Atlantic Monthly Company, Boston, Mass., reprinted with permission; "Space Poem" by T. F. Kline, by permission of the *Bulletin*; "The Other Foot" by Ray Bradbury, dramatized by Martin Walsh, by permission of Harold Matson Company, Inc.; "The Hitch Hiker" by Hugo Williams from *Symptoms of Loss* by Hugo Williams, 1965, by permission of the Oxford University Press; "The Universal Soldier" by Buffy Sainte-Marie by permission of the copyright owners Southern Music Publishing Co. (A/Asia) Pty Ltd; "The Most Dangerous Game" by Richard Connell, copyright © 1924 by Richard Connell, copyright renewed © 1952 by Louis Fox Connell, reprinted by permission of Brandt and Brandt, New York; "The Curse of Kali" by permission of Grace Gibson Radio Productions Pty Ltd; "School in the Holidays" by Stanley Cook from *World of Challenge 3* edited by Marie Sweeney, University of London Press Ltd, 1972, reprinted by permission of Hodder and Stoughton; extracts from the *Sun* newspaper reproduced by permission of John Fairfax and Sons Pty Ltd, Sydney; letter on p. 157 reproduced by courtesy of Mrs Marie J. Munro, Beverly Hills.

We have been unable to locate the copyright owners of "My Country" by Oscar Krahnvohl, "Cats on the Roof" by Edward Harrington, "Hunt the Hunter" by Wallis Peel and "Barney" to obtain permission to reprint this material and would be grateful for any information which could assist us in contacting them.

DUEL
IN
THE
DARK

Gilbert Wright

In my country when two fellows become angry enough to kill the other because of a lady, or some matter, it is the custom to arrange a duel. From such a duel as we arrange, the trouble between these two fellows will be settled, believe me.

The committee for duels prepares a house of one room so that, on the closing of the door, the room is dark. Fine sand, without little stones, is spread over the floor to the depth of a span. The bare feet of a man make not the smallest sound walking on such a floor.

The two fellows are made naked. Each has his knife, nothing more. The committee puts one fellow in a corner of the room and across from him, in that corner, the other fellow. And in one of the other two corners the committee puts a live rattlesnake of good size. The committee retires, the door is shut quickly, the duel now begins.

Outside, the people wait for the half of one minute. If the winner has not come out by that time, the committee piles empty oil cans against the door completely over the top. The people now go about their affairs because it may be many hours, even two or three days, before the winner opens the door and makes the cans crash down. The crashing down of the cans will be heard, day or night, all over the village and the people may now go to see which fellow has come out.

If it should happen that the duel is over in the half of one minute it will be because one of the fellows rushed.

Most often the rush is not made and so the cans are piled up. The duel is now an affair of patience, great care and much thought. Each fellow seeks to find the other without making his own presence known. One smart fellow may think of a method to work a trick on the other, but if the trick is not completely successful it will be the smart fellow who remains behind in the Room of Dark.

Much will depend upon the control of the mind because, after some hours in complete dark, the mind can grow unreliable and a fellow may do something foolish and so inform his enemy of his position. Because of the thirst and the growing bad air, after three days one of the fellows is pretty sure to lose control. He may talk to himself, or even sing. And, should this happen, it will not be that fellow that crashes down the cans.

There are reasons for putting the rattlesnake into the Room of Dark. It is of great danger to both men equally, not caring whom it might bite. We also believe that the snake will make the fellow who is most afraid even more fearful, and many times, we believe, the snake will prevent a duel. Fellows quick to fight if the snake were not there may think of a way to settle their quarrel without the duel.

But if the anger of two fellows to kill the other is strong enough they will duel, even if more than one snake would be put into the room.

Such an anger was between Damundo and Pito. Both these fellows were my cousins because, in our village, if a fellow is not your brother he is certain to be your cousin.

Damundo is a cousin not liked by me and others. He is more than thirty, dark, strong and rough, much hair, and a moustache that he trims like a lady's little eyebrow. Damundo has the strong belief that he is a great victor over men and girls. In this, there is truth.

Five times in not two years he has duelled and each time it was he who crashed down the cans. Never did he receive even a small wound and the times of his winnings were never more than an hour, often less. A thing unheard of in history! He brags that only cowards take the time of two or three days. Ridiculous! Damundo gets hungry! Damundo misses his girl! Every year he goes working on a ship for two months, and on his return from foreign places he brings presents of bracelets, necklaces, shining chains to hang from the waist, ribbons, combs, sweets, lipsticks, perfumes and other delights.

Pito is a cousin much liked by me and others. He is slim and has a moustache of first growth which he does not yet trim or it would be gone. Pito is three years older than me and the feeling has come upon him that he is no longer a boy.

His voice has become deep, but is not yet dependable to remain so. Several girls of our village notice him, but when we all go out upon the beach at low tide to gather the harvest of the shore, Pito digs with Angia and their hands meet together under the sand.

Angia is a bit younger than Pito and has much charm. She smiles softly and does not scream and produce silly laughing like some girls.

This day Pito and Angia and I dug together. Damundo came, looking down at Angia. We did not show we knew that he was there, but dug, putting the small clams into our one basket.

Damundo dropped a little bottle of shining glass and gold into the sand before Angia's hands. She looked at it, but did not look up. She then dug to one side of the little bottle. We dug, putting the clams into our one basket.

Damundo squatted. He took up the bottle and twisted out the stopper. There was a strong, sweet smell; the smell of some foreign flower. Damundo held the little bottle close to Angia.

We stopped digging and sat back from our knees because something would now happen. Angia took the bottle and put back the stopper. Then she gave it to Pito.

Pito stood. Damundo stood. Pito offered him back the little bottle and Damundo struck it from his hand. He said, "I, Damundo, gave that foreign perfume to Angia for a present, little boy."

"I give the presents to Angia," said Pito. "I only." His voice began very deep, but went suddenly like a young boy's. Pito's face was red with shame, but he stood looking Damundo hard in the eyes. Damundo laughed and laughed at Pito. He laughed loud and others around us who were digging looked.

Damundo stopped laughing, his face now strong with anger. "So," he said, "so you think to give the presents to Angia. Only you! Listen, little boy, I will tell you something. Angia has come to the notice of a *man*!"

"I am that man," said Pito, and his voice remained deep.

Pito's mother came hurrying and scolding as if she did not know of the growing trouble. Pito should go to hunt the cow. She took his arm and pulled. "Make haste, my child."

Pito shook away her hand, looking straight at Damundo.

Damundo stepped close to Pito and placed his hand on Angia's shoulder. "So," he said to Pito, "so you are that man?"

Then, as was the custom, a friend of Damundo's led him one way and I, being Pito's friend, led him another way. Angia stood where we had dug, looking down at the little bottle shining in the sand. She put down her hand for it.

I and some of my family were at the house of Pito. I began to sharpen his knife, a thing at which I am good.

Not much was said and the duel, which would begin next day at noon, was not talked of. We had come to be with Pito and his people to show friendship.

Then came Pito's father with three old uncles. Each, long ago, had been winner in a duel and it was hoped that Pito might learn a little from them. You see, it is not right to ask a young man who has crashed down the cans how he did his winning. He may have to fight again and so does not want his method known. But with old men, they will not fight again.

"When the door is shut, Pito," said old Uncle Chaco, who is thin and trembles, "squat down quickly in your corner. Hold your knife point up, thus. If Damundo rushes, the image in his mind will see you standing. He will strike too high. Then you may rise into him."

Old Uncle Cantu, who is blind, said strongly, "No, Pito, you must leave an image of more deception. As the door closes, move the left foot. Damundo will think you are stepping out of your corner. He will rush to the left of it, but you will remain in your corner. You can get him when he arrives."

"Damundo will not rush," said old Uncle Juan, who speaks thick because the right side of his mouth does not move. "Damundo has never rushed."

"But he will do something very soon," said old Uncle Chaco. "He is known for the short times of his winnings. He will not lessen his reputation by delay. Not Damundo."

"Then, if he does not rush," said old Uncle Cantu, "he will come along the wall. He will count his steps by placing his heel and toe together. There are fifteen of such steps to each wall of the room. He will come quickly and without sound. When the count of his steps brings him to where he thinks you to be, Pito, he will strike."

"But because Pito moved his left foot," said old Uncle Chaco, "Damundo will expect him to be a little out of his corner to the left. He will strike at that count. You, Pito, will hear nothing but you may feel the little fan of air stirred up by his empty blow. Strike in the direction of the air. To the right of it, my boy."

"Do not forget the snake," said old Uncle Cantu. "Damundo will not come by way of the corner where the snake lies."

"Never delude yourself, Pito," said old Uncle Juan, "that you know *what* Damundo will do. It is good to leave an image of deception, but how can you know you have left it? The door might close so quickly that the movement of your foot will not be seen by Damundo. My advice to you is to stay close to the wall at all times. Then you will at least know where something is. That will be a comfort."

"What!" said old Uncle Chaco, trembling greatly. "Stay close to the wall? Oh, no! The snake will come along the wall. He will go all the way around the room keeping close to the wall. He seeks a hole through which he may escape. The snake will meet you if you stay close to the wall, Pito. Then he will rattle and Damundo will know your position."

"To see, any eye must have some light," said old Uncle Cantu. "The snake will rattle, not because he sees you, Pito; but because he feels the heat from your naked body. This frightens him and the trembling of his tail sends forth the rattle. At any time you hear the rattle you will know that either you or Damundo is close to the snake."

"This need not be so," said old Uncle Juan. "Lie down, Pito, your feet against the wall and your body into the room. You will know where you are, with your feet against the wall. Now cover your feet, legs, and all but the chest and arms with sand. When the snake comes along the wall he will crawl over you without rattling. The heat of your body will not come through the sand. And, should Damundo be close by the snake will rattle at him."

"More can be done with sand," said old Uncle Chaco. "Mound the sand about one ear. It will happen that if Damundo moves by stepping, crawling or in any manner, he will disturb the grains of sand under his weight. These grains will pass on the disturbance to other grains and they to still other grains so that the disturbance will come to the grains mounded over your ear. You will know that Damundo moves."

"But not *where* he moves," said old Uncle Cantu. "To discover Damundo's direction both ears must be mounded over with sand."

"With both ears in the sand," said old Uncle Juan, "you will not hear the rattle of the snake. His tail is in the air and does not disturb grains of sand. The rattle may bring you information of importance, Pito. Surely, do not cover both ears with sand."

"It is important, Pito," said old Uncle Chaco, "to keep account of the time. This may be done by the sound of the village, cows asking to be milked at sundown, dogs howling at moonrise, roosters calling at dawn. In this way, my winning was helped. After the second calling of the cows I thought it reasonable to try to deceive my enemy by sounds of sleep. I came back along the wall a little way from my corner and, facing the corner, cupped my hand around my mouth and against the wall, leaving a small opening to direct the sound. I made sounds of sleep, not too often, not too loud. The sounds echoed from the opposite wall of my corner. My enemy came to stab there, his knee brushed me. I had no confusion in placing my knife."

"On the second day," said old Uncle Juan, "my enemy began to talk to me in whispers. He said that we were fools. That the trouble between us was not of the importance to cost the life of either. He proposed that we go along the walls, find the door and crash down the cans together. I did not accept his proposal, neither did I altogether reject it. In this way we came to the door and I had my success. I have often wondered if he made his proposal with honest intent."

"Never believe," said old Uncle Cantu, "that the snake must rattle before he strikes. Always, if you move, keep the body low. More heat will go to the snake and he will rattle the sooner. If you move standing, the snake may feel the small, quick heat of your stepping foot and strike before he has time to grow fearful and rattle. I believe it was thus that I came to crash down the cans. Never did I hear the snake rattle, but at the first calling of the roosters I began to hear the dying of my enemy. After some hours these sounds ceased. I came out of the Room of Dark because I no longer had an enemy."

The old uncles thought for a time, thinking if more could be said. By now I had made Pito's knife very sharp with the stone and with the leather. I honed it upon my palm. I looked to see if Pito had received confidence from the wisdom of the uncles. I could not see that he had.

"The boy is young," said old Uncle Cantu. "He has not defiled his body by smoke and drink and the numberless dissipations of Damundo. Pito's senses are alert and clear. In this he has great advantage."

After a long thinking old Uncle Chaco said, "Five times has this Damundo won. Never with a wound. Never with more time than an hour."

After this, the old uncles said nothing, not thinking of more to say. Old Uncle Juan went to sleep a little.

Pito looked to me and we stood and walked away together. I gave him his knife and he whistled at its sharpness. Indeed, I can sharpen a knife. I had twice seen the knife of Damundo, an evil, foreign thing with a jewelled handle and a hooked blade. I told Pito I believed that Damundo would not strike with such a knife, but rip up with the hook. Also, to cheer Pito — and this was true — I said that his knife was longer than Damundo's. By a finger's breadth at least. I was certain of it.

Pito smiled a little. "Of one thing we may be sure, good friend of mine, you have made my knife sharper than any knife in the world."

We came to the tall tree by the village well. Many times I have climbed this tree with Pito. From the high branches one can see the tops of mountains that rise from the far edge of the sea.

"Pito," I said, "do you truly feel yourself to be a man?"

He was angry. "Did I not show it upon the beach?" On the last word his voice changed into the voice of a young boy. Ashamed, Pito ran off.

By noon the committee had prepared the room. The sun was bright and shone fully on the house and all who desired went in and closed the door to inspect if the room was truly dark. Two sparks of sun were seen in the roof and a boy was sent with soft mud to the top of the house.

All came out, saying that the room was now truly dark. A fellow had come with a rattlesnake of good size in a sack. A member of the committee shook the sack roughly. The snake rattled well.

Damundo stood with two friends at the north of the door. He was laughing and talking, so all could hear. He said that he would be glad to go into the Room of Dark. It was cool there, away from the sun. He would take a nap, because he had drunk much the night before. After awakening, he would take a moment for the business of the day, and then crash down the cans. Damundo had plans for the evening.

Pito and his friends stood to the south of the door as was the custom. None of us talked one word.

Angia came, beautiful in her best dress. Naturally, she had not been seen by anyone since Pito had insulted Damundo on the beach. She had remained in her house, as was the custom. But now, it was also the custom that she must come and look, long at Pito and then go and look long at Damundo also.

When she came to Pito she did not come very close. She stood looking at him. And it was as though she had put something in her face for him to understand. There was something there to see, if one knew. I did not. She did not smile. Then she went to Damundo.

Her back was towards us and her face could not be seen as she looked at him. Damundo suddenly smiled big and put both his hands on her shoulders. And she put both her hands on his head. Then she turned and went back to her house.

Damundo called, "Tonight, little one! Do not change your clothes; I like that dress."

We, with Pito, were most sick to the heart. We could not believe what we had seen. On Pito's face was a very strange look. A look of anger, of not believing, of thinking.

For with us, when the man puts his hands on the girl's shoulders and she smooths her hands on his head, it is a greeting of lovers. It means, "I am glad you are here." It can also mean farewell, as when lovers part for a time.

For her to make such a greeting with Pito was expected by all. It was because of his love for her that he was now to fight Damundo. But she had stood back from Pito, then gone to Damundo and made the greeting with him. What thing is a woman! It was bitter to believe what must be believed. Angia, like all of us, thought that Pito would be killed soon. So now, she chose Damundo because it would be he who would come out of the Room of Dark. But what cruelty to let Pito see! Now he must go in with no hope of her, no strength of love to fight with. Pito would be killed for nothing.

Damundo, waving and kissing his hand, went into the room with the committee. Then they came out and put his clothes to the north of the door.

Pito went in, with one smile for his mother and for us. The committee came out and put his clothes to the south of the door.

One man, the head of the committee, now went inside with the snake. Soon he came out and tossed the empty sack aside. He put his hand on the door and called in, "Farewell to one of you." He shut the door.

All waited for the half of one minute. Nothing happened. Then began the piling of the empty cans against the door. But before the cans were halfway, a scream came from the Room of Dark. It was the voice of Pito.

I went away and came to the tree Pito and I had climbed so many times. I looked into the high branches and I swore to the tree that I would kill Damundo. I could kill him when he slept. I could kill him when he lay drunk. I could kill him on a dark path at night. Yes, I would find a way to kill him.

After a time I went back. Damundo had not come out. No one had come out. There had been no more sounds. The cans were now piled fully over the top of the door.

People talked of Pito's scream. Some said that it was a scream of pain. Others were not sure of this. Another boy and I thought that Pito had given more of a yell. A cry of angry hate.

Many people besides Pito's family stayed all night before the door. Angia watched too, but apart from everyone, and no one spoke to her or took notice of her presence.

When morning came, I went with my mother to our house, she to get us something to eat, I to put our cow into the field.

Our house is a little distance from the village, but as I was fastening the wire of the gate I heard the crashing down of the cans.

I ran with all my power, but when I got to the Room of Dark, Pito was already dressed and the committee was examining the method of Damundo.

The handle of his knife was hollow and the jewelled plate at the butt unscrewed. It was in the handle that Damundo kept a light of electricity. The light was no bigger than a thumb, but, in the Room of Dark, strong and blinding. There is no trouble to kill a man if you are behind such a light.

The flashing on of the light had caused Pito to scream out in anger. Then he had reached down quickly and thrown a handful of sand at the light. The sand went into Damundo's eyes. He turned off the light because, being now blinded, the light was of danger to him. Also it was believed that he dropped the light. It was found in another part of the room from where Pito and Damundo at last met.

Of the meeting, Pito had not much to say. The snake had rattled for him, as he thought. He had not moved. The snake went away, not rattling hard. Then suddenly it had rattled loud again. The snake must now be rattling at Damundo. This was all that Pito would say.

"But you were close to the wall, Pito," said old Uncle Juan.

"Your senses were alert and clear," said old Uncle Cantu. "Damundo was close. He moved because of the snake. You heard him."

"It is plain that you were close together and that you knew his direction because of the snake," said old Uncle Chaco. "But how, Pito, could you know just *when* to strike? Just *where* to strike?"

"When I am old, my uncles," said Pito, "I may speak of how I came to crash down the cans if the occasion is of importance. But that will be many years."

He went to where Angia stood, beautiful with smiles, and only I heard what they said.

"It was long, Angia," said Pito, "before it came to my mind why you made the greeting with him." He brought her hands to his face, then smiled. "You have washed them well."

"Very well, man of this heart."

"Good," said Pito. "The perfume of that foreign flower I never want to smell again."

And they walked away towards the sea.

in the dark?

Try getting down to the nitty gritty of the story by answering the following questions on the setting, the characters and the plot.

Setting

1. Diagram A is a simple plan of the duelling room, just four walls and a door space. Diagram B illustrates the objects associated with the room.

  (a) Draw a larger version of the plan in your workbook. Then sketch in the objects so that they are positioned where they should be according to the story.

  (b) Write a sentence about each object, explaining its use in or near the duelling room.

2. What name is commonly used in the village for the place where the duel takes place?

3. Describe in detail the secret of Damundo's dagger.

4. "Pito and Angia and I dug together." What does this and what follows in the story tell us about the location of the village?

5. Pick out three phrases that show that this story has been translated from another language.

Characters

1. How is Damundo able to give exotic presents to his girlfriends?

2. List the presents that Damundo gives to his girlfriends. From the point of view of the story, which present proves to be the most important?

3. What is there about Angia's personality that makes her rather special?

4. What is it about Pito that makes us hope that he, and not Damundo, will win the duel?

5. The uncles try to give Pito the benefit of their experience in duelling. However, they do not get this across very well. Why not?
6. Who tells the story? If you were writing a story like this, would you use an "I" (first-person) point of view? What advantages and disadvantages are there in using a first-person point of view?

Plot

1. "We, with Pito, were most sick to the heart. We could not believe what we had seen." What have they just seen? Why was this important to the story's plot?
2. Angia causes Damundo to lose the duel. Explain how she manages to do this.
3. At what revealing instant in the story does Pito give "a cry of angry hate" and for what reason?
4. When do we discover exactly how Pito came to win the duel? Explain how this discovery clears up earlier doubts and disappointments about Angia.
5. Write a 100-word summary of the plot.

different forms of the same basic word

Look at the word "dark" in this sentence from the story: "The committee for duels prepares a house of one room so that, on the closing of the door, the room is dark." Notice that the word "dark" describes "room" and is therefore an adjective. However, in other contexts the word "dark", or forms of it such as "darkly", "darken" or "darkness", can be used quite differently. Here are the different forms of the word "dark" in table form.

Noun	Adjective	Verb	Adverb	Participle	
				Present	Past
darkness dark	dark	darken	darkly	darkening	darkened

exercise 1

Construct seven sentences using all the forms of "dark" given in the table.

exercise 2

Copy the following table into your workbook and fill in the blank spaces.

Noun	Adjective	Verb	Adverb	Participle	
				Present	Past
confidence		deceive			
	ridiculous				
					received
		trim			

on your mark!

Inverted commas (quotation marks) enclose direct speech (conversation or dialogue) in a piece of writing. There's plenty of direct speech in the story to illustrate the use of inverted commas, so let's look at a few examples.

Example 1

"Do not forget the snake," said old Uncle Cantu.

Note the position of the comma after the last word of direct speech ("snake") — it is inside the inverted commas. Also note that the word "said" does not require a capital letter because there is no full stop preceding it.

Example 2

"So," he said to Pito, "so you are that man?"

· Example 3

"Damundo will not rush," said old Uncle Juan, who speaks thick because the right side of his mouth does not move. "Damundo has never rushed."

Note that, in example 2, the direct speech carries right on after the information about Pito. Also, there's no need for "so" to begin with a capital as the direct speech has merely been interrupted by a piece of description about the speaker.

However, in example 3 there are two sentences involved, so a full stop is needed after "move" and a new sentence starts with "Damundo".

Get the idea? Now try punctuating the following passages from the story. Note that all punctuation marks, including capital letters, have been removed. However, the punctuation marks you need (although not how many of each one) are shown in the brackets at the side of each passage.

```
On your mark
!! ?? ! ? " " " "
      GO
```

1. pito i said do you truly feel yourself to be a man he was angry did i not show it on the beach

$$\begin{bmatrix} `` & " & , \\ ? & . & \end{bmatrix}$$

2. it is plain that you were close together and that you knew his direction because of the snake said old uncle chaco but how pito could you know just when to strike just where to strike

$$\begin{bmatrix} `` & " & , \\ ? & . & \end{bmatrix}$$

3. what said old uncle chaco trembling greatly stay close to the wall oh no the snake will come along the wall he will go all the way around the room keeping close to the wall he seeks a hole through which he may escape the snake will meet you if you stay close to the wall pito then he will rattle and damundo will know your position

$$\begin{bmatrix} `` & " & \\ . & ? & ! \end{bmatrix}$$

4. damundo called tonight little one do not change your clothes i like that dress

$$\begin{bmatrix} `` & " & ; \\ ! & . & \end{bmatrix}$$

5. it was long angia said pito before it came to my mind why you made the greeting with him he brought her hands to his face then smiled you have washed them well

$$\begin{bmatrix} `` & " & , \\ . & , & \end{bmatrix}$$

When you have finished, check your punctuation by looking up the passages in the story.

criss-cross-word — vocabulary

This criss-cross-word deals with words that you should know from the story.

Clues and first letters of the words are given. Simply draw up the criss-cross-word in your workbook and fill it in.

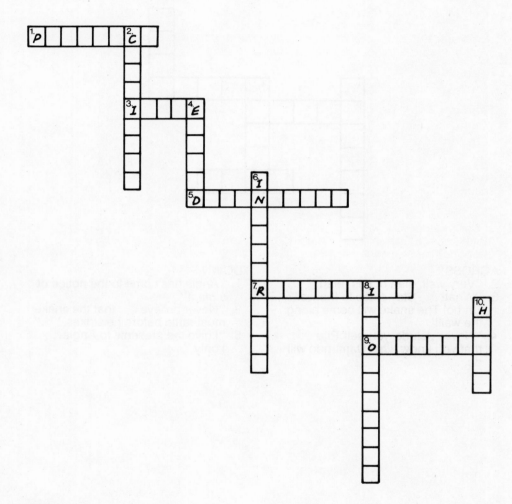

ACROSS
1. In the face of difficulties, you need a lot of ————————
3. Something pictured by the imagination
5. Reliable
7. The good name and character of a person
9. The time when something happens

DOWN
2. A group of people appointed to deal with some special matter
4. When sound is reflected back, it is ——————
6. Countless
8. Knowledge received or acquired
10. Sharpened on a smooth sharpening stone

criss-cross-word — characters

The clues are things said by each of the six characters. All you have to do is work out which character said what in the story, and then fill in the blanks. This time there are no first letters to help you.

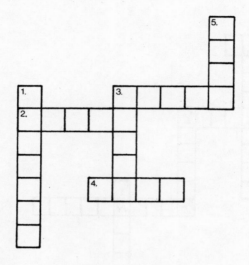

ACROSS
2. "Very well, man of this heart."
3. "What! . . . Stay close to the wall? Oh no! The snake will come along the wall!"
4. "Never delude yourself Pito . . . that you know *what* Damundo will do. . . ."

DOWN
1. "Angia has come to the notice of a *man*!"
3. "Never believe . . . that the snake must rattle before he strikes. . . ."
5. "I give the presents to Angia. . . . I only."

My Country

I love a sunburnt country,
A land of open drains
Mid-urban sprawl expanded
For cost-accounting gains;
Broad, busy bulldozed acres
Once wastes of fern and trees
Now rapidly enriching
Investors overseas.

A nature-loving country
Beneath whose golden wattles
The creek is fringed with newspapers
And lined with broken bottles.
Far in her distant outback
Still whose cities chafe
Find hidden pools where bathing
Is relatively safe.

A music-loving country
Where rings throughout the land
The jingle sweet enjoining
Devotion to the brand.
O, hark the glad transistors
Whence midnight, dawn and noon
Cry forth her U.S. idols
A trifle out of tune.

Brave military pylons
That march o'er scenic hills;
Fair neon lights, extolling
Paint, puppy food and pills!
I love her massive chimneys,
Production's, profits pride,
Interminably pouring
Pollution high and wide.

A democratic country
Where, safe from fear's attacks,
Earth's children all are equal
(Save yellows, browns and blacks).
Though Man in Space adventure,
Invade the planets nine,
What shall he find to equal
This sunburnt land of mine?

Oscar Krahnvohl

how well did you understand the poem?

One of the most popular poems taught in Australian high schools is a poem called *My Country* by Dorothea Mackellar. This is a poem full of praise for the natural beauty and harshness of the Australian landscape. Its most favoured lines are:

"I love a sunburnt country,
A land of sweeping plains,
Of ragged mountain ranges,
Of droughts and flooding rains."

Oscar Krahnvohl has written a new version of *My Country*, but what he depicts is a very different picture from the one given by Dorothea Mackellar.

1. What contrast does the poet give you between Australia today and the Australia of yesterday?
2. The poet suggests that the desire for profits has encouraged the developers. Write down the words that convey this impression.
3. Words not only have a dictionary meaning but can also have "feelings" associated with them. For instance "yellow" can suggest "cowardice", as well as the colour yellow. Write down the negative feelings that you get from these words: "drains", "broken bottles", "chimneys".
4. The word "newspaper" can have positive associations or feelings for us. Used in stanza two, it has negative associations. Explain why this is so.
5. What is the poet's message in the second stanza?
6. In the third stanza, the poet is describing the kind of music that he believes is being played throughout the land. What criticism is he making? Do you think he is exaggerating?
7. Look at the four lines quoted from Dorothea Mackellar's *My Country*. Krahnvohl has deliberately imitated her approach. What has he achieved by doing this?
8. In a democracy, all men should have equal rights. In Australia, the poet is suggesting that coloured races do not have the same rights as white men. Do you think this is a valid criticism? Why?
9. What do you think is the poet's main aim in writing this poem? Do you think he has been successful? Why?
10. Do you think that the mood of the poem is one of despair or anger? Why?
11. The poem is critical of many aspects of the Australian landscape and lifestyle. Draw up the following table in your workbook and, beside each of the headings, write down a phrase or two from the poem that shows this criticism.

My Country

land	
water	
air	
way of life	

National Hero

(An Asian girl, shown a postage stamp with the head of an Australian Aboriginal, asked: "Is he a national hero?")

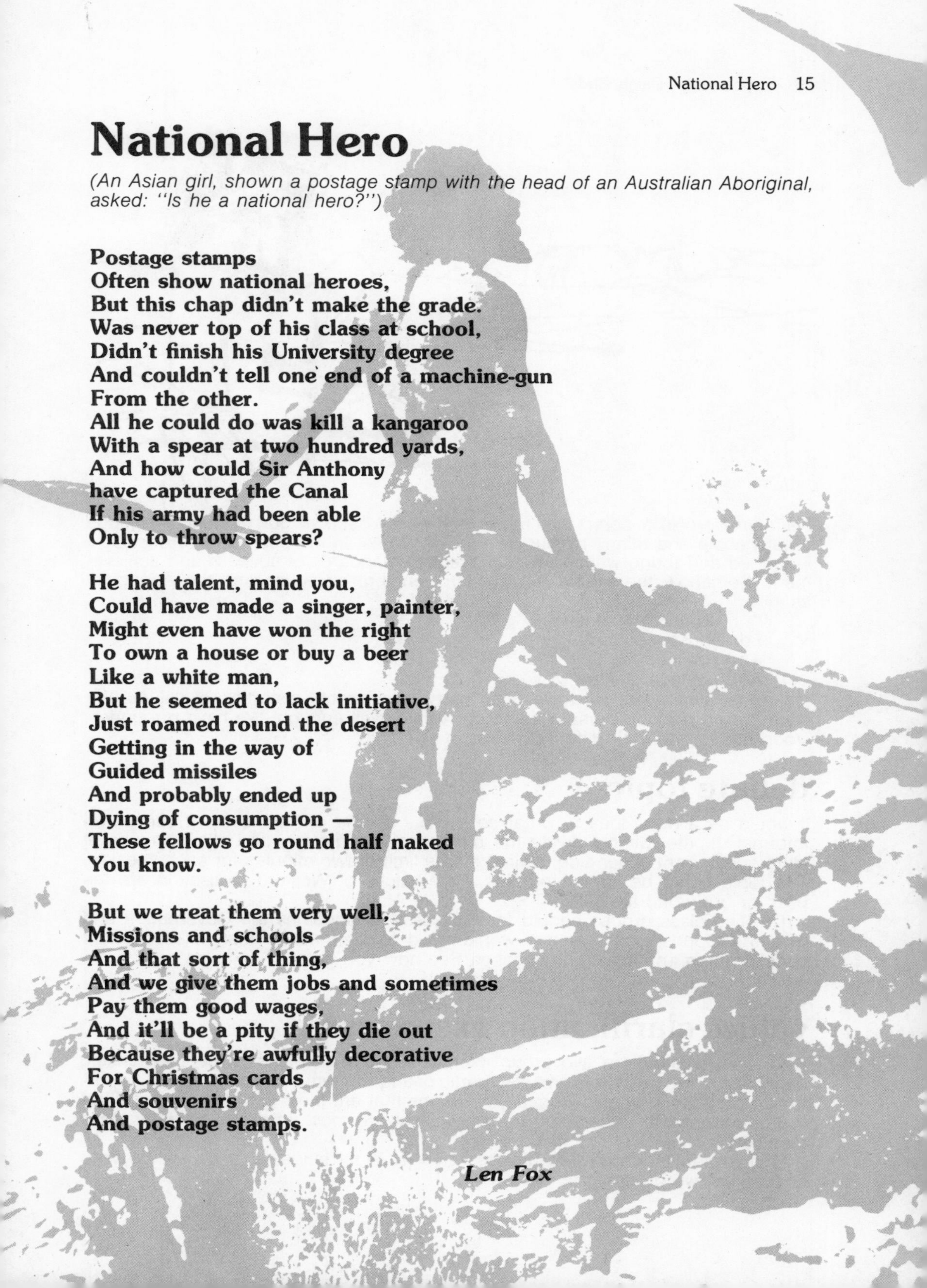

Postage stamps
Often show national heroes,
But this chap didn't make the grade.
Was never top of his class at school,
Didn't finish his University degree
And couldn't tell one end of a machine-gun
From the other.
All he could do was kill a kangaroo
With a spear at two hundred yards,
And how could Sir Anthony
have captured the Canal
If his army had been able
Only to throw spears?

He had talent, mind you,
Could have made a singer, painter,
Might even have won the right
To own a house or buy a beer
Like a white man,
But he seemed to lack initiative,
Just roamed round the desert
Getting in the way of
Guided missiles
And probably ended up
Dying of consumption —
These fellows go round half naked
You know.

But we treat them very well,
Missions and schools
And that sort of thing,
And we give them jobs and sometimes
Pay them good wages,
And it'll be a pity if they die out
Because they're awfully decorative
For Christmas cards
And souvenirs
And postage stamps.

Len Fox

National Hero is a poem that raises the whole issue of our tendency to judge other people and things by our own set of values. In the poem a race of people is judged and found wanting by our Western standards of success and achievement. Somehow the simple but powerful ending, which depicts the Aboriginal as

> ". . . awfully decorative
> For Christmas cards
> And souvenirs
> And postage stamps",

makes us aware that we have been party to a terrible distortion of values. We have not understood ourselves and our values well enough. We have not understood others and their differing values.

debate topic

It would be a good idea to organise a class debate on this issue. It can be an informal debate. Simply divide the class into two groups, and allow anyone at all to speak from either side, setting a time-limit of two minutes for each speaker. The topic could be something like: "The values of Western civilisation are the best for our world today."

The two class groups should toss to see who becomes the Government and who the Opposition. Speakers would need to alternate — first a Government speaker, then an Opposition speaker. See how you go!

values clarification exercises

Here are variations on two group exercises often used to start people thinking about their own value systems. By participating in them you will have the opportunity to clarify in your own mind the things that are most important to you, and the opportunity to understand the things that are most important to other class members.

First, divide the class into groups of six to eight students, and arrange your chairs into two groups.

1. house on fire

Imagine that you have just come round the corner and you are heading up the street towards your house one night, when you see that your house is on fire. The blaze is spreading rapidly. All the people and pets are safe outside. You have time to save just three things from inside the burning house. Take a few minutes silence in your group and think of the three things you would save. Write them down on a piece of paper, and then take it in turns to tell the rest of the group what three things you chose. Explain why you chose those particular things.

2. fall-out shelter*

Nuclear war has broken out and the whole world is involved. Your group is a high-ranking committee meeting in a city that will probably soon be destroyed. It is likely that this war will see the destruction of the whole world.

However, in a distant part of the country, a fall-out shelter exists that may be able to save a few lives. This particular shelter, because of its position, is the one most likely to survive the war, so that those who are saved in it may well be the only ones left to begin a new world. There are ten people in the shelter at the moment, but it is clear that it will only have enough food, water and air to support six people for the length of time necessary for their salvation. Not trusting themselves to make the decision, the ten have contacted your committee by telephone and have asked you to decide who should be the six survivors. They have agreed to abide by your decision.

Here are the ten people, together with all the information you have about each of them.
- a middle-aged book-keeper
- his wife who is six months pregnant
- a football player who is a current state representative
- a middle-aged female concert pianist
- a policeman with a gun (he is not prepared to part with it)
- a third-year medical student, male, Aboriginal
- a forty-year-old minister of religion
- a sixteen-year-old female high-school dropout of doubtful intelligence
- a male industrial chemist
- a fifty-year-old female history teacher

You have 15–20 minutes in which to come up with a group decision on the six people to be saved. At the end of that time each group can share its consensus with the other groups in the class.

*Based on a values-clarification exercise outlined by S. B. Simon, L. W. Howe and H. Kirschenbaum in *Values and Clarification* (New York: Hart Publishing Co. Inc., 1972).

COMPOSE YOURSELF

Look at this cartoon first.

Now, why not let your imagination go to your head? Run your eyes over the smorgasbord of ideas on the next three pages. Select one that appeals to you. Gaze fixedly at it, for, as everyone knows, this will feed it thoroughly into your mental conveyor belt. Press the mental button that starts your pen-toting fingers racing across the paper and — BZZOWNT! With a bit of luck you've tossed off a glowing piece of prose!

Ready? OK, press on!

The day a vending machine gave me exactly what I needed
My enemy the automat
The best thing ever invented was . . .
Don't do what I do — do what I tell you
Getting away from it all — how I managed it
The most surprising thing ever to come through that door was . . .
Too much ability, that's my trouble
Superstrength
Some people who'd never be missed
The place I'd rather be right now
An oldster about youngsters
A youngster about oldsters
My dreamboy
My dreamgirl
My favourite approach to the opposite sex
The ideal home (with plan attached)

Pop! Bridging the (generation) gap

The ideal classroom (with plan attached)

How I'd run a school

Teachers are a funny lot

The worst teacher I have ever known — and why

Teachers are not creatures

What's right with education

When I look around me I see . . . (Describe something or someone in minute
    detail but leave out the name. Give your neighbour your description to read
    and see if he or she can guess whom or what you've described.)

My big moment

How I thought up a completely new record and got myself into the *Guinness
    Book of Records*

My favourite fantasy

The ghost in my life

How to make a fortune honestly in one week

Conformity — good or bad?

Let me make your mouth water

The day Hell came to me!   Auntie Jack! Look out!

I have this secret problem
Hanging five — where and when I did it best
Surf, glorious surf
Horses — how I see them
Dogs — they never give up
The pet(s) in my life
Mmmm, I can tell you a story about that
Doing a little fortune telling — my own
My dream on wheels
Hero of sport (second class) — that's me!
My favourite nightmare
The dentist in my life
Freedom of thought — does it still mean anything?
Conservation — where I believe it's most needed
The problems of old age
Positive thinking about pollution
Of course I'm bitter, I'm an Aboriginal
My thoughts and experiences of poverty
Where would we be without unions?
Confessions of a probable dropout
One wonder of nature I'd like to repeat
What "overseas" means to me
I'm sick of being an Aussie
My job prospects as I see them
It was a bad moment when I came close to being just another statistic
I hope to be reincarnated as a mosquito
The funny side of my family

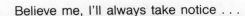

Believe me, I'll always take notice . . .

Mercedes Benz

Oh, Lord, won't you buy me a Mercedes Benz?
My friends all drive Porsches,
I must make amends,
Worked hard all my life-time,
No help from my friends,
So, Lord, won't you buy me a Mercedes Benz?

Oh, Lord, won't you buy me a colour TV?
Dialling for dollars is trying to find me,
I wait for delivery each day until three,
So, Lord, won't you buy me a colour TV?

Oh, Lord, won't you buy me a night on the town?
I'm counting on you, Lord,
Please don't let me down:
Prove that you love me,
And buy the next round,
Oh, Lord, won't you buy me a night on the town?

Oh, Lord, won't you buy me a Mercedes Benz?
My friends all drive Porsches,
I must make amends,
Worked hard all my life-time,
No help from my friends,
So, Lord, won't you buy me a Mercedes Benz?

Janis Joplin
Michael McClure
Bobby Neuwirth

how well did you understand the poem?

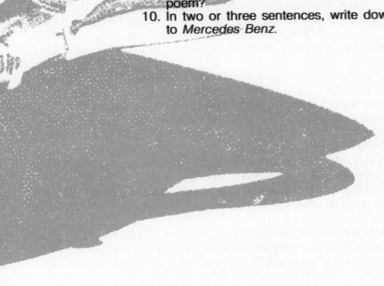

1. It is unusual to find "Mercedes Benz" as the title for a poem. What associations does it bring to your mind?
2. *Mercedes Benz* was a very popular song throughout the English-speaking countries of the world. Can you put forward some suggestions for its popularity?
3. In the poem, the poets ask God not just for an ordinary TV set but for a colour one. What feelings do you associate with colour TV?
4. The poem is written in the form of a prayer to God. Does this technique help or hinder the poets' achievement?
5. What is the poets' reason for asking for a Mercedes Benz? Do you think this kind of prayer is likely to be answered? Why?
6. The words "Mercedes Benz", "Porsche" and "colour TV" are associated with status and wealth. What other words can you think of that are part of the world around you and that have similar associations?
7. What does this poem suggest about modern society and its values?
8. Do you think the poets are being serious in *Mercedes Benz*? Why?
9. Often poets reveal something about themselves in their poetry. What did you learn about the authors of this poem?
10. In two or three sentences, write down your own reaction to *Mercedes Benz*.

The Harry Hastings Method

Warner Law

He didn't have the time to lie in wait for this wily intruder so devised a tricky plan to trap him

Susie Plimson says I should keep on practising my writing. She's been my teacher at Hollywood High Adult Education in the professional writing course and says I am still having trouble with my syntaxes and my tenses, and very kindly gave me private lessons at her place, and she is dark-haired and very pretty and about my age (which is twenty-five).

Susie says if I really want to be a professional writer, I should write about what I really know about — if it is interesting — and while I did do a hitch in the navy some time back, I was on a destroyer tender and never heard a shot fired except in practice, which I don't think is a highly interesting matter to describe.

But one thing I know a lot about is working the houses in the Hollywood hills. The people who live up there are not particularly stinking rich, but then, I've never been interested in valuable paintings or diamond necklaces, anyway, because what do you do with them?

But there are usually portable radios and TV sets and auto tape decks and now and then there is some cash lying around, or a fur, or a few pieces of fairly good jewellery, or maybe a new leather jacket — all things easy to dispose of.

This is an area of winding streets and a lot of trees and bushes, and the houses are mostly set back from the street and are some distance from their neighbours, and so it is an easy vicinity to work.

There's no bus service up there at all, so everybody needs a car or two, and if there is no auto in the carport, you can be pretty sure that no one is home.

There are rural-type mailboxes on the street, and people are always stuffing them with business cards and circulars, like ads for house cleaning and landscaping and such.

So I had a lot of cards printed for various things, like for a house-painting firm, and some for the "Bulldog Burglar Protection Agency", which say we will install all kinds of silent burglar alarms, and bells will ring in our office and we will have radio cars there in a few minutes.

I also have some Pest Control and House Repair cards. None of these firms exists, of course, but neither do the phone numbers on my cards.

But while I drive slowly around the hills in my little VW bus and put my cards in the boxes, I can get a pretty good idea of who is home and who isn't, and who is gone all day, and so forth.

By the way, my truck is lettered with: H. STRUSSMAN INC. GENERAL HOUSE REPAIRS on one side and FERGUSON PEST CONTROL, EVERYBODY LOVES US BUT YOUR PESTS! on the other side.

I make these up myself. My theory is that nobody can ever see both sides of my truck at the same time, which will really confuse witnesses, if there are any. Of course I change the truck signs every week, and every month I paint the truck a different colour.

When I decide that a certain house is ripe for hitting, I go up and ring the doorbell. If I am wrong and someone is home — this is seldom — I ask them if their house happens to be swarming with disease-infested rats. Since there are no rats at all in these hills, they always say no and I leave.

If nobody answers the doorbell, it is, of course, another matter. Most of these houses have locks that could be opened by blindfolded monkeys. Not one of them has any kind of burglar alarm.

There are watchdogs in some houses, but these I avoid, because you never know a friendly dog from a vicious one until you've been chewed up. And, of course, I would not hurt any dog if you paid me.

What I am getting to is about one particular house up there. It's a fairly new one-storey modern style, up a driveway, but you can see the carport from the street below. In casing the place for some time, I figured that a man probably lived there alone.

There was only one car, a great big new Mercedes, and this man drove off every weekday morning at nine. I saw him a few times and he was a nice-looking gentleman of about forty-five. He was always gone all day, so I guessed he had an office job.

So one day, I drove my truck up the driveway and got out and saw a sign: BEWARE OF THE DOG — and, at the same time, this little pooch comes out of a dog door and up to me, and he is a black bundle of hair and the wiggliest, happiest little puppy you ever saw.

I picked him up and let him lick my face and saw that he had a tag on his collar that read: CUDDLES, MY OWNER IS HARRY HASTINGS. There was also a phone number.

I rang the doorbell, but nobody came. The front-door lock was so stupid that I opened it with a plastic card.

Inside — well, you have never seen such a sloppy-kept house. Not dirty — just sloppy. There was five days' worth of dishes in the sink.

I found out later that this Harry Hastings has a maid who comes and cleans once a week, but meantime, this character just throws his dirty shirts and socks on the floor. What a slob.

I turned out to be right about his living alone. There was only one single bed in use — which, of course, was not made, and I doubt if he makes it from one year to the next. There was no sign of any female presence, which I don't wonder, the way this Hastings lives.

One of his rooms is an office, and this was *really* a mess. Papers all over the desk and also all over the floor. This room stank of old cigarette butts, of which smell I am very conscious since I gave up smoking.

From what I found on his desk, I learned that this Harry Hastings is a TV writer. He writes kind of spooky stuff, like this Rodney Serling. I took one of his scripts, to study.

From his income-tax returns, which were lying around for all the world to see, I saw he made nearly $23,000 gross the year before.

But most of the furniture in the house is pretty grubby, and the drapes need replacing, which made me wonder what this character spent all his money on, besides the Mercedes.

He had a new electric typewriter and a great big colour-TV set, which would take four men to move, and a hi-fi, but no art objects or decent silver or gold cufflinks or things like that.

It wasn't till I went through his clothes closet that I found out that most of his bread went into his wardrobe. There was about $5000 worth of new apparel in there, most of it hand-tailored and from places like where Sinatra and Dean Martin get their outfits. Very mod and up-to-date.

I tried on a couple of jackets, and it turns out that this Hastings and me are exactly the same size! I mean exactly. These clothes looked like they had been tailored for me alone, after six fittings. Only his shoes didn't fit me, sad to say.

I was very pleased, indeed, I can tell you, as I have always had trouble getting fitted off the rack. Also, I like to dress in the latest fashion when I take Susie to nice places.

So I took the entire wardrobe, including shirts and ties. I decided to take the typewriter, which I needed for my writing-class homework. The machine I had kept skipping.

But I wanted to try out the typewriter before I took it, and also, I thought I would leave a note for this Hastings, so he wouldn't think I was some kind of crude thug. So I typed:

> Dear Mr Hastings,
>   I am typing this to see if your typewriter works OK. I see that it does. I am not taking it to sell but I need it because I am trying to become a professional writer like you, which I know because I saw your scripts on your desk, and I am taking one to help me with my work, for studying.

I wish to make you a compliment anent your fine wardrobe of clothes. As it happened, they are like they have been made for me only. I am not taking them to sell them but because I need some good clothes to wear. Your shoes do not fit me, so I am leaving them.

I am also not taking your hi-fi, because there is a terrible screech in the treble. I like your dog, and I will give him a biskit.

A Friend

Well, some three months or so now passed, because there was no sense in hitting Hastings's house again until he had time to get a new bunch of clothes together.

But when I thought the time was ripe, I drove by there again and saw a little VW in the carport, and also, there was a big blonde woman shaking rugs.

I drove up and asked her if her house was swarming with disease-infested rats and she said she didn't think so but that she was only the once-a-week cleaning lady. She sounded Scandinavian. I took note that this was a Wednesday.

I went back the next Monday. No car in the carport. But on the way to the house, there was a new sign, hand-lettered on a board, and it read: BEWARE! VICIOUS WATCHDOG ON DUTY! THIS DOG HAS BEEN TRAINED TO ATTACK AND MEAN IT! YOU HAVE BEEN WARNED! PROCEED NO FARTHER!

Well, this gives me pause, as you can well imagine. But then I remember that this Hastings is a writer with an ingenious and inventive mind, and I do not believe this sign for one moment. Cuddles is my friend.

So I start for the house, and suddenly, this enormous alsatian jumps through the dog door and runs straight at me, growling and snarling, and then he leaps and knocks me down, and sure enough, starts chewing me to pieces.

But then out comes Cuddles, and I am sure there is a dog language, for he woofed at this monster dog as if in reproach, as if to say: "Knock it off. This is a friend. Leave him alone." So pretty soon, both dogs are licking me.

But when I get to the front door, I find that this Hastings has installed a new, burglar-proof lock. I walk around the house and find that there are new locks on both the kitchen door and the laundry-room door. They must have set Hastings back about seventy-five bucks.

There are also a lot of sliding-glass doors around the house, but I don't like to break plate glass, because I know how expensive it is to replace.

But I finally locate a little louvred window by the laundry-room door, and I find that by breaking only one louvre and cutting the screen, I can reach through and around and open the door.

Inside, I find that the house is just as messy as before. This guy will *die* a slob.

But when I get to his bedroom, here is this note, taped to his closet door. It is dusty and looks like it has been there for months. It says:

Dear Burglar,
    Just in *case* you are the same young man who was in here a few months ago, I think I must tell you that you have a long way to go before you will be a professional writer.
    "Anent" is archaic and should be avoided. A "wardrobe of clothes" is redundant. It is "biscuit", not "biskit". Use your dictionary!
    I know you are a young man, because both my cleaning woman and a nineteen-year-old neighbour have seen you and your truck. If you have gotten this far into my house, you cannot be stupid. Have you ever thought of devoting your talents to something a little higher than burgling people such as me?

                                Harry Hastings

Inside his closet are two fabulous new suits, plus a really great red-and-blue-plaid cashmere sports coat. I take these and am about to leave when I remember there is something I want to tell Hastings.

In his office, there is a new electric typewriter, on which I type:

> Dear Mr Hastings:
>
> Thank you for your help. In return, I want to tell you that I read the
> script of yours I took and I think it is pretty good, except that I don't
> believe that the man should go back to his wife. I mean, after she tried
> to poison him three times. This is just my opinion, of course.
> I do not have a dictionary, so I am taking yours. Thank you.
>
> A Friend

I, of course, do not take this new typewriter, partly because I already have one
and also because I figure he will need it to make money with so he can replace
his wardrobe again.

Four months go by before I figure it is time to hit the house again. By this time,
my clothes are getting kind of tired, and also the styles have changed some.

This time, when I drive up to the house one afternoon, there is a new hand-lettered
sign: THIS HOUSE IS PROTECTED BY THE BULLDOG BURGLAR PROTECTION
AGENCY! THERE ARE SILENT ALARMS EVERYWHERE! IF THEY ARE TRIPPED,
RADIO CARS WILL CONVERGE AT ONCE! PROCEED NO FARTHER! YOU HAVE
BEEN WARNED!

Come *on* now! I and I alone am the *nonexistent* Bulldog Burglar Protection Agency!
I'd put my card in his mailbox! This is really one cheap stinker, this Harry Hastings.

When I get near the house, the dogs come out, and I give them a little loving,
and then I see a note on the front door:

> Dear Jack,
>
> Welcome! Hope you had a nice trip. The key is hidden where it always
> has been. I didn't have to go to work today. I've run down the hill to
> get some scotch and some steaks. Be back in a few minutes. The gals
> are coming at six.
>
> Harry

Well, this gives me pause. I finally decide that this is not the right day to hit the
house. This could, of course, be another of Hastings's tricks, but I can't be sure.
So I leave.

But a few days later, I come back and this same note to Jack is still on the door,
only now it is all yellowed. You would think that this lame-brain would at least write
a new note every day, welcoming Bert or Sam or Harriet or Hazel or whoever.

The truth is that this Hastings is so damn smart, when you think about it, that
he is actually stupid.

The broken louvre and the screen have by now been replaced, but when I break
the glass and cut the screen and reach around to open the laundry door, I find
that he has installed chains and bolts on the inside.

Well, as any idiot knows, you can't bolt all your doors from the inside when you
go out, so one door has to be openable, and I figure it has to be the front door;
but the only way I can get in is to break a big frosted-plate-glass window to the
left of it and reach through and open the door.

As I said, I'm not happy to break plate glass, but this Hastings has left me no
choice, so I knock out a hole just big enough for me to reach through and open
the door and go in.

This time, there is *another* note on his closet door:

Dear Burglar,

Are you incapable of pity? By now, you must be the best-dressed burglar in Hollywood. But how many clothes can you *wear*? You might like to know that my burglary insurance has been cancelled. My new watchdog cost me one hundred dollars and I have spent a small fortune on new locks and bolts and chains.

Now I fear you are going to start smashing my plate-glass windows, which can cost as much as ninety dollars to replace. There is only one new suit in this closet. All my other clothes I keep now either in my car or at my office. Take the suit, if you must, but never return, or you will be sorry, indeed, if you do. I have a terrible revenge in mind.

Harry Hastings

P.S. You still have time to reform yourself.
P.P.S. I don't like his going back to his poisoning wife, either. But the network insisted on a "Happy Ending".

H.H.

Well, I am not about to fall for all this noise about pity. Any man who has a dog trained to go for me and who uses my own Bulldog Agency against me is not, in my mind, deserving of too much sympathy.

So I take the suit, which is a just beautiful Edwardian eight-button, in grey sharkskin.

Now, quite a few months pass and I begin to feel a little sorry for this character, and I decide to let him alone, forever.

But then, one day, when I am out working, some louse breaks into my own pad, which is three rooms over a private garage in Hollywood. He takes every stitch of clothing I own.

By this time, I am heavily dating Susie Plimson, and she likes good dressers. So, while I am not too happy about it, I decide I have to pay Hastings another visit.

No dogs come out this time when I walk to the front door. But on it is a typed note, which says:

HELGA! DO NOT OPEN THIS DOOR! Since you were here last week, I bought a PUMA for burglar protection. This is a huge cat, a cougar or a mountain lion, about four feet long, not including the tail. The man I bought it from told me it was fairly tame, but it is *NOT*!

It has tried to attack both dogs, who are OK and are locked in the guest room. I myself have just gone down to my doctor's to have stitches taken in my face and neck and arms. This ferocious puma is wandering loose inside the house.

The SPCA people are coming soon to capture it and take it away. I tried to call you and tell you not to come today, but you had already left. Whatever you do, if the SPCA has not come before you, DO NOT UNDER ANY CIRCUMSTANCES OPEN THIS DOOR!!

Well, naturally, this gave me considerable pause. Helga was obviously the blonde cleaning woman. But this was a Tuesday, and she came on Wednesdays. Or she used to. But she could have changed her days.

I stroll around the outside of the house. But all of the curtains and drapes are drawn, and I can't see in. As I pass the guest-room windows, the two dogs bark inside. So this much of the note on the door is true.

So I wander back to the front door, and I think and I ponder. Is there really a puma in there, or is this just another of Hastings's big fat dirty lies?

After all, it is one hell of a lot of trouble to buy and keep a puma just to protect a few clothes. And it is also expensive, and this Hastings I know by now is a cheapskate.

It costs him not one thin dime to put this stupid note to Helga on his front door and, God knows, it would terrify most anybody who wanted to walk in.

Susie told us in class that in every story, there is like a moment of decision. I figured this was mine.

After about five minutes of solid thought, I finally make my decision. There *is* no puma in there. It's just that Hastings wants me to think that there is a puma in there.

So I decide to enter the house, by breaking another hole in the now-replaced frosted-plate-glass window to the left of the front door. So I break out a small portion of this glass.

And I peer through this little hole I've made, and I see nothing. No puma. I listen. I don't hear any snarling cat or anything. No puma. Just the same, there *could* be a puma in there and it could be crouching silently just inside the door, waiting to pounce and bite my hand off when I put it in.

Very carefully, I put some fingers in and wiggle them. No puma. And so I put my arm in and reach and turn the doorknob from the inside and open the door a crack.

No snarl from a puma — whatever pumas snarl like. I open the door a little wider and I call, "Here, pussy-pussy! Here, puma-puma! *Nice* puma!" No response.

I creep in very cautiously, looking around, ready to jump back and out and slam the door on this beast, if necessary. But there is no puma.

And then I realise that my decision was, of course, right, and there is no lousy puma in this damn house. But still, I am sweating like a pig and breathing heavily, and I suddenly figure out what Susie means when she talks about "the power of the written word".

With just a piece of writing, this Hastings transferred an idea from his crazy imagination into my mind, and I was willing to believe it.

So I walk down the hall to his bedroom door, which is shut, and there is *another* typed note on it:

> Dear Burglar,
>
> OK, so there is no puma. Did you really think I'd let a huge cat mess up my nice neat house?
>
> However, I am going to give you a *serious warning*. DO NOT OPEN THIS DOOR! One of the engineers at our studio has invented a highly sophisticated security device and I've borrowed one of his models.
>
> It's hidden in the bedroom and it works by means of ultrasonic waves. They are soundless and they have a fantastically destructive and permanent effect on brain tissues. It takes less than a minute of exposure.
>
> You will not notice any brain-numbing effects at once, but in a few days, your memory will start to go, and then your reasoning powers, and so, for your *own* sake, DO NOT ENTER THIS ROOM!
>
> Harry Hastings

Well, I really had to hand it to this loony character. No wonder he made a lot of money as a writer. I, of course, do not believe *one word* of this, *at all*; therefore, I go into the bedroom and hurry to see if there is any hidden electronic device, but, of course, there is not. Naturally.

Then I see another note, on the closet door, and it says:

> Dear Burglar,
>
> I don't suppose I should have expected you to believe that one, with your limited imagination and your one-track mind. By the way, where do you *go* in all my clothes? You must be quite a swinger.
>
> There are only a few new things in the closet. But before you take them, I suggest you sniff them. You will notice a kind of cologne smell, but this is only to disguise another *odour*. I have a pal who was in chemical warfare, and he has given me a liquid that can be sprayed inside clothing. No amount of dry cleaning can ever entirely remove it.
>
> When the clothes are worn, the heat of the body converts this substance into a heavy gas that attacks the skin and produces the most frightful and agonisingly painful blisters, from the ankles to the neck. Never forget that you have been *warned*.
>
> Harry Hastings

Well, I don't believe this for one moment, and so I open the closet door. All there is is one pair of slacks and a sports coat. But this coat looks like the very same *plaid cashmere* I took before and the rat stole from *me*!

But then I realise this could not be so, but it was just that Hastings liked this coat so much he went out and bought another just like it.

Anyway, I find myself sniffing these. They smell of cologne, all right, but nothing else, and I know, of course, that this kind of gas stuff does not exist at all except in Hastings's wild imagination, which I am coming to admire by now.

As I drive back to my pad, I start to laugh when I think of all the stupid and fantastic things that Hastings has tried to put into my mind today by the power of suggestion, and I realise that he almost succeeded. *Almost*, but not quite.

When I get home and climb the outside stairs to my front door, there are three envelopes taped to it, one above another. There are no names on them, but they are numbered, 1, 2, 3. I do not know what in hell all this could be about, but I open 1 and read:

> Dear Burglar,
>
> The plaid cashmere coat you have over your arm right now is *not* a replacement for the one you stole. It is the *same identical coat*. Think about this before you open envelope 2.
>
> Harry Hastings

Well, of *course*, I think about this as I stand there with my mouth sort of hanging open. All of a sudden, it *hits* me! *Harry Hastings* was the rat who stole all his clothes back! But how did he know where I *live*? How could he know I was going to hit his house *today*? My hands are all fumbles as I open 2. Inside it says:

> Dear Burglar,
>
> To answer your questions: On your *third* visit to my house, my young neighbour saw you and followed you home in his car, and so found out just where you live. Later, in my own good time, I easily entered this place with a bent paper clip and retrieved my own clothes. Today, my neighbour called me at my office and said you were inside my house again.
>
> Later, I phoned him and he said you had come out, with my coat. So I've had time to come here and write and leave these notes. I also have had time to do something else, which you will read about in 3.
>
> Harry Hastings

I open this third envelope very fast indeed, because I figure that if Hastings knows all this, the fuzz will be along any minute. In it I read:

> Dear Burglar,
>
> I got the puma idea from a friend out in the valley who has one in a large cage in his yard. Long ago, I asked him if I might borrow this huge cat for a day sometime, and he said yes and that he didn't like burglars, either. He has a large carrying cage for the puma. I called him this morning the moment I heard you were inside my house, and he drove the puma right over *here*, and we released the huge cat inside your place. She is now in there, wandering around loose.

I have done this partly because I am vengeful and vindictive by nature and partly because I've made my living for years as a verisimilitudinous (look it up later) writer, and I deeply resent anyone I cannot fool. The puma that is now inside is my childish way of getting even.

This is no *trick* this time! If you have any brains at *all*, DO NOT OPEN THIS DOOR! Just get out of town before the police arrive, which will be in about half an hour. Goodbye.

Harry Hastings

P.S. The puma's name is Carrie — as if that would help you any.

Well, I read in a story once where somebody was called a "quivering mass of indecisive jelly", and that is what I was right then. I simply did not know *what* to think or believe. If this was any door but mine, I could walk away. But all my *cash* was hidden inside, and I *had* to get it before I could leave town.

So I stand there and I sweat and I think and I think and after a long time, it comes to me that *this* time, Hastings is finally telling the *truth*. Besides I can hear little noises from inside. There *is* a puma in there! I know it! But I have to get *in* there, just the same!

I finally figure that if I open the door fast and step back, Carrie might just scoot past me and away. But maybe she will attack me.

But then I figure if I wrap the sports coat around one arm and the slacks around the other, maybe I can fend off Carrie long enough to grab a chair and then force her into my bathroom, the way lion tamers do, and then slam the door on her, and then grab my cash and run out of there, and the police can worry about her when they come.

So this is what I decide to do, only it is some time before I can get up the nerve to unlock the door and push it open. I unlock the door and I stand there. But finally, I think, "Oh, hell, you *got* to do it, sooner or later," and so I push my door open and stand back.

No puma jumps at me. Nothing happens at all. But then I look around the corner of my door and *Harry Hastings* is sitting inside. Not with a gun or anything. He is sitting very calmly behind the old card table I use as a desk, with a cigarette in his mouth and a pencil in his hand, and I see one of my stories in front of him.

I walk in and just stand there with my face on and cannot think of any clever remark to make, when he says: "Tell me one thing. *Did* you or did you *not* really believe there was a puma in here?"

If I remember right — I was pretty shook up then — I nodded and I said, "Yes, sir. Yes. I really did."

Then he smiled a big smile and said, "Well, thank heavens for *that*, I was beginning to think I was losing my grip. I feel a little better now. Sit down. I want to talk to you. By the way, your syntax is terrible and your grammar is worse. I've been making some corrections while waiting for you. However, that's not what I want to talk to you about. Sit down. Stop trembling, will you, and sit down!"

I sat.

As I write now, I am the co-owner and manager of the Puma Burglar Protection Agency. Harry Hastings is my silent partner and he put up two thousand dollars for financing. Susie helps me with my accounts. I have 130 clients now, at five dollars a month each.

The reason it's so cheap is that we use the Harry Hastings Method. That is, we don't bother with burglar alarms or things like that, I just patrol around and keep putting up and changing signs and notices and notes on front doors. Already, the burglary rate in my area has been cut by two-thirds.

This very morning, I got a little letter from Harry Hastings with two new ideas for front-door notes. One is: CLARA! I HAVE ALREADY CALLED THE POLICE AND THEY WILL BE HERE IN MINUTES! DO NOT CALL THEM AGAIN! GEORGE IS LOCKED IN THE BATHROOM AND CAN'T GET OUT, SO WE WILL BE SAFE TILL THEY GET HERE!

The second one is: NOTICE! BECAUSE OF A FRIGHTFULLY CONTAGIOUS DISEASE, THIS HOUSE HAS BEEN EVACUATED AND QUARANTINED. IT MUST ABSOLUTELY NOT BE ENTERED UNTIL IT HAS BEEN FUMIGATED!

Harry Hastings says that I should be sure to warn the householder to remove this notice before any large parties.

how well did you understand the story?

1. What was the basis of the Harry Hastings Method?
2. What, according to Susie, is the key to being a good writer?
3. Why does the burglar find the Hollywood hills area particularly good for his work?
4. What motivates the burglar to disperse his printed cards throughout the neighbourhood?
5. Why does the burglar have different signs on each side of his truck?
6. Can you find evidence to suggest that the burglar is quite intelligent? Explain your answer.
7. With whom do you sympathise — Harry or the burglar? Why?
8. How do you know that the burglar really believed that there was a puma in his flat?
9. Why does Harry Hastings ask the burglar, "Tell me one thing. *Did* you or did you *not* really believe there was a puma in here?"
10. What comment would you make about Harry Hastings's treatment of the burglar at the end of the story?

Copy the following story evaluation sheet into your workbook, and then fill in the answers.

evaluation sheet

Title of the story: ....

Author's name: ....

Plot (Write a brief summary of what the story is about): ....

....

....

....

....

Realism (Is the story realistic? What methods does the writer use to make his story realistic?): ....

....

....

Humour (How does the author make his story humorous?): ....

....

....

....

Characters (Do the characters ring true? Why?): ....

....

....

Conclusion (Is the conclusion a good one? Why?): ....

....

....

....

the burglar's vocabulary

Harry Hastings is indeed correct when he tells the burglar that his "syntax is terrible" and his "grammar is worse".

Rewrite in formal English the following sentences, which have been taken from the story.
1. "It wasn't till I went through his clothes closet that I found out that most of his bread went into his wardrobe."
2. "I tried on a couple of jackets, and it turns out that this Hastings and me are exactly the same size!"
3. "They [the new locks] must have set Hastings back about seventy-five bucks."

4. "Four months go by before I figure it is time to hit the house again."
5. "Well, I am not about to fall for all this noise about pity."
6. "But then, one day, when I am out working, some louse breaks into my own pad. . . ."
7. "After all, it is one hell of a lot of trouble to buy and keep a puma just to protect a few clothes."
8. "I figure that if Hastings knows all this, the fuzz will be along any minute."

the character of Harry Hastings

We learn a lot about the character of Harry Hastings before we actually meet him. What comments would you make about his character from the following statements? Copy the following table into your workbook and fill in the spaces.

Information and comments supplied by the young burglar	Your evaluation
"There was five days' worth of dishes in the sink."	
"There was about $5000 worth of new apparel in there, most of it hand-tailored and from places like where Sinatra and Dean Martin get their outfits. Very mod and up-to-date."	
"A 'wardrobe of clothes' is redundant. It is 'biscuit' not 'biskit'. Use your dictionary!"	
"HELGA! DO NOT OPEN THIS DOOR! Since you were here last week, I bought a PUMA for burglar protection."	
"He is sitting very calmly behind the old card table I use as a desk, with a cigarette in his mouth and a pencil in his hand, and I see one of my stories in front of him."	
"Harry Hastings is my silent partner and he put up two thousand dollars for financing."	

jumbled events

The following events from the story are listed in the wrong order. Arrange them in their correct order.

1. "I picked him up and let him lick my face and saw that he had a tag on his collar that read: CUDDLES, MY OWNER IS HARRY HASTINGS."
2. "As I write now, I am the co-owner and manager of the Puma Burglar Protection Agency."
3. "But one thing I know a lot about is working the houses in the Hollywood hills."
4. "No puma jumps at me. Nothing happens at all."
5. "When I decide that a certain house is ripe for hitting, I go up and ring the doorbell."
6. "I called him this morning the moment I heard you were inside my house, and he drove the puma right over *here*, and we released the huge cat inside your place."

find the word in the story to match the meaning

The meaning of the missing word is on the right-hand side. Some of the letters of the missing word are on the left-hand side. Find the word.

s–n–ax	the grammatical arrangement of words in speech or writing
r–r–l	of the country(side)
–pp–r–l	clothing
re–r–ach	rebuke
l–c–t–	discover exact place of
–ed–n–ant	not needed, more than enough
ver–s–m–l–t–d–n–u–	seeming true
q–i–er–n–	trembling
–on–a–ious	infectious
ar–h–ic	no longer in common use
–ua–an–i–e	isolation to prevent spread of contagious disease

Ever feel like giving up on a cold, becoming totally immobile and letting the TV do all the work? Read on.

A Winter Scene

The noses are running at our house.
Like faucets. Wild horses.
Otherwise it is quiet here,
There is nothing afoot except Lassie who is running
Hastily through a TV pasture in quest of a
TV doctor, while we
Who are not running (except for our noses)
Vegetate (off TV) with Vicks and prescriptions
In an atmosphere so sedentary that if
We ever get well and get up and regain the potential
For running again with more than just our noses,
We may not.
          I mean it is possible
That when we get well we will not undertake to run
Or even to walk (though we'll be able to),
But will hold firm to our sofas and spread our Vicks
Even more thickly over our throats and chests, letting Lassie
And such other TV characters as may follow
On Channel Five
Do all our running, walking, barking, thinking
For us, once even our noses
Have stopped their incessant running and it is quiet here.

Reed Whittemore

Did you notice that the poem really has two parts? The first part is all about what is happening in the lounge room at the *present time*. This part goes down to "We may not". The second part is all about *what might possibly happen* in the lounge room. It begins, "I mean it is possible".

exercise (to be completed in your workbook)

Answer these questions about the lounge room of the present and the what-might-possibly-happen lounge room. Pay attention to the directions in brackets.
(a) What's showing on the TV (quote)? What's going on in the lounge room (in your own words)?
(b) What's possibly going to happen in the lounge room (in your own words)? What extra duties might the TV possibly have to take over (quote)?

questions

1. The stifling atmosphere of the sick room is suggested in a number of ways. See if you can spot them.
2. If you were to enter the lounge room, which two pieces of furniture would immediately catch your eye?
3. What sounds would immediately trouble your ears?
4. What smell would predominate (or be most powerful or dominating)?
5. Why is the title of the poem a bit of a surprise?
6. What connection is there between running noses and wild horses?
7. There is one word, besides "running", that ties up the start of the poem with the ending. What is it?

vocabulary (to be completed in your workbook)

Find the words in the poem that correspond to the following meanings.

Meanings	Word (initial letter given)
sitting idly, sluggish, inactive	s_____
possessing the possible power	p_____
plumbing fixtures	f_____
never ceasing	i_____
to live like a vegetable	v_____
pharmaceutical preparations	p_____
the feeling of the place	a_____

UNHOLY MARRIAGE

Police are seeking to identify the pillion rider who was also killed

Her mother bore her, father cared
And clothed her body, young and neat.
The careful virgin had not shared
Cool soft anointment of her breast
Or any other sweet,
But kept herself for best.

How sweet she would have been in bed,
Her bridegroom sighing in her hair,
His tenderness heaped on her head,
Receiving benediction from her breast
With every other fair
She kept for him, the best.

Who she is now they do not know
Assembling her body on a sheet.
This foolish virgin shared a blow
That drove her almost through a stranger's breast
And all her sweet
Mingles with his in dust.

Unwilling marriage, her blood runs with one
Who bought for a few pounds and pence
A steel machine able to "do a ton",
Not knowing at a ton a straw will pierce a breast:
No wheel has built-in sense,
Not yet the shiniest and best.

And so, "doing a ton", in fog and night
Before he could think, Christ! or she could moan
There came a heavy tail without a light
And many tons compressed each back to breast
And blood and brain and bone
Mixed, lay undressed.

Anointed only by the punctured oil
Poured like unleashed wind or fire from bag
Sold by some damned magician out to spoil
The life that girded in this young girl's breast
Now never to unfurl her flag
And march love's happy quest.

Her mother hears the clock: her father sighs,
Takes off his boots: she's late tonight.
I hope she's a careful virgin: men have eyes
For cherished daughters growing in the breast.
Some news? They hear the gate —
A man comes: not the best.

David Holbrook

how well did you understand the poem?

1. It seems peculiar for the poet to refer to the death of the young girl pillion rider and her boyfriend as a "marriage". Why does he do this?
2. Why is this marriage "unholy"?
3. The girl is referred to as a "foolish virgin". Why "foolish"?
4. The girl's purity is stressed in this poem. Jot down some of the words the poet uses to achieve this.
5. Why is the union between the girl and the driver of the bike "unwilling"?
6. How does the poet bring out the horrible aspects of the accident?
7. What do you think is the poet's main reason for writing this poem?
8. What is the prevailing mood that runs through this poem?
9. Explain the meaning of
    "Now never to unfurl her flag
    And march love's happy quest."
10. Why are the girl's mother and father important in the poem? Comment particularly on the last stanza.

MY
FATHER'S
HANDS

Big and competent, they served him well — in all respects but one

Calvin Worthington

His hands were rough and exceedingly strong. He could gently prune a fruit tree or firmly wrestle a stubborn mule into harness. He could draw and saw a square with quick accuracy. He had been known to peel his knuckles on a tough jaw. But what I remember most is the special warmth from those hands soaking through my shirt as he would take me by the shoulder and, squatting beside my ear, point out the glittering swoop of a blue hawk, or a rabbit asleep in its lair. They were good hands that served him well and failed him in only one thing: they never learnt to write.

My father was illiterate. The number of illiterates in the country has steadily declined, but if there were only one I would be saddened, remembering my father and the pain he endured because his hands never learnt to write.

When he started school, the remedy for a wrong answer was ten ruler strokes across a stretched palm. For some reason, shapes, figures and recitations just didn't fall into the right pattern inside his six-year-old tow-head. Maybe he suffered from some type of learning handicap such as dyslexia. His father took him out of school after several months and set him to a man's job on the farm.

Years later, his wife, educated to the fourth year of primary school, would try to teach him to read. And still later I would grasp his big fist between my small hands and awkwardly help him trace the letters of his name. He submitted to the ordeal, but soon grew restless. Flexing his fingers and kneading his palms, he would eventually declare that he had had enough and would depart for a long, solitary walk.

Finally, one night when he thought no one saw, he slipped away with his son's second-grade reader and laboured over the words, until they became too difficult. He pressed his forehead into the pages and wept. "Jesus — Jesus — not even a child's book?" Thereafter, no amount of persuading could bring him to sit with pen and paper.

From the farm to road building and later factory work, his hands served him well. His mind was keen, his will to work unsurpassed. During World War II, he was a pipefitter in a shipyard and installed the complicated guts of mighty fighting ships.

His enthusiasm and efficiency brought an offer to become a foreman — until he was handed the qualification test. His fingers could trace a path across the blueprints while his mind imagined the pipes lacing through the heart of the ship. He could recall every twist and turn of those pipes. But he couldn't read or write.

After the shipyard closed, he went to the cotton mill, where he laboured at night, and stole from his sleeping hours the time required to run the farm. When the mill shut down, he went out each morning looking for work — only to return night after night and say to Mother as she prepared his dinner, "They just don't want anybody for the job who can't take their tests."

It had always been hard for him to stand before a man and make an X mark for his name, but the hardest moment of all was when he placed "his mark" by the name someone else had written for him, and saw another man walk away with the deed to his beloved farm. When it was over, he stood before the window and slowly turned the pen he still held in his hands — gazing, unseeing, down the mountainside. I went out to the barn that afternoon and wept for a long, long while.

Eventually, he found another cotton-mill job, and we moved into a millhouse village with a hundred look-alike houses. He never quite adjusted to town life. The blue of his eyes faded; the skin across his cheekbones became a little slack. But his hands kept their strength, and their warmth still soaked through when he would sit me on his lap and ask that I read to him from the Bible. He took great pride in my reading and would listen for hours as I struggled through the awkward phrases.

Once he had heard "a radio preacher" relate that the Bible said, "The man that doesn't provide for his family is worse than a thief and an infidel and will never enter the Kingdom of Heaven." Often he would ask me to read that part to him, but I was never able to find it. Other times, he would sit at the kitchen table leafing through the pages as though by a miracle he might be able to read the passage should he turn to the right page. Then he would sit staring at the Book, and I knew he was wondering if God was going to refuse him entry into heaven because his hands couldn't write.

When Mother left once for a weekend to visit her sister, Dad went to the store and returned with food for dinner while I was busy building my latest homemade wagon. After the meal he said he had a surprise for dessert, and went out to the kitchen, where I could hear him opening a can. Then everything was quiet. I went to the doorway, and saw him standing before the sink with an open can in his hand. "The picture looked just like pears," he mumbled. He walked out and sat on the back steps, and I knew he had been embarrassed before his son. The can read "Whole White Potatoes", but the illustration on the label did look a great deal like pears.

I went and sat beside him, and asked if he would point out the stars. He knew where the Big Dipper and all the other stars were located, and we talked about how they got there in the first place. He kept that can on a shelf in the woodshed for a long while, and on several occasions I saw him turning it in his hands as if the touch of the words would teach his hands to write.

Years later, when Mum died, I tried to get him to come and live with my family, but he insisted on staying in his small weatherboard house on the edge of town with a few farm animals and a garden plot. His health was failing, and he was in and out of hospital with several mild heart attacks. Old Doc Green saw him weekly and gave him medication, including nitroglycerin tablets to put under his tongue should he feel an attack coming on.

My last fond memory of Dad was watching as he walked across the brow of a hillside meadow, with those big, warm hands, now gnarled with age, resting on the shoulders of my two children. He stopped to point out to them, confidentially, a pond where he and I had swum and fished years before. That night, my family and I flew to a new job and new home, overseas. Three weeks later, he was dead of a heart attack.

I returned alone for the funeral. Doc Green told me how sorry he was. In fact, he was bothered a bit, because he had just written Dad a new nitroglycerin prescription, and the chemist had made it up. Yet the bottle of pills had not been found on Dad's person. Doc Green felt that a pill might have kept him alive long enough to summon help.

An hour before the chapel service, I found myself standing near the edge of Dad's garden, where a neighbour had found him. In grief, I stopped to trace my fingers in the earth where a great man had reached the end of life. My hand came to rest on a half-buried brick, which I aimlessly lifted and tossed aside, before noticing underneath it the twisted and battered, yet unbroken, soft plastic bottle that had been beaten into the soft earth.

As I held the bottle of pills, the scene of Dad struggling to remove the cap and in desperation trying to break the bottle with the brick flashed painfully before my eyes. With anguish I knew why those big warm hands had lost in their struggle with death. For there, imprinted on the bottle cap, were the words, "Child-Proof Cap — Push Down and Twist to Unlock." The chemist later confirmed that he had just started using the new safety bottle.

I knew it was not a purely rational act, but I went straight to town and bought a leather-bound pocket dictionary and a gold pen set. I bade Dad goodbye by placing them in those big old hands, once so warm, which had lived so well, but had never learnt to write.

how well did you understand the story?

(a) The author's outstanding memory of his father's hands was
  1. watching them pruning fruit trees;
  2. their warmth on his shoulder as his father pointed things out to him;
  3. their quickness and accuracy in drawing and sawing out a square;
  4. seeing them fighting other men.

(b) The father's education was
  1. terminated at the fourth year of primary school;
  2. something he never mentioned;
  3. brief — only a few months when he was six years old;
  4. unfortunately in the wrong kind of school system.

(c) The father would go for long solitary walks after attempts at writing because
  1. he got discouraged and just felt the need to be alone for a while;
  2. he liked plenty of exercise;
  3. walking cleared his head and enabled him to try again;
  4. walking gave him time to revise the material he had been learning.

(d) The father finally gave up trying to read because
  1. even his wife and son were better at it than he was;
  2. he felt he had dyslexia and would never learn;
  3. he couldn't even read a child's reader;
  4. he no longer had time.

(e) Having a son who could read
  1. hurt him, because he could not read himself;
  2. made him aware of the importance of education;
  3. spurred him to try even harder to learn;
  4. filled him with pride.

(f) When the incident with the can of potatoes took place, the author went and sat by his father. He asked his father to point out the stars
  1. because he wanted to take his father's mind off the shame of not being able to read;
  2. because he knew that astronomy was something his father knew a lot about;
  3. so that he could learn more about astronomy;
  4. because he wanted to take his father's mind off the wasted money.

(g) The fact that the father stayed on at his own small home after his wife's death, instead of moving in with his son, shows
  1. his fear of having to make new changes;
  2. his independent spirit;
  3. his unspoken dislike of his son's family;
  4. his shame at still being illiterate.

(h) The father finally died of a heart attack when
  1. his family deserted him and moved overseas;
  2. he lost his bottle of heart tablets somewhere in the garden;
  3. his body was too old to fight any more;
  4. he was unable to open the new bottle containing his life-saving tablets because he could not read the instructions on the label.

(i) The son bought a dictionary and a gold pen set, and had them interred with his father's body, because
  1. he himself was a writer and they were a gift from him;
  2. they were the most expensive gifts he could find;
  3. they represented another gift that his father would so dearly have loved;
  4. he was not completely rational.

crossword

Draw the following crossword in your workbook and then answer the clues. The answers are all taken from *My Father's Hands*.

ACROSS

4. First part of the name of the tablets prescribed by Dr Green
5. A position the father missed out on because of his illiteracy
8. He would often sit .... through the pages
9. What he thought were the contents of the can he bought
10. The father's reaction to being unable to read the child's school book

DOWN

1. He worked as a .... in a shipyard
2. One of the words on the can of potatoes
3. Something he never quite adjusted to (two words)
6. Children were hit with this when the father was at school
7. One word used to describe the father's hands (reversed)

fixing the facts

Arrange the following facts into the order in which they occur in the story.

He worked at a mill at night and on his farm during the day.
His wife and son tried to teach him to read and write.
He bought a can of potatoes thinking they were pears.
He began work at another cotton-mill job.
He had a few months of schooling.
He died of a heart attack.
He lost his farm.
He took his two grandchildren for walks.
He worked at a shipyard.
He lived on in his small weatherboard cottage after his wife's death.
The son used to read to him from the Bible.
His father took him out of school.
The reason for his death was discovered.

using descriptive words

Words that describe people, places, objects or qualities are known as adjectives. The sensible and sensitive use of adjectives in writing can help the reader a great deal to imagine the things described. Of course, if adjectives are over-used they can become a distraction and break the flow of a story but, used wisely, they can be most effective.

Look carefully at the use of descriptive words (or adjectives) in the opening paragraph.

"His hands were *rough* and exceedingly *strong*. He could gently prune a fruit tree or firmly wrestle a *stubborn* mule into harness. . . ."

1. Find adjectives used in the rest of the story to fill in the following blanks.

.... heart attacks
.... warmth from father's hands
.... village
.... ships
.... jaw
.... phrases
.... bottle
.... farm
.... walk

".......... .... Potatoes"
.... houses
.... reader
.... hands
.... guts
.... wagon
.... house
.... memory

2. The hands of different people are listed below. Make up two adjectives that you feel would appropriately describe their hands.

.... hands of a concert pianist
.... hands of a coal miner
.... hands of a tiny baby
.... hands of a surgeon
.... hands of a wealthy socialite
.... hands of an aged person
.... hands of a house painter
.... hands of a policeman

words in context

In these four passages from the story, key words have been removed and placed conveniently in frames at the side. Bracketed meanings have been inserted in place of the missing words.

Rewrite each of the passages in your workbook, replacing the bracketed meanings with words from the frames. This puts key words back into context. As you finish rewriting each passage, check for accuracy by finding the passage in the story.

Passages	Key words
1. My father was (unable to read or write). The number of (people unable to read or write) in the country has steadily (gone down), but if there were only one I would be saddened, (recalling) my father and the pain he (put up with) because his hands never learnt to write.	remembering endured illiterate declined illiterates
2. He (surrendered or yielded) to the (trying experience), but soon grew (impatient). (Bending) his fingers and (pressing and massaging) his palms, he would (finally) declare that he had had enough and would (leave) for a long, (lonely) walk.	depart solitary submitted kneading ordeal eventually flexing restless
3. His (keenness) and (competence) brought an (invitation or proposal) to become a (overseer) — until he was handed the (standard of ability) test. His fingers could (follow) a path across the (plans) while his (intellect) imagined the pipes lacing through the heart of the ship. He could (remember) every twist and turn of those pipes.	recall qualification mind enthusiasm trace offer blueprints efficiency foreman
4. As I held the bottle of pills, the (picture) of Dad (battling) to (take off) the cap and in (hopelessly struggling) trying to break the bottle with the brick (came suddenly like a burst of light) painfully before my eyes. With (agony) I knew why those big warm hands had lost in their (fight) with death.	scene struggling flashed remove anguish desperation struggle

debate topic

"In our world today, nothing is more important than being able to read and write."

words and meanings

Show that you understand the meaning of the following words (all taken from
My Father's Hands) by linking each word with its proper meaning.

aimlessly	picture
unsurpassed	secretly
medication	den or hiding place
relate	difficulty in reading and forming words
embarrassed	without purpose
illustration	tell
gnarled	to feel self-conscious
confidentially	curative preparation
dyslexia	sensible or completely reasonable
rational	knobby and twisted
lair	unequalled

Ted Hughes creates a great and amusing mystery about holes in this poem, which has a rather unexpected title.

My Father

Some fathers work at the office, others work at the store,
Some operate great cranes and build up skyscrapers galore,
Some work in canning factories counting green peas into cans,
Some drive all night in huge and thundering removal vans.

But mine has the strangest job of the lot.
My Father's the Chief Inspector of — What?
O don't tell the mice, don't tell the moles,
My Father's the Chief Inspector of HOLES.

It's a work of the highest importance because you never know
What's in a hole, what fearful thing is creeping from below.
Perhaps it's a hole to the ocean and will soon gush water in tons,
Or maybe it leads to a vast cave full of gold and skeletons.

Though a hole might seem to have nothing but dirt in
Somebody's simply got to make certain.
Caves in the mountain, clefts in the wall,
My Father has to inspect them all.

That crack in the road looks harmless. My Father knows it's not.
The world may be breaking into two and starting at that spot.
Or maybe the world is a great egg, and we live on the shell.
And it's just beginning to split and hatch: you simply cannot tell.

If you see a crack, run to the phone, run!
My Father will know just what's to be done.
A rumbling hole, a silent hole,
My Father will soon have it under control.

Keeping a check on all these holes he hurries from morning to night.
There might be sounds of marching in one, or an eye shining bright.
A tentacle came groping from a hole that belonged to a mouse,
A floor collapsed and Chinamen swarmed up into the house.

A Hole's an unpredictable thing —
Nobody knows what a Hole might bring.
Caves in the mountains, clefts in the wall;
My Father has to inspect them all!

Ted Hughes

Do you agree that this is a very humorous poem? Why is it so funny?

First, Ted Hughes proceeds to inform us about one particular job that happens to be more important than all others, the Chief Inspector of Holes. ''Pull the other leg,'' you bellow. Yes, indeed. On the surface, an Inspector of Holes appears to be just about as important as the swaggies' traditional job of Milestone Inspector. However, Hughes, tongue-in-cheek, produces scary but persuasive evidence to show that a Hole Inspector is a serious and nationally important job because — wait for it — holes are really sinister and perhaps even world-shattering objects. They are not nothings after all.

Find the answers to these questions in the poem.
1. At first glance, what do holes seem to have in them?
2. What is the one word that sums up the element of the unexpected in all holes?
3. Is the world really in any danger of splitting in two? Quote the line that informs us of this possibility.
4. In your opinion, what is the most bizarre hole possibility that is conjured up?

the big hole

Here's a big hole filled with the following:
- things that come up from holes
- sounds heard coming from holes
- actions and movements linked with holes
- types of holes
- what the inspector does to holes
- what other fathers do
- where other fathers work

FLOOR COLLAPSED   OFFICE   CREEPING
WATER   SILENT   GROPING   MOUSE
FACTORIES   RUMBLING   MARCHING
STORE GOLD   WORK   SKELETONS   GUSH
HURRIES   CRACK   CLEFT   OPERATE
CHINAMEN   FEARFUL THING
VANS   SWARMING   INSPECTS
KEEPS A CHECK   TENTACLE   SKYSCRAPERS
BUILD UP   OCEAN   HARMLESS (?)   CAVE

Draw up seven columns in your workbook to correspond with the seven categories. Use these categories as headings for your columns. Slot into the columns all the items from the big hole.

where does it lead?

The final destinations of five holes are more or less described in the poem. We can depict them as they are shown in this diagram.

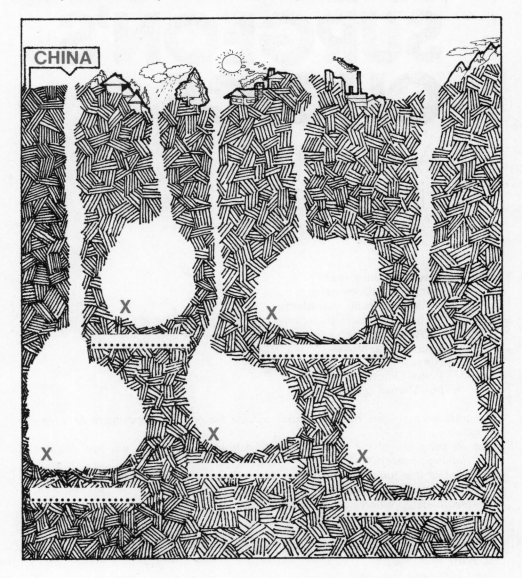

1. Sketch holes like these in your workbook and see if you can signpost each one (the first has been done as an example).
2. Draw your impression of each cave's final destination at the places marked X.
3. Quote the relevant line from the poem beside your drawing.

THE SURGEON'S CHOICE

A Matter of Life or Death

CAST: Joe, *ambulance man*
Harry, *ambulance man*
Dr John Morton, *anaesthetist*
Dr Edna Samuels, *physician*
Dr Andrew Fraser, *surgeon*
Loudspeaker Voice
Nurse
Police Officer
Mrs Pastelli (and son)

(An ambulance, engine running, stands outside the casualty department of a big city hospital)

HARRY *(leaning out of the ambulance window):* Joe, hurry it up, will you! *(Sound of running footsteps)*

JOE: Coming! *(He jumps in the ambulance and slams the door; tyres screeching, the ambulance races away)*

JOE *(breathlessly):* Where's the duty physician?

HARRY: He's already inside.

JOE: What's the call?

HARRY: Car smash on Highway 202. The police phoned through.

JOE: Bad?

HARRY: Two dead, they said.

JOE: Morgue been alerted?

HARRY: Yeah. Yeah.

JOE: OK. So what's the hurry now?

HARRY: Maybe the police were wrong. Maybe there's still somebody alive. Traffic up ahead. Let's have some noise. *(He flips a switch and the siren wails)*

(The next scene takes place at the city hospital. Drs Morton, Samuels and Fraser are playing cards in the Medical Officers' Lounge. Dr Morton steps forward)

DR MORTON: My name is Morton — Dr John Morton. I'm an anaesthetist. I was on duty the night of the smash on Highway 202. Here at City Hospital, where I work, there are never less than three doctors on house duty. At the weekend we work eight-hour shifts — a physician, an anaesthetist, and a surgeon. When things are quiet, we mostly sit around the Medical Officers' Lounge, maybe playing cards or reading or talking. And always with one ear listening to the loudspeaker system. It never rests and it never allows you to relax fully. After a while, it seems as though the voice doesn't belong to anyone. You begin to believe that it comes from no human person — just a voice, no feeling, no character — just a metallic voice.

LOUDSPEAKER: Nurse Thomson, please contact Number Three Ward immediately.

DR MORTON: This voice destroys your privacy. It even destroys your very thoughts. You turn into a robot, obeying only commands of the voice from the void. *(He returns to the card game)*

LOUDSPEAKER: Nurse Thomson, contact Number Three Ward immediately!

DR SAMUELS *(shuffling and dealing)*: One of these days I'm going to rip out the entire loudspeaker system. I think I'll do it on the day I retire.

DR MORTON *(fanning his hand)*: Ace! That's just the card I've been waiting for! *(He throws down his cards; they all throw down their cards)*

DR MORTON: Now let me see. Mmm. That's one million eight hundred and forty thousand dollars you owe me, Dr Fraser, sir!

DR FRASER *(laughing)*: Well, the moral is — never play cards with an anaesthetist. *(Putting on a snobbish voice)* You'll take my personal cheque, of course?

DR MORTON *(laughing):* No, Andy, but I'll give you a chance to win it all back tomorrow night.

DR FRASER: Oh no you won't, John. My holidays start in exactly thirty-six minutes from now.

DR SAMUELS: Lucky devil.

DR FRASER: A fortnight's peace and quiet. Caroline and the boy will be calling for me in half an hour. And then it's Gold Coast here we come!

DR MORTON: You're travelling tonight?

DR FRASER: Oh no. We're only going as far as the Harbour. Caroline's folks live there. Should make it by about ten o'clock and then we'll make an early start in the morning.

DR SAMUELS: You're driving up?

DR FRASER: Oh, sure. We'll take it nice and easy. Caroline's bringing the car.

LOUDSPEAKER *(cuts in):* Duty Sister Frobisher, call Reception, please.

DR SAMUELS: Just think of it. A fortnight without listening to old "golden voice" there. *(They laugh)*

DR MORTON: Carlton relieving you early then, Andy?

DR FRASER: Yes, he said he'd get here at seven-thirty . . .

LOUDSPEAKER: Stand by, Emergency Ambulance Crew!

DR SAMUELS: Oh no . . .

LOUDSPEAKER: Dr Samuels, please report to Ambulance Bay. Stand by, Casualty Reception. This is an emergency!

DR SAMUELS *(going out the door):* Fourth emergency tonight. No rest for the wicked.

DR MORTON: Keep your fingers crossed, Andy. *(Pause)*

LOUDSPEAKER: Prepare Emergency Operating Theatre. Dr Fraser and Dr Morton, report to the Theatre. Stand by, Operating Staff.

DR MORTON *(sighs):* Yes, I thought we wouldn't get out of it. Come on *(getting up).* Never mind, Andy. Maybe it's a false alarm. Maybe we'll be through by 7.30.

DR FRASER: Yeah, and maybe elephants will start flying.

DR MORTON: If it's a broken arm or anything like that, Edna and I can look after it.

DR FRASER: It'll be just my luck for it to be an acute appendix.

LOUDSPEAKER: Stand by, Casualty Reception Ward. Stand by to admit and prepare a minimum of three patients for operation . . .

DR MORTON: Andrew Fraser and I prepared for an emergency. The theatre staff busied themselves preparing for any possibility. Of course, at this stage we had no idea of what to expect. Perhaps it was the victims of a fire, perhaps a car smash — almost anything. It is during this period that you have time to think — and wonder. It is now that the tension starts to mount. Now — as we wait for the ambulance to return . . .

DR FRASER: Should be here any second. Reception'll have prepared the patient.

DR MORTON: Anaesthetic machine ready, Andy. Pentothal and morphia in the tray.

DR FRASER: Good. Thanks, John.

NURSE: Your mask and gown, Doctor.

DR FRASER: Thank you, Nurse.

NURSE: And the Theatre's ready. Everyone's standing by.

DR FRASER: Good.

DR MORTON: Now all we have to do is wait.

LOUDSPEAKER: With reference to Emergency Call at 6.55. Ambulance returned. Patients dead on arrival. Emergency Operating Theatre return to normal routine. *(Dr Morton sighs)*

DR FRASER: And that would seem to be that.

DR MORTON: Poor devils.

DR FRASER: Wonder what it was?

DR MORTON: At this time of night? Car smash probably. Come on.

DR FRASER: Twenty-six minutes to go — and then Carlton can have my job!

DR MORTON: I hope the weather stays good for you, Andy.

DR FRASER: For the first three or four days I won't care. I think I'll spend the whole of that time in bed.

LOUDSPEAKER: Pathology Department, blood grouping in Number Eight Ward.

DR MORTON *(small laugh):* It's a good job there are no loudspeakers in the wards. We'd have every patient in the hospital going round the bend.

DR FRASER: Yep. *(Suddenly)* Oh, before I forget. I must ring through to the hall porter. Tell him to let me know as soon as Carlton arrives — and Caroline. 'Scuse me a sec, John.

DR MORTON: Sure, Andy. *(Fraser leaves)*

DR SAMUELS: Hey, John.

DR MORTON: Eh? Oh, hello, Edna.

DR SAMUELS *(obviously distressed):* John, I must talk to you for a minute.

DR MORTON: You look as white as a ghost. The emergency?

DR SAMUELS: Yes.

DR MORTON: Bad one, eh? What was it?

DR SAMUELS: Car smash. But there's worse to come.

DR MORTON: What d'you mean?

DR SAMUELS: Where'd Andy go?

DR MORTON: Gone to telephone ...

DR SAMUELS: He's bound to know sooner or later. Maybe I should tell him now — of all the rotten — God, it's awful.

DR MORTON: Edna ...

DR SAMUELS: The dead-on-arrivals, John. The victims of the car smash — you know who they were? Caroline and Tommy!

DR MORTON *(after horrified pause):* You mean — Andy's Caroline?

DR SAMUELS: Yeah! I've never had such a shock. It completely knocked me cockeyed. They must have been on their way here to pick him up! They were dead when we got there — I don't think they suffered.

DR MORTON *(deeply shocked):* He was devoted to them. One of us'll have to break it to him. One minute everything's fine — the next ...

DR SAMUELS: Yes, and there's something else ...

DR MORTON *(suddenly):* Shh! Here he comes.

DR FRASER *(entering):* Hi, Edna. *(Gently)* Had a bad spin?

DR SAMUELS *(after pause):* Yes, Andy. Yes, very bad.

DR MORTON *(after pause):* Andy, let's go to the lounge.

DR FRASER: No, you'll have to excuse me. Carlton will be here in a minute and I have to get ready.

DR MORTON *(almost harshly):* Come into the lounge, Andy.

DR FRASER: Huh? What's the matter?

DR MORTON: We have to talk to you.

LOUDSPEAKER *(cuts in):* Stand by, Casualty Reception. Police ambulance coming in. Stand by, Emergency Operating Theatre Staff. Dr Fraser and Dr Morton, please report to the Theatre.

DR FRASER *(with disappointment):* Oh, no! With just a few minutes more to go. Why couldn't Carlton have arrived?

DR SAMUELS *(quickly):* Maybe you should wait for him and not go to the Theatre ...

DR FRASER: No, that wouldn't be fair. *(Sighs)* Well, come on, John. It was a waste of time leaving the Theatre..

DR SAMUELS *(in a low voice):* John ...

DR MORTON: We can't tell him now! We'll have to wait till after the op.

DR SAMUELS: Yes, but ...

DR MORTON: See you after this is over.

(The next scene takes place in the Operating Theatre)

DR MORTON: What's the emergency, Nurse?

NURSE: Bullet wound, Dr Morton. Bullet lodged in the lung. It's going to be a difficult one, I think. Reception says that the patient's more dead than alive. Some gangster, they said.

DR MORTON: I see.

LOUDSPEAKER: Mr Seers, report to Reception. Blood plasma needed for emergency. Reception will give you details and grouping.

DR FRASER: It's going to be a nasty one, John. He's in a terrible mess. I think he must've been beaten up before he was shot. Where did they pick him up?

DR MORTON: Haven't any idea.

NURSE: Police Department have asked if they can keep an officer on duty outside the Theatre.

DR FRASER: Yes, all right.

DR MORTON: Big shot, huh?

DR FRASER: I'll just make a final check.

DR MORTON: I watched as Andrew Fraser walked into the Theatre. Right at that minute the most important thing in his entire life was the dying gunman. But had he known — had I been able to tell him that less than ten minutes ago his wife and child had been killed on the road — now it was impossible. The shock would come later after all this was over. We'd tell him then. I went into the Theatre Ante-room. And for a second stood looking at the still form on the stretcher. Here lay a gunman. Lodged deep in a lung there was hidden the bullet that had toppled him — and Dr Fraser must probe and search for it. I got down to the job in hand. I checked the hundred and one things I must know before I could give an anaesthetic. Must know whether or not the shock might kill him before Fraser had a chance to use his skill ...

DR SAMUELS *(in a low voice):* John.

DR MORTON: Come to give us a hand, Edna?

DR SAMUELS: John, I didn't have a chance to tell you the rest about what happened.

DR MORTON: Listen, I've got to get this patient ready for the op.

DR SAMUELS: It's about him! It was *his car that crashed into Caroline's!* He caused the smash-up!

DR MORTON: What?

DR SAMUELS: Apparently there'd been a shooting. He'd been shot but was trying to make his getaway. He must have been weak — couldn't have had much control over the car. A witness said it was weaving all over the road. On top of that the police were chasing him. They said he made no effort to miss Caroline's car. When straight into it — but he was thrown clear! Caroline and Tommy died!

DR FRASER: Say that again, Edna.

DR MORTON *(in horror):* Andy!

DR SAMUELS: Y-you heard?

DR FRASER: Yes. You said — Caroline and Tommy were dead. You said this man killed them.

DR MORTON: Listen, Andy, we were going to tell you after ...

DR FRASER *(dazed):* Caroline and Tommy died on their way to fetch me, that's what you said, wasn't it?

DR SAMUELS: I swear to you they couldn't have suffered, Andy.

DR FRASER *(shocked, uncomprehending):* But a few minutes more and we'd have been on our way to the Gold Coast ...

DR MORTON: You can't do this op. now, Andy. Listen, go along to the lounge. Edna, go with him. Carlton will be here soon.

DR FRASER: There's no time ... the patient's dying ... We have to operate right away ... no time to lose ...

DR MORTON: We'll wait for Carlton.

LOUDSPEAKER: Dr Fraser, please call Reception.

DR SAMUELS: I'll get it. *(She goes to the telephone and rings)*

DR MORTON: Perhaps we can rustle up a brandy ...

DR FRASER *(in a monotonous voice):* Is the patient ready for an anaesthetic, John?

DR MORTON: Andy, listen to me. There's no need for you to go in there. Take your gown off. Edna'll stay with you in the lounge. You've had a bad shock. Look at your hands. They're shaking like fury. You couldn't even hold a scalpel, let alone probe for a bullet.

DR FRASER: Ask the nurse to wheel the patient in.

DR MORTON *(fiercely):* You can't do it, Andy!

DR SAMUELS *(calling from telephone):* He'll have to.

DR MORTON: What is it, Edna?

DR SAMUELS: Dr Carlton phoned. He's been held up. He can't get here for at least half an hour.

DR FRASER *(quietly):* Ask the nurse to wheel the patient into the Operating Theatre.

DR MORTON: So now there was no turning back. Now Andy Fraser *had* to operate on the gunman who lay so close to death. A gangster who'd caused the death of his wife and son. And now the scalpel would cut deep into his flesh. It would be so easy for Fraser to make a slip — so very easy. How often during the next vital few hours would Andy see in his mind's eye the mangled and mutilated bodies of those he loved? I tried to pull all these thoughts out of my mind. I concentrated on the dials of the anaesthetic machine. Concentrated on maintaining pressures and watching pulse beats — watching as death hovered close by . . .

DR FRASER *(tersely):* Artery forceps.

NURSE: Artery forceps.

DR FRASER: Swabs.

NURSE: Swabs. Two.

DR FRASER: Pulse rate, John?

DR MORTON: Steady — but slow, Andy. We'll have to watch for shock.

DR FRASER: Uh huh. Probe.

NURSE: Probe.

DR MORTON: I'm increasing the oxygen.

DR FRASER: Yes, all right. Clip.

NURSE: Clip.
DR FRASER: Artery forcep.
NURSE: Artery forcep.
DR MORTON: Pulse decreasing again.
DR FRASER: Swabs.
NURSE: Swabs. Two.
DR FRASER: Scalpel again.
NURSE: Scalpel.

(Outside the Operating Theatre)
POLICE OFFICER *(angry at himself):* I shouldn't have allowed it.
DR SAMUELS: Your man would have died.
POLICE OFFICER: It seems to me he's going to die anyway. That doctor isn't going to let him live after what's happened!
DR SAMUELS: Fraser'll do everything in his power to save him.
POLICE OFFICER: Yeah, who are you trying to kid? Put yourself in his position. He has the man helpless on the table there. Helpless and unconscious. The man responsible for killing his wife and child. A vicious thug. No, a slip of the scalpel — no jury in the world would convict. Huh, I know what I'd do!
DR SAMUELS: If you'll forgive me, Officer — you aren't a doctor. There comes a point for a doctor where you have no feelings. They just cease to exist. Everything you've been trained to do — everything years of training has taught you — takes over.
POLICE OFFICER: But this is different. You said he shouldn't've gone on with the operation.

DR SAMUELS: Yes, I know. It's not fair to put the man under such a strain. It'll hit him afterwards — after it's all over. If Carlton had been able to get here . . .

POLICE OFFICER: Why didn't they send for another surgeon?

DR SAMUELS: Your prize patient would have been dead by then.

POLICE OFFICER *(tense)*: He mustn't die — he's too important. He can give us enough information to put a dozen of the top boys behind bars. You see how important it is? If that crim lives, we can put paid to half the rackets in this town. If he dies — then we're right back where we started.

DR SAMUELS: Fraser'll do his best.

LOUDSPEAKER: Sister Carnegie, contact the X-ray Department immediately.

POLICE OFFICER: Doesn't that thing get on your nerves?

DR SAMUELS: Yes, constantly.

POLICE OFFICER: So you think Fraser'll patch him up okay, huh? You think he'll be able to patch him up enough for us to bring him to court?

DR SAMUELS: I think so.

POLICE OFFICER: And after that, you know what'll happen? He'll spend the rest of his life in prison. It's crazy, isn't it?

DR SAMUELS: Yes. Yes, it's crazy. But it happens often enough. You fight for a life that must soon end — or be wasted. Yes, it's crazy . . .

(Scene changes to Operating Theatre)

DR FRASER *(in a monotonous tone)*: Scalpel.

NURSE: Scalpel.

DR FRASER: I'm making the final incision now. Swabs, Nurse.

NURSE: Swabs. Two.

DR MORTON *(low — urgent)*: You'll have to work fast, Andy. He's failing.

DR FRASER: Just a few more minutes. Try to hold him a few more minutes. Artery forceps.

NURSE: Artery forceps.

DR FRASER: Bring that light farther. down. I need more light. Yes, that's better. Clips.

NURSE: Clips.

DR MORTON *(suddenly)*: Andy!

DR FRASER: Yes, I'm hurrying. I'm going as fast as I can.

DR MORTON *(urgent)*: Andy, stop! Stop, it's no good.

DR FRASER: Wha . . .

DR MORTON: He's gone into shock!!!

DR MORTON: Shock! Every danger signal was present. The pulse rate had fallen suddenly and then it had started to race as the heart fought desperately to send blood through the veins. But then it faltered — and finally stopped! To all intents and purposes the patient was dead! But the fight wasn't ended as far as Andy was concerned. Operating on the lung, he had easy access to the heart. He quickly, calmly, cut deeper. With instinct born of training, the theatre staff prepared for his every move. They knew this was the last desperate resort. This was the cardiac massage!

POLICE OFFICER *(on telephone outside, exasperated)*: Yeah. Yeah, I know the time. No, they're still working on him. No, I can't go in there! Listen, I'm sitting out here with a doctor and even she won't go in. I've got no idea what's happening, Inspector. No idea at all. I don't even know whether he's alive or dead! Yeah. Yeah, well if I can . . .

LOUDSPEAKER *(cuts in):* Early menus and special . . .

POLICE OFFICER *(he hates that voice):* Hold it a second.

LOUDSPEAKER: . . . diets are now ready for collection at the kitchens.

POLICE OFFICER: Okay now! Yeah, it was the loudspeaker system . . . uh huh. Okay. Yeah, I won't move — and I'll let you know as soon as there's some news.

DR SAMUELS: Headquarters getting nervous?

POLICE OFFICER: Jumpy, I guess. What's the time now?

DR SAMUELS: 3.18.

POLICE OFFICER: Seven hours! He's dead. He must be dead.

DR SAMUELS: We'd know immediately if he was.

POLICE OFFICER: That other doctor's here now. Why doesn't he go in and help?

DR SAMUELS: Carlton couldn't help any. Nobody can — except Fraser. *(Dr Fraser comes out of the Operating Theatre)*

DR SAMUELS: Andy . . .

POLICE OFFICER: Dr Fraser, how's . . .

DR FRASER *(desperately tired):* It's all over. It's all finished.

POLICE OFFICER: He's — dead?

DR FRASER: No. Oh, no. We saved him. He's going to live.

DR SAMUELS *(quietly):* Well done, Andy.

NURSE: The patient's ready to go to the ward now, Doctor.

DR FRASER: Thank you. I want a special twenty-four hour watch, Nurse — and quarter-hour pulse-and-respiration chart maintained.

NURSE: Yes, Doctor.

POLICE OFFICER *(apologetically):* I'll go along with him — keep an eye on him. Er — we're very grateful, Doctor. I guess it was — we're very grateful.

DR SAMUELS: Sit down, Andy. Here, cigarette? *(Dr Fraser draws heavily on cigarette — very slow, long puff out)*

DR SAMUELS *(pause):* Bad, huh?

DR FRASER *(speaking as though in a daze):* He went into shock, Edna, and I thought he was gone.

DR SAMUELS: Yeah.

DR FRASER: I never fought so hard for anyone's life before. I read a story about a knife-thrower once. His wife used to work as his living target. One day he made up his mind to kill her during the act. No one could have proved anything against him. One of his knives would just — go astray. An accident. But when he tried to do it — he just couldn't. He tried hard to send a knife into her heart. But he couldn't. His every instinct revolted — and the knife would thud harmlessly near her. You see, he'd trained himself for years to make his knives miss. And when the time came — he just couldn't make them kill her!

DR SAMUELS *(in a calming voice):* Take it easy, Andy.

DR FRASER: Perhaps I wanted the patient to die. I don't know. But I know I couldn't kill him! I knew I couldn't cut too deeply or slip in any way. And then he went into shock — and I gave a cardiac massage. He was as close to death as anyone could be. In actual fact he died on that table! But I brought him back to life! And now I'm tired. I'm desperately tired.

DR MORTON *(warmly):* Congratulations, Andy. That was as fine a piece of work as I've seen.

DR FRASER: Uh huh.

DR SAMUELS *(low):* I think we should give him a shot of something. He's on the verge of cracking.

LOUDSPEAKER: Dr Samuels, please report to the morgue.

DR FRASER *(after pause):* The morgue? Edna, it's for them, isn't it?

DR SAMUELS *(with difficulty):* Their death certificates — I have to make them out.

DR FRASER: May I come?

DR SAMUELS: No, Andy. It's best you don't see. *(Dr Fraser moans. Dr Samuels can hardly get the words out as she excuses herself and leaves.)*

DR FRASER *(to himself):* I saved the life of a murderer — but they didn't give me the chance to help Caroline and the boy.

DR MORTON: Easy, Andy.

DR FRASER *(recovers):* Carlton came?

DR MORTON: Hours ago.

DR FRASER: It'd be all right for me to leave now.

DR MORTON: If you want to.

DR FRASER: It's getting light outside. We must have been in there a long time.

DR MORTON: Yes, we were.

LOUDSPEAKER: Dr Fraser, please call Reception.

DR FRASER: Damn that voice!

DR MORTON *(quietly):* Call Reception, Andy. Here, I'll get them for you. Here you are.

DR FRASER: Fraser here. Yes ... yes ... yes, I'll contact them. *(To Dr Morton)* It's the Harbour — Caroline's parents. They want to know what's — *(his voice breaks)* — holding us up ...

DR MORTON: Come on to the lounge, Andy.

DR FRASER: I have to tell them what happened. *(As he fights for control, a woman hurries up with a young boy at her side)*

MRS PASTELLI: Dr Fraser?

DR FRASER: Yes, I'm Fraser.

MRS PASTELLI *(controlling her emotion):* Doctor, my name is Pastelli. Yvonne Pastelli. I am the wife of the man whose life you just saved.

DR FRASER: Yes ...

MRS PASTELLI: I wanted to thank you — I just wanted to thank you so much.

DR FRASER *(after pause):* Is that your child?

MRS PASTELLI: Yes

DR FRASER: He's — he's a fine-looking fellow.

MRS PASTELLI: Yes, he's a good boy. I'm going to make sure he never gets into the same sort of trouble as his father.

DR FRASER *(after pause):* Yes, do that, Mrs Pastelli. Yes, make sure he doesn't get into the same trouble.

MRS PASTELLI: Thank you again, Doctor. *(Turns to leave)*

DR FRASER: Pastelli. Funny, isn't it? *(Slowly)* I never even knew his name. *(Mrs Pastelli walks away)*

LOUDSPEAKER: Stand by, Emergency Ambulance Crew. Dr Graham, report to Ambulance Bay. Prepare Emergency Operating Theatre. Dr Carlton and Dr Winters, report to the Theatre.

DR MORTON *(after pause):* Andrew Fraser and I walked away from the voice. For us the day's work was over — and for Andrew another life must start. I looked at his face. His eyes reflected the sorrow and loneliness that was now his. But in his hands there rested an abundance of skill. Skill that could even bring a dead man back to life. At that moment, more than ever, I was proud of my friend, and of my profession — I was proud to call myself a doctor.

the characters

We learn a good deal about the characters by what they say and do. What do you learn about each of the following characters from the words below? Write your judgments in your workbook.

Character	Words	Your judgment
Dr Fraser	There's no time . . . the patient's dying . . . We have to operate right away . . . no time to lose . . .	
Police Officer	He mustn't die — he's too important. He can give us enough information to put a dozen of the top boys behind bars.	
Dr Samuels	I think we should give him [Andy] a shot of something. He's on the verge of cracking.	
Mrs Pastelli	Yes, he's a good boy. I'm going to make sure he never gets into the same sort of trouble as his father.	
Dr Morton	I looked at his face. His eyes reflected the sorrow and loneliness that was now his. But in his hands there rested an abundance of skill. Skill that could even bring a dead man back to life.	

an article on page one

Imagine you are a newspaper reporter who has arrived at the hospital where Dr Fraser has just saved the life of Pastelli, the gangster. Interview (in front of the class) the following characters:

● Joe and Harry
● Dr John Morton
● Dr Edna Samuels
● Dr Andrew Fraser
● Police Officer
● Mrs Pastelli

Perhaps various members of the class could take turns at being the reporter. After the interviews have been conducted, the whole class could attempt to write a story about the incident for page one of the newspaper.

emotions, feelings, attitudes

1. What is Dr Samuels's attitude to the loudspeaker?
2. What are Dr Fraser's feelings about going to the Gold Coast?
3. What is Dr Morton's reaction when he is told about the dead-on-arrivals?
4. What is Dr Morton's attitude to the wounded gunman?
5. What are Dr Fraser's feelings about the wounded gunman?
6. What are your feelings while the operation is in progress?
7. How does the police officer react when he learns that Dr Fraser is performing the operation?
8. What comments would you make about Dr Fraser's treatment of Mrs Pastelli?

exercise

Write down the following emotions in your workbook. Next to each one, put a suitable incident from the play.

Emotions	Incident
annoyance	
determination	
love	
sadness	
gratitude	
worry	
happiness	
amazement	

conflict

Conflict in drama often takes place when two or more characters clash with each other because of differences in their ideas, personalities or actions. However, in *The Surgeon's Choice* the action revolves around a different kind of conflict. What is the conflict that is the central issue in *The Surgeon's Choice*? Who or which events caused it? What is the final outcome?

WATER SKIER

Water fans apart and gasps
beneath the skier's blade-swift skill
and even the river's wading reeds
gasp semaphores of praise at all

this rippling youth's display and ease.
Firm and tanned beneath day's curve
of sky the dexterous rider patterns
river-long his rapid love,

alive and flashing in the summer
reach; and all his triumph is
this moment's mastery of flesh.
And here his only conquest lies.

Spelling the symbols of his pride
in water's manuscript, he grooves
a trembling chapter with his skis
which, even as he laughs, dissolves.

Thomas W. Shapcott

Note: semaphores — signals sent by waving flags;
dexterous — skilful;
reach — straight section of a river.

---

how well did you understand the poem?

1. The water skier is so expert that even nature seems to admire his skill. Jot down two lines in the poem that show this.
2. Why do you think the poet has called the water skier "rippling"?
3. Much of the poem expresses admiration for the water skier. See how many phrases you can find that praise him.
4. Shapcott often uses the repetition of certain consonants or sounds to make the picture he is describing seem more vivid. Find some examples of this technique and try to explain how they help the picture to come alive, for example, "the *sk*ier's blade-*sw*ift *sk*ill".
5. Write down some phrases from the poem showing that the water skier enjoys what he is doing.
6. Explain how the water skier has "mastery of flesh".
7. In the last stanza, the water skier is compared with the writer of a book. Jot down the words that suggest this image.
8. The poet suggests in the last stanza that the water skier's achievement is not permanent. Write down the words that the poet uses to suggest this idea.
9. Does this poem appeal to you? Why?
10. What is the poet's purpose in this poem? Is he trying only to describe the water skier or does he have some special message for us?

THE MULLET RUN

All night steady rain, and the wind strong —

Now in the morning, the river orange
with mud, right up Mooney Creek.
Our trawler shifting
the mudbanks under us as we move.
Thousands of mullet trapped
in Dead Horse Bay, and the net's so full now
corklines sink under the weight.
The net-board stained black with night's
            smashed catfish,

and a great ray whipping its tail about below

too many fish for the co-op,
even if half of them rot before we get back,
we'd glut the markets.

I take net-ropes and start dragging.
The fish in the belly kicking
at the mesh, ropes greasy in fine drizzling rain.
And the smell of jewfish
            everywhere.

Robert Adamson

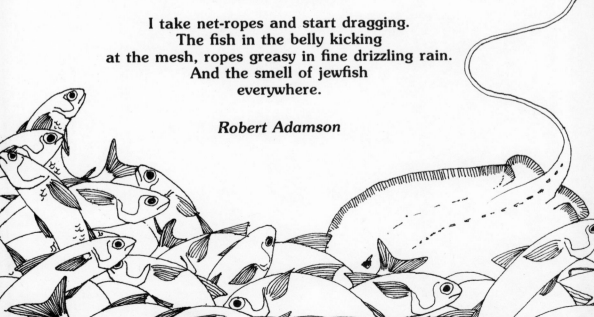

looking at the poem

This seems to be an enjoyable, descriptive poem. The poet is just wrapping words around the experience of one incredible night's fishing. There's a flood, winds, everything to suggest that fishing would be useless but they take an unbelievable haul of trapped mullet, the sort of catch you dream about.

Notice the way the poet savours each sensation, each aspect, each memory. He's written it in the present tense, and it's clear that he really is reliving it! It's happening again for him, right now.

Select from the poem:
1. a sight that remains vivid in the poet's memory of that night;
2. a sound that is re-created in his memory;
3. a sensation of touch that has remained with him;
4. a smell that he recalls.

write-a-memory

Every one of you must have been fishing or hunting at some time or other. Cast back into your memory and try your hand at re-creating the experience in a poem. It might not have been the incredible success that this particular fishing expedition was — it might have been a total failure — yet the memories will be there if you can only tap them. Use the present tense as Robert Adamson does, and try to recapture some of the incidents — the sights, sounds, touches and smells that made up the experience. If you can make it come alive again for yourself, then it should be quite an effective poem for others to read also.

Share your efforts with the class.

The Crabs

Richmond Lattimore

There was a bucket full of them. They spilled,
crawled, climbed, clawed: slowly tossed
and fell: precision made: cold iodine colour of
  their own
world of sand and occasional brown weed,
  round stone
chilled clean in the chopping waters of their
  coast.
One fell out. The marine thing on the grass
tried to trundle off, barbarian and immaculate
  and to be killed
with his kin. We lit water: dumped the living
  mass
in: contemplated tomatoes and corn: and with
  the good cheer of civilised man,
cigarettes, that is, and cold beer, and chatter,
waited out and lived down the ten-foot clatter
of crabs as they died for us inside their boiling
  can.

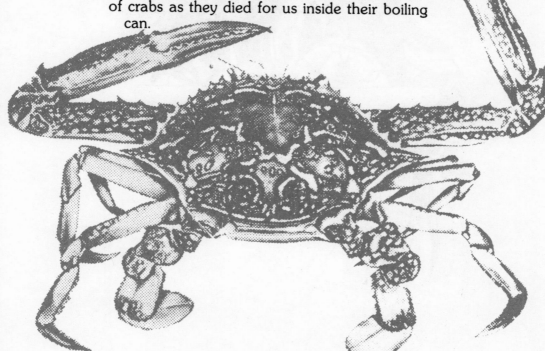

how well did you understand the poem?

1. Why does the poet refer to the crabs as "precision made"?
2. In the words "crawled, climbed, clawed" what is the effect of the repetition of the hard "c", the "l", and the "aw" sounds?
3. What idea does the poet convey to his reader by the words "the marine thing on the grass" and "barbarian"?
4. What does the word "dumped" suggest about the attitude of the people?
5. Comment on the poet's use of the word "civilised".
6. Discuss the effect of rhyming sounds in the last four lines, for example, "man", "chatter", "clatter", "can".
7. What is the poet's attitude to the crabs?
8. What is the poet's attitude to himself ("us") in the poem?
9. Explain what the poet means by "they died for us".
10. What do you think is the poet's message in the poem?

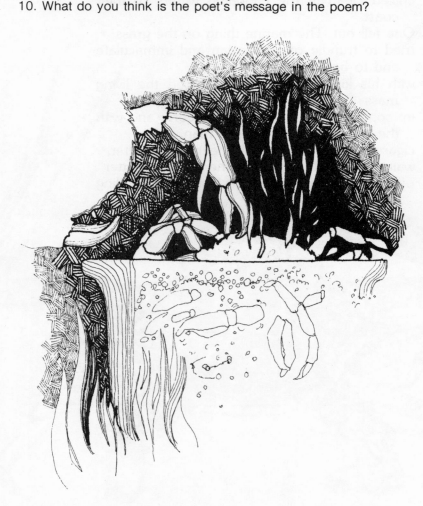

HUNT THE HUNTER

Wallis Peel

The scent of blood could mean the end of both of them . . .

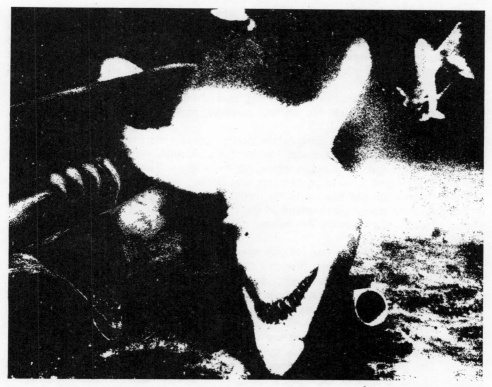

The shark was hungry again. It was always hungry and spent its life continually searching for food. It scavenged remorselessly and ate anything that came its way. Best of all, it liked meat. Good, red meat. Living meat where the blood still pulsated.

Like most of its species it was aggressive without reason. All of its Australian breed were ferocious to the extreme, quite without fear and a terror to all in the sea except the killer whale.

The shark wanted meat — now. It swam around in agitation. Its progress a small circle. Its senses tantalised by the scent. Somewhere, not far away, was meat. Living meat, too!

The current wafted the blood scent nearer and the shark pinpointed the meat's direction. With a powerful thrust of its tail, it reversed its circling and shot away to one side. Small, piggy eyes searched. Keen nostrils dissected the sea and homed the shark on a correct course.

With unerring precision, the shark increased speed, its progress effortless. It cut through the water with dorsal and tail fins beautifully balanced, giving a rapid, streamlined progression.

The swimmer was preoccupied with the matter at hand. He had one spear left for his gun and no fish yet to show for his sport. He was so totally occupied with hunting that he had not felt the tear in his skin where the coral had snagged his leg. The pain was non-existent. The skin-cut small. The blood loss minute but enough to reach the shark's uncanny nostrils and trigger off a hunt.

The hunter was about to turn into the hunted. The vicious shark with its puny brain against the intelligent man with his weak body.

The shark decreased speed and slowed into a cruising circle while it considered the situation. The blood-scent tantalised its ravenous appetite but, as yet, the shark was not angry enough to attack without surveying the scene. It wanted to weigh up the opposition. Its temper not quite demoniacal. Once that stage had been reached the opposition's strength was of no consequence. Only the attack and feast would matter.

The swimmer saw a fat fish move nearby and carefully lined up his gun. One finger took up the trigger's slack. He sighted carefully, making allowance for the water's deflection.

He was on the verge of firing when death rippled cold fingers along the length of his spine. In the warm, tropical sea his body shivered with a chill deep enough to penetrate his guts. His finger came off the trigger. The fish swam lazily away. The shark appeared in view on its narrowing circle.

The swimmer felt gall rise up in his throat. He almost gagged on his mouthpiece as his grey eyes stared mesmerised at the sheer size of the whaler shark. The most wicked of all the sharks in the Australian coastal waters and this was the Grand-daddy of them all!

What should he do? He had his one spear left and a mere fifteen minutes oxygen in his cylinders. This gave him precious little margin for safety.

He was only at a depth of twenty feet and the shoreline was not much farther away than that, but the greatest danger would be in the ascent. Two retreating human feet would goad any shark into a frenzied attack let alone a whaler which usually required little excuse to kill a man.

The shark's circle decreased as the thin vapour-trail of blood tickled the beast's ever shrunken stomach. The beady eyes decided this meat would be good and easy to take. The sweet allure of the blood was triggering the temper fuse in the shark's small brain into a state of explosive ferocity. Here was the wanted meat! Good, living meat! Now to take it!

The dorsal fin altered its angle a fraction. The shark's body changed course. The great rudder of a tail thrashed left and then right sending the huge torpedo-shaped body forward in the first probing attack.

The swimmer circled on his axis. Spear gun at the ready. His heartbeats drummed in his ears. They reached such a pitch that it required rigid self-discipline to concentrate and breathe in the steady rhythm necessary to gain the best from his oxygen cylinders. He must not panic! It would be fatal to swim wildly or breathe too quickly — but the time! Those precious minutes ticking away. The shore was so near — and yet so far!

The shark churned straight at the swimmer. Three feet away it rolled on its back. Exposing a pale-coloured belly. Gills, slit, open jaws and rows of razor-sharp retracting teeth. Terrible teeth which, once they had gripped anything, could not let go without taking flesh with them.

The swimmer had anticipated the shark's classical attack. At the last second he thrust back with his flippered feet and moved out of range. He took care to keep the spear gun before his body. His fingers itched to fire. His mind ordered restraint. This one shot must be perfect. The shark had a tough skin. There would be no second chance.

Baulked by the swimmer's action the shark churned past, turned, and charged again. The great jaws opened, slashing at an arm. The spear gun jabbed hard in the shark's eye. The sudden pain blunted the whaler's venom temporarily.

The swimmer anxiously looked at his watch. Seven minutes left! He must surface soon! He scanned the sea, peering intently through his goggles and thought he saw other shapes appearing in the distance.

He made up his mind. It was now or never! He lined up his spear gun, finger again on the trigger. The next charge would be the last — for himself or the shark.

The shark broke from its circle and headed into the attack again. Equally determined to end this before other predators appeared and expected part of the meal.

The swimmer kept himself as still as possible. Flippered feet moved gently, maintaining an upright stance in the water. The shark was a terrifying sight as it headed as straight as an arrow but the swimmer was suddenly unafraid now. The time for that was past.

The spear gun was lifted an inch. A sight was taken on the head. As seconds ticked by the swimmer felt cool anger sweep through him. The shark bellied over again for its usual attack. This was it!

With steady hands the swimmer pressed the trigger. The spear shot free and plunged in the shark's exposed under-belly. It disappeared half way up its length.

The shark jerked sideways, rolling over wildly, trying to snap at the thing lodged in its vitals. The water heaved and boiled as the huge tail thrashed in wild contortions.

The swimmer fled. He thrust upwards. A snap glance at his watch had shown just two minutes air left. He discarded his gun. Peered around as arms and legs pushed him to the surface. There were other forms appearing. Ugly, dark torpedoes who were moving in. Converging on a point where the water was stained and boiled in a cauldron.

His head broke surface and the swimmer flung himself into the fast and powerful Australian trudgeon crawl. The shore! Those rocks. Ten feet to go! Was anything coming after his feet? He spat out his useless mouthpiece and gasped wildly. His lungs straining under the cruel effort required for such a pace.

One sun-tanned hand grasped a rock. The other pulled. Within four seconds he was out of the water and safe on the rock of the shoreline. He collapsed. His body shuddered from goggled eyes to rubber-shod feet.

Slowly he sat up and slipped the useless oxygen cylinders from his brown back. He rubbed his neck and only then noticed the cut on his leg. A wry grimace crossed his face as understanding dawned. It had been such a near thing.

Twenty feet away and ten feet below the surface the water spewed in a mixture of white, blue and red. Objects churned frantically until the sea appeared to be having a paroxysm.

The swimmer stood and watched. The pack of tiger sharks were as relentless as the whaler had been. Blood flowed! Meat was for the taking! They converged upon the dying whaler and tore him to shreds.

Once again the hunter had become the hunted.

how well did you understand the story?

1. How does the opening paragraph effectively arouse your interest and point out the elements that are to be stressed in the story?
2. How does the author give the impression that the shark is designed for its environment?
3. Why did the swimmer consider that the ascent to the surface would be so dangerous for him?
4. In dealing with the shark, what special disadvantages did the swimmer have to contend with?
5. What effect did the appearance of the shark have on the swimmer?
6. The author maintains that the shark's brain was "puny". What evidence can you find in the story to support this view?
7. Why does the author refer to the shark's nostrils as "uncanny"?
8. Explain why it would have been fatal for the swimmer "to swim wildly or to breathe quickly"?
9. What finally prompted the swimmer to shoot the shark?
10. Explain the significance of the final statement, "Once again the hunter had become the hunted."

word pictures

Write down the missing words in your workbook. The first letter has been provided to help you.
1. The shark's tail is likened to a boat's r−−−−−.
2. The sharpness of its teeth is compared to that of a r−−−−.
3. The eyes of the shark are described as b−−−− or p−−−−.
4. The shape of the shark is likened to that of a t−−−−−−.

movement and action words

1. Write down a list of words that describe the movements and actions of the shark in the water. Some words with missing letters have been given to start you off, but there are others you can find yourselves.
    (a) cr−−s−−g (b) th−−sh−− (c) ch−−n−− (d) sla−−ing (e) be−−ied
    (f) j−−ked (g) he−−ed
2. Now write down a list of words that describe the movements and actions of the swimmer in and out of the water.
    (a) shi−−red (b) cir−−ed (c) thr−−− (d) p−−ring (e) sc−−−−ed
    (f) ga−−ed (g) sh−dd−−ed (h) c−ll−−sed

sentence beginnings

Complete the following sentences in your own words.
1. "The shark decreased speed and slowed into a cruising circle while it considered the situation."
   Decreasing speed and slowing into a cruising circle ....
2. "The current wafted the blood scent nearer and the shark pinpointed the meat's direction."
   As the current wafted ....
3. "With a powerful thrust of its tail, it reversed its circling and shot away to one side."
   Powerfully ....
4. "The blood-scent tantalised its ravenous appetite but, as yet, the shark was not angry enough to attack without surveying the scene."
   Even though the blood-scent...
5. "The shark was a terrifying sight as it headed as straight as an arrow but the swimmer was suddenly unafraid now."
   The swimmer was suddenly unafraid now of ....
6. "Baulked by the swimmer's action the shark churned past, turned, and charged again."
   Although the swimmer's action baulked the shark...
7. "He had his one spear left and a mere fifteen minutes oxygen in his cylinders. This gave him precious little margin for safety."
   Since he had only his one spear left...
8. "The swimmer kept himself as still as possible. Flippered feet moved gently, maintaining an upright stance in the water."
   With his flippered feet...

feelings and physical attributes

Write down a sentence or two from the story to illustrate the attributes listed in the left-hand column of the table. One example has been done to help you, but you will find some others as well.

THE SHARK

Attribute	Answer
hunger	It scavenged remorselessly and ate anything that came its way.
speed	
size	
sense of smell	

THE SWIMMER

Attribute	Answer
calmness and control	
fear	
determination	
intelligence	
anticipation	

word meanings

The words in the left-hand column below have been taken from the story. Write them down and then match them with the correct meaning in the right-hand column.

converged	without making a mistake
wafted	hindered
unerring	bile
baulked	twisted
predator	in a kind of trance
gall	tormented
wry	came together
mesmerised	conveyed
tantalised	a fit
paroxysm	one who preys on others

adjectives and adverbs

Write down the following sentences. Then insert in the blank spaces the correct adverb or adjective from the rectangle.

> dying, temporarily, continually, exposed,
> anxiously, wildly, beady, useless

1. The swimmer .... looked at his watch.
2. They converged upon the .... whaler and tore him to shreds.
3. Slowly he sat up and slipped the .... oxygen cylinders from his brown back.
4. The spear shot free and plunged in the shark's .... under-belly.
5. The sudden pain blunted the whaler's venom ....
6. The shark jerked sideways, rolling over ...., trying to snap at the thing lodged in its vitals.
7. It was always hungry and spent its life .... searching for food.
8. The .... eyes decided this meat would be good and easy to take.

"CALL MY BLUFF"

ABC radio listeners may occasionally have heard the humorous pro-gramme *Call My Bluff*. In this half-hour panel game, teams of three members are given a fairly obscure word taken from the dictionary. Two team members each make up a false definition for the word and one team member gives the correct definition. The opposing team has to identify the correct definition before its members take their turn at offering three definitions for their word. Teams win a point either by successfully identifying the correct definition, or by fooling the oppo-sing team into picking a false definition instead of the correct one.

You can modify *Call My Bluff* to suit your classroom, and have a lot of fun at the same time. Here's the procedure.

teacher

1. Make a selection of suitable words from the *Shorter Oxford English Dictionary*. (Use the list below as a guide.) Write each word on a separate piece of paper.

claquer	mondaine	mongcorn
derf	suttle	light-bob
embay	tweeny	imbroglio
gyromancy	zho	gerah
jacare	snood	footrill
infra dig.	prog	éclat
spoony	phiz	applot
hobbledehoy	necromancy	deave
nog	nabs	tipper

2. Divide the class into groups of three.
3. Give each group a slip of paper with their word on it.

students

1. Look up the correct meaning of your word.
2. Assign one group member to prepare an explanation of the meaning of the word, using the correct definition.
3. Assign the other two group members to each prepare a "bluff" definition for the word. This sort of planning can be done cooperatively to aid the flow of ideas. The important thing is to be creative with the made-up definitions, but not to go overboard, otherwise the class members will easily identify them as bluffs.

When preparations are complete, the teacher writes the word on the blackboard. One at a time, the three team members offer their definitions as convincingly as possible. Finally, the class members take a vote to see if they can pick out the correct definition from the bluffs.

example

See if you can pick the correct definition. The word is "fairing".

First group member

Well, believe it or not, a "fairing" is simply a place where you pick a lot of mushrooms. This particular word was originally formed by the compounding of two words, "fairy" and "ring". In the mythology of fairies it was believed that, when the moon was at its highest, fairies would dance in a ring in certain spots throughout the countryside. These "fairy rings" could later be identified by the large numbers of mushrooms growing there. The word "fairing" eventually came to be used to describe these places instead of "fairy ring".

Second group member

I certainly hope you won't be fooled by that particular definition. Here's the real one. If you want to get in sweet with your girlfriend or boyfriend, a fairing is the thing to get. It's simply a gift — a present that's intended as a compliment for someone. It can be anything at all, from a bunch of pansies to a pendant — but not a set of bagpipes! A "fairing" is a complimentary gift, and the word comes from the word "fair", because it was at fairs that most gifts were bought during the sixteenth century.

Third group member

Very impressive bluffs, but I certainly hope you don't believe a word of them. The truth is that a "fairing" would probably be considered very interesting today, but a century ago it would have been put to death soon after it was born. They were hard times! The word is a colloquial expression, used in the Midlands in England in earlier years to describe a rare albino sheepdog, a genetic throwback with white hair all over, very pink skin and poor vision. Because they were delicate and useless as sheepdogs, "fairings" were usually killed pretty young. The name "fairing" was coined because of their fair colour.

Well, how did you go? Did you separate the true meaning of "fairing" from the bluffs? If you chose the second definition you were right! You can check it in this extract from a dictionary.

Now try your own classroom game of *Call My Bluff.*

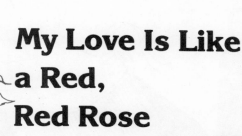

My Love Is Like a Red, Red Rose

Probably no half-hour team-comedy show on radio is better known than the BBC's My Word, starring Frank Muir and Denis Norden. The highlight of the show is the "story time", when these two compete with each other in telling an outlandish story they have concocted, leading up to a quotation they have been assigned. The stories always end in some quite outrageous pun.

Here is an example — a story by Frank Muir leading up to the quotation "My love is like a red, red rose".

Are you there Jimmy Young? You of the cheerful chatter and the gramophone records and the recipe of the day? I have been a staunch listener this many a year, Jimmy Young, and I have just tried out one of your recipes so I thought perhaps you might like to know how it turned out.

I did everything exactly as you said, picking up pad and pencil exactly when you told me — I had to steer with my teeth — and I obeyed the recipe to the letter.

You do an awful lot of recipes, usually for strange delights like Savoury Baked-bean Meringues or Pilchard Tartlets, so you probably don't remember mine offhand — but it was for a Farmyard Cottage Loaf. Good, old-fashioned home-made bread.

You began by asking me to grab hold of two pounds of "plain" flour. You kept repeating that it must be "plain" flour but you didn't spell the word "plain". Well, Jim, I live quite near the airport so I dropped in on the way home. Do you know something? They don't bake on planes. Those ice-cold sandwiches they hand round are not made on board; the bread is baked on the ground. So I bought some flour which the grocer said was "self-raising"; it seemed the next best thing.

Then you said "take a pint of water". Bit of a problem there because the bathroom scales only work in stones and pounds. But I found a quart bottle, took this round to the pub and asked the barman to put a pint of draught in it. Once home I got a milk bottle of water and measured how much water I had to add to the beer to fill the bottle. I then emptied the bottle and poured in this same, measured, amount of water. The empty space in the bottle now represented exactly one pint. All I had to do then was fill the bottle and measure how much water it took and I had my pint. As a point of interest, Jim, a pint is roughly the amount contained in a small milk bottle.

Next you said salt — a pinch. No problem; the kitchen window next door was open.

Then came yeast — a lump the size of a walnut — which you said could be obtained from any Baker. I tooled straight round to my nearest Baker, Ernie Baker who mends bicycles, but he'd never heard of the stuff. Luckily I managed to pick up a knob from the cakeshop. It's a sort of yellow dough, Jim, and it stinks.

You then told me to put the flour, yeast, salt and water into a bowl, which I did. You then said that for twenty minutes it had to be kneaded. That was a tricky business, Jim, and I have a couple of hints which you might give your listeners if you repeat this recipe some time in the future. When kneading it is advisable to roll the trousers up first. If you forget to do this and you can't get the dough off with hot water or petrol quite a good tip is to burn the trousers. I found the most practical way of kneading was to divide the dough into two large bowls, put these on the floor and use one knee to each bowl, hanging on the edge of the kitchen table for balance. Another advantage to this method is that if, as happened to me, the vicar calls in the middle of the process, you can make your way slowly to the front door, Toulouse-Lautrec style, without interrupting the process.

Your next instruction, Jim, was to find a warm place, about 80 degrees Fahrenheit, and put the bowl in to prove it. I found a nice warm spot under the dog and put the bowl in but it didn't prove anything to me. Could have been 20 degrees or 100 degrees, Jim. So I took the bowl out again.

Next I had to grease my baking tin. Now that was something I did know a little about. Out to the garage for the grease-gun. Pump-pump. Done.

Finally you told me to put the dough into the greased tin, press it down well, and bake it in a low oven for four hours. Oh, Jim, that was a tricky one to be faced with right at the end of the recipe. You see, our stove is a pretty old one and it is up on cast-iron legs; the oven is at least eight inches off the ground. But — you wanted a low oven so a low oven you had to have. It took me about twenty minutes to hacksaw off each leg; but I managed it, and in went my bread.

I will be frank with you, Jim, and confess that when I took my loaf out four hours later I was disappointed. It did not even look like a loaf. It was sort of black and blistery and it sat very low in the tin. Nor did it smell like a loaf. It smelt like an Italian garage on a hot day. And I couldn't get it out of the tin. I remember you saying to pass a knife round the edge and shake it out but the knife wouldn't go in. Eventually I drilled a hole in the crust of the loaf, inserted the end of a crowbar and, using the edge of the tin as a fulcrum, threw all my weight on the other end with the object of prising the loaf out. It sort of worked. There was a splintering noise, the crust gave way and I was flat on my back. There was no sign of the interior of the loaf.

I found the interior of the loaf the following morning. On the ceiling. A great lump of semi-cooked, rancid dough had hit the ceiling, started to droop, and then congealed into a cross between a gargoyle and one of those conical plaster ceiling-fittings which electric lights used to hang from.

Far be it from me to criticise, Jim, but are you sure that your recipes aren't a wee bit complicated? I happen to be a handy, practical sort of chap, but many of your listeners are women, Jim, and how some of them would have coped...

Well, you said at the end of the recipe that you would like to hear how our bread has turned out so I am only too happy to oblige:

My loaf is like a weird, weird rose.

Frank Muir

creative writing

Look at the following ten quotations. You can probably add to them by choosing strange, interesting or well-known quotations from the works of poets, playwrights and authors with which you are familiar. Let each student choose a quotation and then set about writing a story in the *My Word* style leading up to the quotation. It won't matter if more than one student works on the same quotation.

When everyone has finished the writing task, let students read their efforts to the class and the class can then decide which is the best *My Word* story.

suggested quotations

"Man is born unto trouble as the sparks fly upwards" — the Bible
"I met a man with funny feet" — C. J. Dennis

"If music be the food of love, play on" — William Shakespeare
"These yellow cowslip cheeks are gone" — William Shakespeare
"Camillo has betray'd me" — William Shakespeare
"Poor Tom's a-cold" — William Shakespeare
"The colt from Old Regret had got away" — A. B. Paterson
"I hail the superman" — W. B. Yeats
"What will the spider do . . .?" — T. S. Eliot
"O for rhubarb to purge this choler!" — John Webster

We often hear of people having such different points of view that they are cut off from one another. This poem offers an example of lack of communication.

GUTTER PRESS

News Editor: Peer Confesses,
Bishop Undresses,
Torso Wrapped in Rug,
Girl Guide Throttled,
Baronet Bottled,
J.P. Goes to Jug.

But yesterday's story's
Old and hoary.
Never mind who got hurt.
No use grieving,
Let's get weaving.
What's the latest dirt?

Diplomat Spotted,
Scout Garrotted,
Thigh Discovered in Bog,
Wrecks Off Barmouth,
Sex In Yarmouth,
Woman In Love With Dog,
Eminent Hostess Shoots Her Guests,
Harrogate Lovebird Builds Two Nests.

Cameraman: *Builds two nests?*
Shall I get a picture of the lovebird singing?
Shall I get a picture of her pretty little eggs?
Shall I get a picture of her babies?

News Editor: No!
Go and get a picture of her legs.

Beast Slays Beauty,
Priest Flays Cutie,
Cupboard Shows Tell-Tale Stain,
Mate Drugs Purser,
Dean Hugs Bursar,
Mayor Binds Wife With Chain,
Elderly Monkey Marries For Money,
Jilted Junky Says "I Want My Honey".

Cameraman: *"Want my honey?"*
Shall I get a picture of the pollen flying?
Shall I get a picture of the golden dust?
Shall I get a picture of a queen bee?

News Editor: **No!**
Go and get a picture of her bust.

Judge Gets Frisky,
Nun Drinks Whisky,
Baby Found Burnt in Cot,
Show Girl Beaten,
Duke Leaves Eton —

Cameraman: *Newspaper Man Gets Shot!*
May all things clean
And fresh and green
Have mercy upon your soul,
Consider yourself paid
By the hole my bullet made —

News Editor (*dying*): **Come and get a picture of the hole.**

                              Paul Dehn

questions

1. Suddenly, at one point in the poem, the Cameraman switches over to the News Editor's staccato (sharp, abrupt) style. Quote the line where this occurs. Why does the Cameraman do this?
2. What are the News Editor's hard-hitting lines supposed to remind you of?
3. Quote a line that reveals the News Editor as a gutter-press man to the end.
4. Why is the poem called *Gutter Press*?

debate topic

Argue for and against the existence of a gutter press in a democracy.

press on with your own "gutter press"

For you

Devise gutter-press headlines to be spoken by the News Editor, for example, "Pop Star Wrinkled". Also, pay attention to the two kinds of rhyme schemes used in the poem for the News Editor.

```
1. . . . a        2. . . . a
   . . . a           . . . a
   . . . b           . . . b
   . . . c           . . . c
   . . . c           . . . c
   . . . b           . . . b
                     . . . d
                     . . . d
```

For your neighbour

Write lines for the Cameraman, seizing on the last words of the last line spoken by the News Editor. Use a different style of lettering, for example, *italic* (slanting type), as is done in the poem. Write four lines for him, then switch back to the News Editor for a crushing reply.

For both of you

When you have finished, you and your neighbour should read your gutter-press effort to the rest of the class with appropriate gestures. For example, use hand movements to fill out the News Editor's headlines (perhaps abrupt, violent gestures) with gentle and artistic gestures for the Cameraman.

The Possum

The possum (as you know)
has a peculiar habit
of using his tail
to toss him-
self (with much
clapping of leaves)
from branch
to branch.
Like the metaphorical man-on-the-trapeze,
with the greatest of greatest of ease,
is the possum.

People (on the other hand)
live in hutches
like the eunuch rabbits
and, losing
the use of their tails,
never know, never
know the applauding
leaves, the breathless
agitation of the branches.
Like a circus of performing fleas,
with mechanic unthinking ease
people live in their houses,
and imagine they're living.

Ray Mathew

how well did you understand the poem?

1. What words does the poet use to suggest the freedom of the possum?
2. The title of the poem is *The Possum,* but the poet does more than merely describe the possum's activities. What else has the poet communicated to the reader?
3. The poet has used three similes in the poem:
    "Like the metaphorical man-on-the-trapeze,
        with the greatest of ease",
    "like the eunuch rabbits" and
    "Like a circus of performing fleas".
    (a) Why does he compare the possum with the man on the flying trapeze?
    (b) The word "eunuch" tends to suggest "not fertile", yet rabbits are famous for their capacity to reproduce. Why does the poet compare people with "eunuch rabbits"?
    (c) Why does the poet liken people to "a circus of performing fleas"?
4. When an object takes on human qualities, we have what is known as "personification"; for example, "Fire walked across the hill." Find at least one example of personification in *The Possum.*
5. What point is the poet trying to make when he talks of people living in "hutches"?
6. What point is the poet making when he talks of people "losing their tails"?
7. What criticism is the poet making about people when he uses the words "with mechanic unthinking ease"?
8. Animals have often been used by writers in poetry and novels to teach people a lesson about life. Explain how the poet has used the possum to try to teach us the error of our ways.

"Why did they knock down the trees, Daddy?"

It's a question of standards, boy; standards of living.
It's cars, you see, that give us a high level of living —
help, so to speak, to set the thing in motion —
and if they also give us a high level of dying
that's incidental, a fringe benefit, a lottery
likely to hand out unexpected promotion.

Without cars, let's face it, a nation is under-developed,
And these days it's bad to be under-developed in anything at all —
Bust, thighs, muscles, sex or ego,
it's a competitive world, son.

The trees? Oh, well they have to go
on the advice of Big Brother
so that the cars can have a better chance
of hitting one another.

Colin Thiele

analysis

1. "It's a question of standards" might be described as a kind of adult-world cliché (fairly meaningless words strung together) to answer (or avoid *really* answering) questions put by a child. Select three other phrases from the poem that you could call adult-world clichés.
2. What is a "fringe benefit"? Explain how the "high level of dying" can be seen as a "fringe benefit".
3. In your own words describe what is meant by the phrase "it's a competitive world, son".
4. What does the speaker in this poem mean by "on the advice of Big Brother"? Who is "Big Brother"? Why are capital letters used?
5. What is the last stanza meant to achieve in this poem? What does it tell you about the speaker?
6. In your opinion, is this poem a success or a failure? Try to explain your feelings.

creative writing

1. Try your hand at writing your own poem to answer the question "Why did they knock down the trees, Daddy?" It could take similar lines to Colin Thiele's poem, or you could make it quite different.

OR

2. Imagine that you are the child in this poem. You have asked your father the question "Why did they knock down the trees, Daddy?" and have received this poem as an answer. Try your hand at shaping your thoughts now into a brief poem — one that expresses some of your feelings and thoughts as a result of what your father has just said.

Don't forget to share your efforts with the class.

The Man Who Sold Rope to the Gnoles

Idris Seabright

The gnoles had a bad reputation, and Mortensen was quite aware of this. But he reasoned, correctly enough, that cordage must be something for which the gnoles had a long unsatisfied want, and he saw no reason why he should not be the one to sell it to them. What a triumph such a sale would be! The district sales manager might single out Mortensen for special mention at the annual sales-force dinner. It would help his sales quota enormously. And, after all, it was none of his business what the gnoles used cordage for.

Mortensen decided to call on the gnoles on Thursday morning. On Wednesday night he went through his *Manual of Modern Salesmanship,* underscoring things.

"The mental states through which the mind passes in making a purchase," he read, "have been catalogued as: (1) arousal of interest, (2) increase of knowledge, (3) adjustment to needs ..." There were seven mental states listed, and Mortensen under-scored all of them. Then he went back and double-scored No. 1, arousal of interest, No. 4, appreciation of suitability, and No. 7, decision to purchase. He turned the page.

"Two qualities are of exceptional importance to a salesman," he read. "They are adaptability and knowledge of merchandise." Mortensen underlined the qualities. "Other highly desirable attributes are physical fitness, a high ethical standard, charm of manner, a dogged persistence and unfailing courtesy." Mortensen underlined these too. But he read on to the end of the paragraph without underscoring anything more, and it may be that his failure to put "tact and keen power of observation" on a footing with the other attributes of a salesman was responsible for what happened to him.

The gnoles live on the very edge of Terra Cognita, on the far side of a wood which all authorities unite in describing as dubious. Their house is narrow and high, in architecture a blend of Victorian Gothic and Swiss chalet. Though the house needs paint, it is kept in good repair. Thither on Thursday morning, sample case in hand, Mortensen took his way.

No path leads to the house of the gnoles, and it is always dark in that dubious wood. But Mortensen, remembering what he had learned at his mother's knee concerning the odour of gnoles, found the house quite easily. For a moment he stood hesitating before it. His lips moved as he repeated, "Good morning, I have come to supply your cordage requirements," to himself. The words were the beginning of his sales talk. Then he went up and rapped on the door.

The gnoles were watching him through holes they had bored in the trunks of trees; it is an artful custom of theirs to which the prime authority on gnoles attests. Mortensen's knock almost threw them into confusion, it was so long since anyone had knocked at their door. Then the senior gnole, the one who never leaves the house, went flitting up from the cellars and opened it.

The senior gnole is a little like a Jerusalem artichoke made of India rubber, and he has small red eyes which are faceted in the same way that gemstones are. Mortensen had been expecting something unusual, and when the gnole opened the door he bowed politely, took off his hat and smiled. He had got past the sentence about cordage requirements and into an enumeration of the different types of cordage his firm manufactured when the gnole, by turning his head to the side, showed him that he had no ears. Nor was there anything on his head which could take their place in the conduction of sound. Then the gnole opened his little fanged mouth and let Mortensen look at his narrow, ribbony tongue. As a tongue it was no more fit for human speech than was a serpent's. Judging from his appearance, the gnole could not safely be assigned to any of the four physio-characterological types mentioned in the *Manual*; and for the first time Mortensen felt a definite qualm.

Nonetheless, he followed the gnole unhesitatingly when the creature motioned him within. Adaptability, he told himself, adaptability must be his watchword. Enough adaptability, and his knees might even lose their tendency to shakiness.

It was the parlour the gnole led him to. Mortensen's eyes widened as he looked around it. There were whatnots in the corners, and cabinets of curiosities, and on the fretwork table an album with gilded hasps; who knows whose pictures were in it? All around the walls in brackets, where in lesser houses the people display ornamental plates, were emeralds as big as your head. The gnoles set great store by their emeralds. All the light in the dim room came from them.

Mortensen went through the phrases of his sales talk mentally. It distressed him that that was the only way he could go through them. Still, adaptability! The gnole's interest was already aroused, or he would never have asked Mortensen into the parlour; and as soon as the gnole saw the various cordages the sample case contained he would no doubt proceed of his own accord through "appreciation of suitability" to "desire to possess".

Mortensen sat down in the chair the gnole indicated and opened his sample case. He got out henequen cable-laid rope, an assortment of ply and yarn goods, and some superlative slender abaca fibre rope. He even showed the gnole a few soft yarns and twines made of cotton and jute.

On the back of an envelope he wrote prices for hanks and cheeses of the twines, and for fifty and hundred-foot lengths of the ropes. Laboriously he added details about the strength, durability, and resistance to climatic conditions of each sort of cord. The senior gnole watched him intently, putting his little feet on the top rung of his chair and poking at the facets of his left eye now and then with a tentacle. In the cellars from time to time someone would scream.

Mortensen began to demonstrate his wares. He showed the gnole the slip and resilience of one rope, the tenacity and stubborn strength of another. He cut a tarred hemp rope in two and laid a five-foot piece on the parlour floor to show the gnole how absolutely "neutral" it was, with no tendency to untwist of its own accord. He even showed the gnole how nicely some of the cotton twines made up in square knotwork.

They settled at last on two ropes of abaca fibre, $\frac{3}{16}$ and $\frac{5}{8}$ inch in diameter. The gnole wanted an enormous quantity. Mortensen's comment on those ropes, "unlimited strength and durability", seemed to have attracted him.

Soberly Mortensen wrote the particulars down in his order book, but ambition was setting his brain on fire. The gnoles, it seemed, would be regular customers; and after the gnoles, why should he not try the Gibbelins? They too must have a need for rope.

Mortensen closed his order book. On the back of the same envelope he wrote, for the gnole to see, that delivery would be made within ten days. Terms were thirty per cent with order, balance upon receipt of goods.

The senior gnole hesitated. Shyly he looked at Mortensen with his little red eyes. Then he got down the smallest of the emeralds from the wall and handed it to him.

The sales representative stood weighing it in his hands. It was the smallest of the gnoles' emeralds, but it was as clear as water, as green as grass. In the outside world it would have ransomed a Rockefeller or a whole family of Guggenheims; a legitimate profit from a transaction was one thing, but this was another; "a high ethical standard" — any kind of ethical standard — would forbid Mortensen to keep it. He weighed it a moment longer. Then with a deep, deep sigh he gave the emerald back.

He cast a glance around the room to see if he could find something which would be more negotiable. And in an evil moment he fixed on the senior gnole's auxiliary eyes.

The senior gnole keeps his extra pair of optics on the third shelf of the curiosity cabinet with the glass doors. They look like fine dark emeralds about the size of the end of your thumb. And if the gnoles in general set store by their gems, it is nothing at all compared to the senior gnole's emotions about his extra eyes. The concern good Christian folk should feel for their soul's welfare is a shadow, a figment, a nothing, compared to what the thoroughly heathen gnole feels for those eyes. He would rather, I think, choose to be a mere miserable human being than that some vandal should lay hands upon them.

If Mortensen had not been elated by his success to the point of anaesthesia, he would have seen the gnole stiffen, he would have heard him hiss, when he went over to the cabinet. All innocent, Mortensen opened the glass door, took the twin eyes out, and juggled them sacrilegiously in his hand; the gnole could feel them clink. Smiling to evince the charm of manner advised in the *Manual*, and raising his brows as one who says, "Thank you, these will do nicely," Mortensen dropped the eyes into his pocket.

The gnole growled.

The growl awoke Mortensen from his trance of euphoria. It was a growl whose meaning no one could mistake. This was clearly no time to be doggedly persistent. Mortensen made a break for the door.

The senior gnole was there before him, his network of tentacles outstreched. He caught Mortensen in them easily and wound them, flat as bandages, around his ankles and his hands. The best abaca fibre is no stronger than those tentacles; though the gnoles would find rope a convenience, they get along very well without it. Would you, dear reader, go naked if zippers should cease to be made? Growling indignantly, the gnole fished his ravished eyes from Mortensen's pockets, and then carried him down to the cellar to the fattening pens.

But great are the virtues of legitimate commerce. Though they fattened Mortensen sedulously, and, later, roasted and sauced him and ate him with real appetite, the gnoles slaughtered him in quite a humane manner and never once thought of torturing him. That is unusual, for gnoles. And they ornamented the plank on which they served him with a beautiful border of fancy knotwork made of cotton cord from his own sample case.

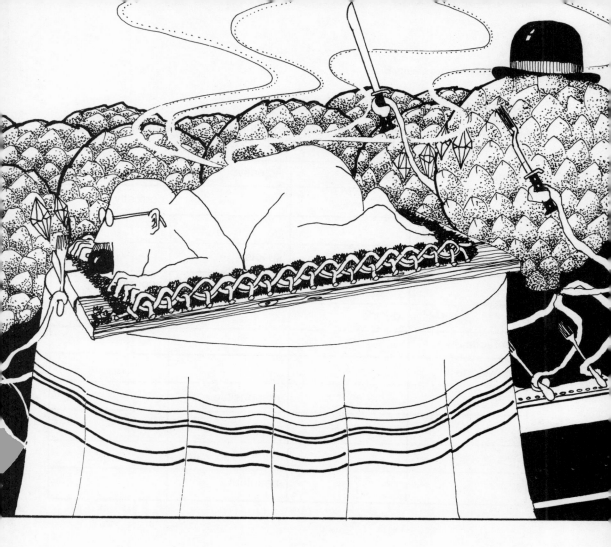

how well did you understand the story?

1. Why did Mortensen find it difficult to communicate with the senior gnole?
2. What evidence can you find in the story to show that Mortensen lacked "tact"?
3. How do you know that Mortensen did not have keen powers of observation?
4. What was it about the chief gnole's appearance that prevented him from being assigned by Mortensen to any of the four types of character mentioned in the manual?
5. Why didn't Mortensen accept the smallest of the emeralds from the gnole?
6. How is Mortensen led to his doom by following the instructions of the manual?
7. Do you think Mortensen's horrible fate was justified? Why?
8. What comments would you make about the character of the gnoles?
9. Can you find evidence in the story to suggest that the writer is anti-salesmen?
10. Why didn't the gnoles torture Mortensen?

fill in the table

All the words in the following table are from the story. Draw up a similar table in your workbook and then fill in the blanks.

Noun	Verb	Adjective	Adverb
			correctly
triumph			
		special	
	—		enormously
	decide		
appreciation			
knowledge			
		responsible	
			easily
		different	
		beautiful	

sentence structures

There are many ways of writing sentences. Take each of the sentences below and see whether you can rewrite them with the new beginnings given.
1. "Mortensen sat down in the chair the gnole indicated and opened his sample case."
   Mortensen, having ....
2. "The gnole's interest was already aroused, or he would never have asked Mortensen into the parlour."
   Mortensen believed that he had been asked into the parlour.........................
3. "Then the gnole opened his little fanged mouth and let Mortensen look at his narrow, ribbony tongue."
   Having opened his little fanged mouth ....
4. "Nor was there anything on his head which could take their place in the conduction of sound."
   On his head there was ....
5. "The gnoles were watching him through holes they had bored in the trunks of trees."
   He was being watched ....

6. "'Other highly desirable attributes are physical fitness, a high ethical standard, charm of manner, a dogged persistence and unfailing courtesy.'"
"Physical fitness, ... "
7. "The gnoles had a bad reputation, and Mortensen was quite aware of this."
Mortensen was quite aware ....
8. "As a tongue it was no more fit for human speech than was a serpent's."
The tongue was as fit for ....

forming nouns

All these words are taken from the story. Turn them into nouns; for example, "suitable" becomes "suitability".

suitable, satisfy, busy, manage, mental, fit, persist, courteous, fail, observe, require, confuse, assign, adapt, curious, assort, ambitious, receive, succeed, convenient.

the character of Mortensen

We learn about a character from what he does and says, and from what others say about him. Draw up the following table in your workbook and explain what you learnt about the character of Mortensen from each of the statements in the left-hand column.

Statement in the story	Your judgment
"The district sales manager might single out Mortensen for special mention at the annual sales-force dinner."	
"And, after all, it was none of his business what the gnoles used cordage for."	
"Nonetheless, he followed the gnole unhesitatingly when the creature motioned him within."	
"Smiling to evince the charm of manner advised in the Manual, and raising his brows as one who says, 'Thank you, these will do nicely,' Mortensen dropped the eyes into his pocket."	
"The gnoles, it seemed, would be regular customers; and after the gnoles, why should he not try the Gibbelins? They too must have a need for rope."	

creative writing — the sales pitch

Rope is a fairly difficult product to sell and Mortensen had his problems. Select any product you like and then write a sales pitch for it. When you have done this, come out to the front of the class and read or act out what you have written. If you can't think of any products, the following list may give you some ideas. Remember, you have to convince people to buy your product.

- your house
- your father's car
- a brand of lipstick
- sports equipment
- clothes
- pet food
- a movie you have just seen
- a record that you like
- a drink of some kind

The woman of the future is still a child in this poem.

Woman of the Future

I am a child.
I am all the things of my past.
I am the freckles from my mother's nose.
I am the laziness of my dad
   Resting his eyes in front of the television.
I am all I see.
   Boys doing Karate Chops.
   Rubens' lovely ladies,
   Fat and bulging.
   TV ads of ladies who wear lipstick in the laundry.
   And worry about their hands
   And their breath.
   Madonnas with delicate faces holding little bundles of Jesus.
I am all I hear.
   "Look after him. You're his sister."
   "Come and get your hair done."
   "Rack off, Normie!"
   Waves lapping or crashing at the beach.
   And the wind in trees and telegraph wires.
I am all I feel and taste.
   Soft and glossy mud on toes.
   Hairy insect legs
   Slippery camphor laurel leaves
   The salty taste of fish and chips on my tongue
   And the watery melting of iceblocks.
And all I remember.
   A veranda shaded by grape vines,
   Where I stepped off the edge and flew
   Like Superman.
   And waking up in the cold in a car where dad changed a tyre.
   And being lost in the zoo with my cousin.
I am all I've been taught
   "I" before "E" except after "C".
   "Smoking is a health hazard."
I am all I think.
   Secrets.
   Deep down inside me.
I am all those things.
I'm like a caterpillar
And these things are my cocoon.
But one day I'll bite my way out
   And be free
   Because
I'm the woman of the future.

Cathy Warry

People are simply the sum of their experiences. Does it come as a surprise that the girl in the poem ardently desires to reach beyond them? She accepts the fact that the past and the present are part of her — but she also thinks of them as a prison.

Look at the outline that follows. Inside, there is a mass of generalities. They represent things that have influenced the child and made her what she is.

boys doing karate chops

violence

boys

innermost feelings

the pleasant past

heredity

tangs

formal learning

art

pleasant memories

textures

nature

unpleasant memories

religion

media

unpleasant memories

the unpleasant past

responsibility

exercise

Copy the outline and its mass of generalities into your workbook. From each generality draw an arrow going outside the outline and beside each arrow note the particular instance (or instances) of the child's contact with the generality. One instance has been put in to help you.

questions

1. For a girl looking forward to becoming something new and bright, the woman of the future, why is the image of a caterpillar in a cocoon particularly apt?
2. Quote two examples of a simile from the poem. (A simile is a figure of speech that compares one idea to another, using the words "like" or "as".)
3. Can you suggest why Cathy Warry devotes only two lines to what she's been taught at school when she has surely been at school for some years?
4. Who are the individuals in the poem who seem to clash with their surroundings?
5. What sort of attitude would you say the girl in the poem has to her childhood?

clustering responsibilities

Eventually, every child becomes an adult. Then he or she faces further experiences and responsibilities, such as a job and marriage.

Of course, many experiences and responsibilities can be thought of as *either* freedoms *or* restrictions, depending on which way you look at them. Let's try putting some of them down.

(to be completed in your workbook)

Here are two intersecting responsibilities.

```
HOME
   A
   R
   R
   I
   A
   G
   E
```

See how many more you can build from this beginning. There is only one rule: make sure there is a clear one-letter space between all words.

exercise 2

When you have thought of a whole cluster of responsibilities, select one of them and write a paragraph about how it really has two sides — freedom and restriction — depending on your point of view.

your own effort

Using Cathy Warry's poem as a model, write a poem about your own family, feelings, experiences, memories, secrets and whatever you are looking forward to being — the future you.

They aren't all they seem to be — or are they?

SPLENDID GIRLS

Those splendid girls at the wheels of powerful cars,
Sheer mechanism setting off slender charms.
I glimpse daredevil smiles as they whip past.

What are they all eager for, driving so fast
That I see them only momentarily? They are
Wholly desirable for half a heart-beat.

They have such style, such red nails! They are so neat!
But though they appear to drive at a dangerous speed
They do not do anything at random, that's for sure.

So keep your shirt on, they are spoken for.
They are as bright and lively as advertisements
For cigarettes or petrol or soap.

But there is no danger, and there is no hope.
Those reckless smiles have been carefully painted.
They are that sort of doll.

Everything, but everything, is under control.

John Normanton

a closer look at the poem

Just like the girls themselves, this poem seems much less controlled than it really is. Have a look at the rhyming scheme, for instance. At first glance there doesn't seem to be any, but there is.

1. Using a new letter of the alphabet for every new rhyme that emerges, detail the rhyming scheme of the poem. For example, the first line ends with "cars" so that will be "a". The second line ends with "charms", a different rhyme, so we'll call that "b". The third line is different again — "past"; we'll call it "c". The whole rhyming scheme for the first stanza is thus abc. Now go through each stanza and assign the rhyming scheme.
2. To add to this picture of planning and structure, look carefully at the adjectives or describing words used in the first stanza. Just one is used with each object, for example, "*splendid* girls" and "*powerful* cars". Find the other three adjectives in this stanza.
3. What two meanings does the word "slender" have in the first stanza?
4. Comment on the use of the words "wholly" and "half" in the line "Wholly desirable for half a heart-beat".
5. What is meant by "keep your shirt on" and "they are spoken for"? How does the use of phrases like this provide a balance to the other emphasis in this poem (the carefully-planned, very correct emphasis)?
6. Comment on the use of the word "splendid". Is it a very common word in daily usage? Why has the poet chosen it for the title?
7. "But there is no danger, and there is no hope." What effect does the repetition of the phrase "there is no . . ." have? What "hope" is he talking about?
8. "They are that sort of doll." Why has the poet used the word "doll"? Is it just used here as a slang word for a girl, or does it have other connotations as well?

Here is a simple, beautifully controlled descriptive poem. There is no attempt to play too heavily on our heart-strings. The poem is a brief description of an incident, built around the image (word picture) of the "first frost". If the poet intended to arouse a response in us, perhaps he would be satisfied with: "Yes, I've been there. I know what he means. I've been in that situation."

Anyway, read it through, and see if *you* have been there.

FIRST FROST

A girl is freezing in a telephone booth,
huddled in her flimsy coat,
her face stained by tears
and smeared with lipstick.

She breathes on her thin little fingers.
Fingers like ice. Glass beads in her ears.

She has to beat her way back alone
down the icy street.

First frost. A beginning of losses.
The first frost of telephone phrases.

It is the start of winter glittering on her cheek,
the first frost of having been hurt.

Andrei Voznesensky

how well did you understand the poem?

1. Why has the poet chosen the image of the first frost to describe this particular incident? What points of similarity are there between the incident and the image used?
2. Select four words from the poem that seem to you to be very well chosen in terms of the poet's purpose.
3. What does the poet mean by "telephone phrases"?
4. Why are the beads in her ears "*glass* beads"? How does this word "glass" fit so well into the poem?
5. What has happened to the girl? What do you think the incident is all about?

calling all poets!

Why not try your own hand at creative writing? Pick one of the following incidents and try to find an image that evokes the feeling or atmosphere of the incident. Use the same structure as *First Frost*.

Structure

1. Four lines of initial description of the incident.
2. A single action or aspect — two lines of description.
3. The image evoked by the incident, which in turn should evoke the incident — expand it a little.
4. A short explanation of why the image seems appropriate.

Here are your suggested incidents. Away you go!
- a hang-glider's first flight
- a person's first full-blooded gallop on a horse
- a person's first experience of falling in love

The TELL-TALE HEART

(based on the supernatural story by Edgar Alan Poe)

CAST: Narrator
Phillip Ranger
Gideon Mansell
Ruth Parry
Inspector of Police
First Warder
Second Warder

Sound effects note: It would be an advantage to have a tape recorder or drum or some other instrument to produce a muffled, thudding sound like the beat of a human heart amplified many times.

NARRATOR: Midnight ... midnight in Broadmoor Asylum for the criminally insane. A place of echoing corridors, constricting bars, shadows, and half-human sounds and sighs. In a small ante-room at the end of a passage, two stolid, middle-aged warders sit. One smokes quietly; the other reads. Presently the latter puts down his newspaper and speaks ...

FIRST WARDER: Number Fifteen's pretty quiet tonight.

SECOND WARDER: The night ain't over yet, Bert.

FIRST WARDER: Know somethink? It would 'ave been much kinder to let him swing for what he did.

SECOND WARDER: We'd have got a more peaceful life, anyway. Just as if this place ain't bad enough — without 'im screamin' his head off all night and wakin' ... *(Interrupting him comes a long, moaning scream of terror. It breaks into a terrified babbling)*

PHILLIP: The heart — the beating heart! Stop the beating, for heaven's sake. Stop it! Stop it!

SECOND WARDER *(resigned):* There 'e goes again.

PHILLIP *(screaming):* It's in my brain ... inside my head ... stop it ... for pity's sake ... Aaahh! *(His scream of terror dies away)*

FIRST WARDER *(uncomfortable):* Crikey ... he's even worse tonight.

SECOND WARDER: Full moon — that's why.

FIRST WARDER: Better go down and quieten him. Rouse the whole bloomin' place with them screams he will.

SECOND WARDER: I'll go now. *(His footsteps go ponderously down the long corridor. Phillip's mad babbling comes closer. There is a jingle of keys. A heavy door creaks open)*

PHILLIP *(in terror):* Who's that?

SECOND WARDER *(soothingly):* Now, now, it's only me.

PHILLIP *(relieved):* Warder — thank heaven you've come. It was so loud I couldn't hear you. Listen to it, Warder.

SECOND WARDER: Listen to what?

PHILLIP *(panting):* The heart — *his* heart. Uncle Gideon's. They say I murdered him, but how can he be dead when I can still hear the beating of his heart?

SECOND WARDER: There ain't a sound in the place.

PHILLIP *(slowly):* You're like the rest of them. You think I'm mad, don't you? Like Ruth and the Inspector. But I'm not, I'll swear I'm not. Let me try to convince you — I'll tell you all about it.

SECOND WARDER: Now, just a minute ...

PHILLIP *(eagerly):* It won't take long, Warder! It's such a simple story, really. You see, I had an uncle, Gideon Mansell, one of the richest men in Surrey. He lived alone, except for his housekeeper, in a ruined old mansion on the downs, where I used to visit him. It was during one of my visits that it happened. In the great library, where the floor boards were rotting away so that you could lift them out quite easily. I remember it was night time and Uncle Gideon sat crouched over the dying embers of a fire as I spoke to him, and I remember his reply...

MANSELL *(aged and cantankerous):* No, Phillip!

PHILLIP *(young and confident):* But Uncle ...

MANSELL: You'll not get so much as a farthing of my money.

PHILLIP: How can you say that with five thousand pounds locked away in that chest.

MANSELL *(chuckling):* Ten thousand, Phillip. I know, because I've counted every one of them.

PHILLIP: And for me, fifty pounds might mean the difference between freedom and a prison sentence.

MANSELL: You need a lesson, Phillip. Do you imagine that just because I've always paid your gambling debts before, I'll go on doing it?

PHILLIP *(pleading):* But this is the last time. Pay this account for me and I promise I'll get a job somewhere — then — then I'll save and pay back every penny I owe you.

MANSELL *(sneering):* Do you expect me to believe that? You *won't* work. I know you. You'd rather sit around waiting for a dead man's shoes.

PHILLIP *(sullenly):* Even you can't live forever.

MANSELL *(thinly):* Come here, Phillip, come closer. Now put your hand on my heart, feel it beating, pounding — strong and vigorous.

PHILLIP *(softly):* Yes.

MANSELL: Does that sound like the heart of a man near death?

PHILLIP: There are other things beside sickness, Uncle. You might meet with an accident, like tripping over those rotten floor boards.

MANSELL: And you think you'd benefit by that? Oh, no. Should I die suddenly, every penny I possess goes to your cousin.

PHILLIP: To Ruth?

MANSELL: Yes! What's more, she knows it. I've made it my business to tell her.

PHILLIP *(angrily):* Uncle, it isn't fair.

MANSELL: That's enough. It's late and the fire's almost out. It's long past my bedtime.

PHILLIP *(slowly):* You're trembling, Uncle. Is it the cold of this old room? Let me stir the fire for you.

MANSELL: I can help myself!

PHILLIP: No, the fire-iron is heavy. You mustn't strain that stout heart of yours. Let me use the fire-iron. *(Rattle of fire-iron)* It is weighty, Uncle. Too heavy for you. This heavy iron poker could quite easily end your life.

MANSELL *(afraid):* Phillip . . .

PHILLIP *(slowly and cruelly):* It could so easily stop that beating heart, Uncle.

MANSELL: Phillip, no, put that iron down! *(His voice rises in terror)* Phillip, don't strike! No! *(There is the thud of a fire-iron, a groan from Mansell and the thud of a body)*

PHILLIP *(softly):* Dead! And now for your grave — safe, secret. I know the place, the very place. *(He laughs softly)* And while you sleep, Uncle Gideon, I shall watch over you.

(Three days later . . .)

RUTH: Really, Phillip, I don't understand it at all.

PHILLIP: My dear cousin, it's all so perfectly simple.

RUTH: You say that three days ago Uncle Gideon asked you to come here to his house and said he was going away?

PHILLIP: He did.

RUTH: He told you to dismiss his housekeeper and the servants, and take care of this house while he was absent?

PHILLIP: Exactly.

RUTH: And he didn't even mention where he was going?

PHILLIP: No, he did not.

RUTH: What did he say about my *(pause)* financial arrangements?

PHILLIP: He mentioned nothing about those — nothing at all.

RUTH: Did you know that Uncle gave me an allowance every month? He used to take it out of a locked chest in his bedroom.

PHILLIP: Then he must have taken it with him. There's certainly no chest in the bedroom now. *(Very softly a muffled, rhythmic thudding begins to sound. Neither Ruth nor Phillip hears it: boom-bup-boom-bup-boom-bup-boom-bup)*

RUTH: I think there's something very wrong here, Phillip. I have the strangest premonition that Uncle is dead.

PHILLIP *(taken unaware):* What nonsense you talk, Ruth! Why, here in this very room three days ago, he asked me to feel his heart. It was as healthy and strong as my own.

RUTH: Phillip ...

PHILLIP: Yes?

RUTH: That chest I mentioned — there was a fortune in it — ten thousand pounds. My inheritance!

PHILLIP: Uncle told you that?

RUTH: Yes.

PHILLIP: Then he was having some game with you. There isn't even a chest, let alone any money. Uncle was really poor — that's why he lived in this mouldy old ruin. He just pretended to be a rich man because he liked to fool ... *(He breaks off suddenly)* Listen! *(The beating is slightly louder: boom-bup-boom-bup-boom-bup-boom-bup. The thudding continues, gradually growing louder as they speak)*

PHILLIP: Ruth. That sound, that dull, rhythmic thudding ...

RUTH *(impatient)*: Don't try to sidestep, Phillip. I want the truth about that money.

PHILLIP *(stammering)*: I — I've told you the truth ...

RUTH: Then why do you falter? Why are you so pale?

PHILLIP: Ruth — that sound! I've recognised it. It's like the beating of a heart!

RUTH: I don't hear anything — neither do you. This is a trick to switch the subject.

PHILLIP: Never mind the money. Surely you can hear that sound? It's so plain. It seems to fill the whole room.

RUTH: There is no sound in this room.

PHILLIP: But there is! Listen . . . *(Louder: boom-bup-boom-bup-boom-bup-boom-bup)*
RUTH: No sound at all.
PHILLIP: You're lying, lying. Just saying that to frighten me.
RUTH: And why should I want to frighten you, Phillip?
PHILLIP *(panting):* Because you think I'll confess . . .
RUTH *(sharply):* Confess what? Phillip, what have you done?
PHILLIP: Nothing.
RUTH: Then why talk of confession?
PHILLIP: I — I don't know what you're talking about. I'm confused, I don't know what I'm saying. It's this — this beating in my ears. I can't think. *(Louder: boom-bup-boom-bup-boom-bup-boom-bup)*
RUTH *(relentless):* Phillip, where is Uncle Gideon?
PHILLIP: Ask the housekeeper.
RUTH: You dismissed the housekeeper and the servants. You were here alone with Uncle. No one has seen him since! Phillip, don't stand there with your hands over your ears. Listen to me. Where is he? *(Louder: boom-bup-boom-bup-boom-bup-boom-bup.)*
PHILLIP *(sweating):* Ruth, have pity on me. Stop the sound.
RUTH: There is no sound, Phillip. What you hear may be the beating of your own heart, your own — or the heart of an old man. *(Very loud: boom-bup-boom-bup-boom-bup-boom-bup)*
PHILLIP *(screaming):* No — no! How can a man's heart beat when he is dead?

RUTH: Dead?

PHILLIP: Yes, Ruth — dead. Do you understand — dead? How can a heart live on, even the strongest and most vigorous heart, when the body is already decaying? Yet why can I hear it? Why does it beat and thud in my brain? I must get away from it — away from this room and its hellish owner. *(He rushes out, slamming the door. Immediately the thudding ceases. There is complete silence)*

RUTH *(quietly):* Poor Phillip. What are you — murderer or madman? *(She goes out)*

(In the library, several hours later. The door opens; Phillip shows in a police inspector)

PHILLIP: And this is the library, Inspector. It was in this room that I said goodbye to my uncle.

INSPECTOR: I'm sorry to bother you, Mr Ranger.

PHILLIP: Not at all, Inspector.

INSPECTOR: It was just that earlier this evening we had a call from your cousin, a Miss Parry. She seemed to fear that your uncle had met with foul play.

PHILLIP: What an extraordinary idea, Inspector.

INSPECTOR *(smiling):* I don't suppose you've been burying any bodies out in the garden have you?

PHILLIP: Good heavens, Inspector . . .

INSPECTOR: Only my little joke, Sir. But this young lady — she — well, she hinted . . .

PHILLIP: That I'd done away with my uncle?

INSPECTOR: Well, she did have this funny notion, Sir. I was rather sharp with her, I may say. I told her that before we could arrest anyone for murder, we'd have to have a body . . . *(Boom-bup-boom-bup-boom-bup-boom-bup. The beating starts again — soft at first, then rising to a gradual crescendo. The Inspector talks over it)* . . . and that she was making a pretty serious statement when . . . *(he stops)* Mr Ranger?

PHILLIP: Listen. It's starting again.

INSPECTOR: What is, Sir?

PHILLIP: You can hear it, can't you? Ruth said she couldn't, but she was lying. I'm not mad, am I? Tell me I'm not mad.

INSPECTOR: Well now, look here, Mr Ranger. *(Boom-bup-boom-bup-boom-bup-boom-bup)*

PHILLIP *(eagerly):* You do hear it, don't you?

INSPECTOR: Hear what?

PHILLIP: The beating of his heart — the monstrous, pounding thud of a heart that can never be stilled. Listen, it's getting louder and louder. *(Very loud: boom-bup-boom-bup-boom-bup-boom-bup)*

INSPECTOR: There's nothing . . .

PHILLIP: There is. You *can* hear it! But you won't admit it. No, I don't believe you can. Then . . . it's only me. That's his revenge.

INSPECTOR: Your uncle's?

PHILLIP *(wildly):* Yes. I'll confess it now. Anything to stop the pounding — this beating in my brain. I'll confess — I killed him.

INSPECTOR *(concerned):* Mr Ranger, you're not well. *(The beating swells louder — filling the entire room: boom-bup-boom-bup-boom-bup-boom-bup)*

PHILLIP *(screaming):* You don't believe me? You think I'm mad? I'll show you that I'm sane — sane as anyone. I killed him, I tell you. Killed him and hid him under these rotten floor boards. You think I'm mad, do you? Well, look for yourself.

(With a grinding wrench he tears up the floor boards) There he lies, three days dead. Only his heart still lives — that strong, vigorous heart beating eternally, the heart that can never die. Ahhh. *(His scream dies in a moan. A thud as he falls. The beating stops. The door flies open)*

RUTH: Inspector, what's happened?

INSPECTOR *(quietly):* He's collapsed, Miss Parry. Offhand I'd say he's had some kind of a brainstorm.

RUTH: And my uncle?

INSPECTOR: Murdered. No doubt about that. But this poor devil will never climb the gallows. You see — he's raving mad.

who was it?

1. This person believed Phillip would never hang for his crime.
2. This person was supposed to inherit a fortune.
3. This person made his presence felt even after death.
4. This person had been known to pay other people's gambling debts.
5. This person made others suspicious by talking of confession.
6. This person felt it would have been better for Phillip if he had been hanged.
7. This person was known sometimes as ''Number Fifteen''.
8. This person listened to Phillip's story in the Broadmoor Asylum.
9. This person was present when the murderer experienced his first delusion.
10. This person felt that a full moon had a bad effect on Phillip's illness.

what kind of a person?

Every play is built around characters, people who interact with each other and have effects on one another. One of the areas of primary interest to students of drama is the study of the characters involved. Think over the characters in this play. The three main characters are Phillip Ranger, Gideon Mansell and Ruth Parry. What sort of person is each one of them? What facts are there in the play that help us to understand each of them? What do we learn about them from their actions, their words and the way they react to other people?

Write a paragraph describing in your own words how you see the characters Gideon Mansell and Ruth Parry. Support your claims by referring to things they say and do.

clinical diagnosis

What kind of person is Phillip Ranger?

Imagine that you are a psychiatrist who has been given the task of diagnosing Phillip Ranger's particular mental illness in order to help him.

1. Your first job is to find an answer to the question at the beginning of this section — just what makes Phillip ''tick''? You ask him to tell you about himself and he tells you his story — the same story that he told the Second Warder, the story that forms our play. With all this information you now set out to write

down your summary of this man's character. You will be drawing conclusions from what he has said and done, continually referring to his story (the play) to back up your conclusions. Go ahead and write down *your* summary of Phillip Ranger's character. Build on the following table.

> PATIENT'S NAME: Phillip Ranger
> CASE NOTES: Phillip Ranger seems to be..
> ....
> ....
> ....

2. Now you are required to weigh up the evidence and make your diagnosis. You believe you know the sort of person he is and the symptoms he manifests. You decide he is schizophrenic. (A schizophrenic person is not a "split personality" or person who acts like two different people at different times; he is, rather, a person whose personality has split or fractured so that he has lost touch with the real world.) Phillip Ranger's personality is fractured — his thinking and emotions have lost contact with the real world, and are more affected by a fantasy world of fears and guilt feelings. Below is a list of symptoms of schizophrenia. Select those that are present in Phillip Ranger and list them. Cite evidence from the play to prove that each symptom you list *is* present in Phillip.

> ### Common Symptoms of Schizophrenia
>
> The patient is usually young, not older than the late thirties.
>
> Usually a precipitating incident has caused the onset of schizophrenia.
>
> The patient complains that the world appears distorted.
>
> The patient has delusions of persecution by others and a belief that others have formed a conspiracy against him or her.
>
> The patient has delusions of grandeur and a belief that he or she is possessed of great power and importance.
>
> The patient has visual hallucinations.
>
> The patient has auditory hallucinations.
>
> The patient's emotional behaviour is unpredictable and extreme.
>
> The patient's verbal behaviour is bizarre.
>
> The patient has poor ability to concentrate.

use of the "flashback" technique

The flashback technique is a frequently used technique in stories, films and dramas in which the actual chronology (order in which things happen in time) is altered. Instead of events being described in the exact order in which they occurred, the stories start with the present and then "flashback" to events in the past before building slowly back to the present. The technique may be used once or many times in the same work.

discussion

1. At what point in this play is the flashback technique used?
2. Why *is* the flashback technique used so often by writers? What advantages are there in using this technique?
3. What dangers, if any, can you see in using the flashback technique? Are there precautions that should be taken when using it?
4. Is its use suitable in this play?
5. Try to think of other books, films or plays you have read or seen that employ this technique. Comment on its use in these instances.

creative writing

One scene that is not described at all for us is the scene in the courtroom at Phillip Ranger's trial. Imagine that you have been asked to write such a scene to link the rest of the flashback to the opening part of the play.

Here is a suggested opening. Try to build on it in some exciting way. Recall as much as you can of TV shows, films or books in which courtroom scenes have been portrayed so that your scene will seem authentic. Use the hallucination of the beating heart to bring your scene to its climax.

Suggested opening

COURTROOM OFFICER: Silence please. This court is now in session.

Away you go!

costume

If you were faced with the task of staging this play, what costumes would your characters wear? Think through the part played by each of the following characters, and suggest detailed costuming for each of them.

First Warder
Gideon Mansell
Phillip Ranger (before his arrest)
Ruth Parry
Phillip Ranger (in the asylum)

The Salmon Rule

The silken surface of the river pool
above the salmon weir
(soft gravel pool)
is stretched out tight;
stretched out and pegged into each bank
by lank
smooth stems of willow saplings,
white
in warm November evenings.

But
under the taut surface
there is eager movement,
excitement through the water.
Salmon on their spawning run
have obeyed the ancient salmon rule
and come
home
to the soft gravel pool
above the salmon weir,
as they have done each year
since years began.

Fires of desire quiver
the cock-fish
as the female cuts her bed
in the soft river-gravel:
jerking, curling, curving,
twisting with spasms
at last she crouches to lay her eggs.
Then, drawn by some strange ecstasy,
the male moves over
to cover
with her the gravel bed.
Eggs trickle from her,
strings of translucent bubble beads,
seeds
for next year's parr.
His milt flows,
clouding the water — Milky Way.

Soon he lies spent;
strength drawn from him
in the act of giving life.
The estuary is far;
deep Atlantic farther,
farther, perhaps, than he will ever travel.

Year, year after year,
alevins* rise
from the soft gravel
in the river pool
above the salmon weir.
They feed in its water;
learn its taste and smell.
No other river, no other pool
will call to them,
when, as running salmon,
year, year after year
they will obey the ancient salmon rule;
return home to spawn
in the soft gravel pool
above the salmon weir.

F. J. Teskey

* Note: alevins — young fish

evaluation sheet

Poem's title: ....

Poet's name: ....

Content (what the poem describes): ....
....
....
....

Message (the main idea the poet is trying to communicate to the reader): ....
....

Word choice (write down some of the words in the poem that convey the idea of movement, calmness and tiredness): ....
....
....
....

Your reaction (explain what aspects of the poem you like and/or dislike): ....
....
....
....

Foxes Among
the Lambs

Each morning there were lambs with bloody mouth,
Their tongues cut out by foxes. Behind trees,
Where they had sheltered from the rainy South,
They'd rise to run, but fall on wobbly knees.
And knowing, though my heart was sick,
That only death could cure them of their ills,
I'd smash their heads in with handy stick
And curse the red marauders from the hills.

Each afternoon, safe in a sheltered nook
Behind the smithy, I'd prepare the bait;
And I remember how my fingers shook
With the half-frightened eagerness of hate
Placing the strychnine in the hidden rift
Made with the knife-point in the piece of liver;
And I would pray some fox would take my gift
And eat and feel the pinch and curse the giver.

Each night I'd lay abed sleepless until,
Above the steady patter of the rain,
I'd hear the first sharp yelp below the hill
And listen breathless till it rang again,
Nearer this time; then silence for a minute
While something in me waited for the leap
Of a wild cry with death and terror in it;
And then — it strikes me strange now — I could sleep!

Ernest G. Moll

how well did you understand the poem?

1. What feelings do you have for the lambs when you read the following?
    ". . . lambs with bloody mouth,
       Their tongues cut out by foxes."
2. What is your attitude towards the foxes when the poet describes the dying lambs as they "fall on wobbly knees"?
3. Poetry tells us about many aspects of life. One aspect that comes up from time to time is that of suffering. The lambs, the foxes and the poet himself all suffer in different ways in this poem. Draw the following table in your workbook and fill in phrases from the poem that describe the suffering of each.

	Suffering
lambs	
foxes	
the poet	

4. What do you think was the poet's main purpose in writing this poem?
5. In this poem the poet reveals to us much about his own character. What are some of the things you learn about him?
6. Did you feel that the poet was justified in killing the foxes in the way he did? Could he have done anything else?
7. What picture comes to you in the words "a wild cry with death and terror in it"?
8. Why does the poet say "it strikes me strange now — I could sleep!"?

CATS
ON THE ROOF

The street where I board is a forest of flats,
And it's cursed by a plague of most insolent cats.
As soon as the sun has sunk down in the west
They all sally forth on an amorous quest.
A tomcat will call from the top of a roof,
A second will answer from somewhere aloof;
Then others arrive, and the concert begins
As they slither and slide on the tiles and the tins.

Cats on the roof,
Cats on the roof,
Amorous, clamorous
Cats on the roof,
White ones and yellow ones,
Black-as-Othello ones,
Oh, the Devil's in league with the cats on the roof.

They talk of the need for our country's defence,
But it wouldn't involve a great deal of expense
To put on the market some new sort of bombs
To hurl at the tabs and the turbulent toms
Who gather in numbers that nightly increase
To shatter our slumber and slaughter our peace.
An inventor will surely make plenty of oof
Who can deal with the menace of cats on the roof.

They climb and they clamber, they hiss and they wail,
And they go up and down on the musical scale.
A shy young soprano will start on a note
While the ardent old tenor is clearing his throat.
Then off they will go on a dainty duet,
And the bass will come in when the tempo is set;
And any young student of sharps and of flats
Can learn quite a lot from a chorus of cats.

Then all of a sudden the tempo will change —
They really possess a most wonderful range
From alto, contralto, falsetto and bass;
Caruso and Melba are not in the race.
The tenor will rise on a note of his own
And the bass will die off to a horrible moan.
Oh, I doubt if the patience of Job would be proof
'Gainst amorous, clamorous cats on the roof.

A lull may occur when the midnight is past,
And you think you are set for some slumber at last,
But just as you're dozing, your face to the wall,
The concert will end in a general brawl.
And you'll turn on your pillow and mentally vow
To kill every cat that you meet with from now,
Till morning comes in with a dusting of mats,
And another night's rest has been ruined by cats.

Cats on the roof,
Cats on the roof,
Amorous, clamorous
Cats on the roof,
White ones and yellow ones,
Black-as-Othello ones,
Oh, the Devil's in league with the cats on the roof.

Edward Harrington

how well did you understand the poem?

1. Do you think that the poet really wants
   "... some new sort of bombs
   To hurl at the tabs and the turbulent toms"?
2. Have you noticed in the poem that the poet often uses words beginning with the same consonant? (A consonant is any letter in the alphabet except a, e, i, o, u.) Repetition of an initial sound is called alliteration. Look at the following line closely and say it over in your mind:
   "As they slither and slide on the tiles and the tins."
   Which consonants are being repeated? Did you notice that the poet also repeats some vowel sounds? Which are these? What kind of picture and sound is the poet trying to present?
3. Find two or three other examples of repetition of the same consonant in the poem. Then explain what picture, mood, feelings or action the poet has created by his use of repetition.
4. An example of vowel repetition (assonance) in *Cats on the Roof* occurs in the line " 'Gainst amorous, clamorous cats on the roof." Here the poet has repeated the "a" sound. What picture and feelings about the cats does this assonance conjure up in your mind?
5. Some words suggest the picture they are describing by their very sound, for example, "thump", "bump", "thud", "smash", "fizz". This is called onomatopoeia. Find two or three examples in the poem.
6. A simile compares one idea to another using the words "like" or "as". A metaphor likens one idea to another without using "like" or "as"; in fact, in this sort of comparison, one thing is treated as if it *were* the other.
   Look at this line of poetry:
   "The moon was a ghostly galleon tossed upon cloudy seas."
   Here the poet is likening the white moon with the clouds passing beneath it to a ghostly galleon sailing on the sea. In the first line of *Cats on the Roof*, the poet says, "The street where I board is a forest of flats." What impression does he give us of the street and the flats by using the word "forest"?
7. What does the poet tell us about the nature of the cats' singing?
8. What comments would you make about the mood of the poem? Is it sad, serious, happy or something else? Give reasons for your point of view.

Hawkins's Pigs

Brian James

Some of Davie's early years were spent on the Brush Farm. Of his life there Davie hardly spoke at all, but one was able to gather that the experience had not soured him. After that had come employment with Hawkins — Hawkins of the many pigs. The terms of that employment are not so clear, though Davie understood well enough that it was a form of slavery very thinly disguised. Another Brush Farm boy shared in this slavery.

Hawkins was a bachelor. He was a man of considerable possessions, and owned many acres of good land, many cows, and very many pigs. Pigs were his chief interest. Davie intimated that a vague feeling of kinship, as it were, made them so. Certainly, he was far more considerate towards his pigs than he was towards "those blessed Brush Farm boys".

Once Hawkins's lordly boar had seized Davie by the thigh and made a wound that kept Davie in hospital for months and months. Davie would recount all this in quiet, level tones, and then with startling suddenness he would undress sufficiently to show the wound. And say, "Look!"

Davie was almost childishly proud of that wound. Perhaps he should have been, for it was larger than a man's hand, and curiously resembled a relief map of the Balkans.

"Fifty-four stitches — and no compensation either! That's Hawkins's boar for you!"

That he didn't get compensation Davie viewed quite philosophically — as one might view a hailstorm that destroyed a neighbour's crop.

Then Davie would dress again and describe how Hawkins often leaned on the fence to watch his pigs grazing and grunting on the rich creek flat or waddling to and fro — heads weaving to left and right, tails crisply curled, little wicked eyes glancing in contempt at all things.

Most prized of all these pigs was the lordly Berkshire boar from Bimlow, and the saddleback sow from Appin. Hawkins was unduly vain that he owned such pigs. For the rest, his pride lay in their numbers and their condition.

One Saturday Hawkins was to set out for Penrith. Before he left he said to the boys, "You two! Look after things till Monday." It was more of a threat than an order. They had no names with Hawkins — they were just "You!" or "You two!"

Then followed detailed orders — or threats. As an addition to routine the boys were instructed to clean out the lofts of the barn. "Clean out all the rubbish!" was the command, "And then sweep them lofts as clean as dancing floors." Hawkins didn't dance, but he had an idea that very clean floors were needed for the exercise. Hawkins left.

The barn was long and high, and had lofts at each end, with a wide unlofted section in the middle. This part was open on one side to the yard, and in it the pigs were free to roam and grunt and squabble. On a ladder, Davie and his mate climbed to the separated lofts and started operations. They hurled much dusty litter to the floor below — boxes, clothes, twine, withered turnips, rats and mice in mummy and skeleton form. ... In a half-broken box in a corner Davie came upon a large quantity of yellow-grey objects, round and bigger than marbles.

"Hey, Brid!" he yelled. "What are these?"

"What are what?"

"These?" Davie held up some.

"What do I care!" said Brid. "Toss them out!"

Davie, for some reason, was not certain. What the balls were he didn't know, but he had some sort of intuition that they were wrong. But what odds! Orders were to sweep all as clean as a dancing floor. He tipped the box of yellowish balls over the edge. It crashed on the earth floor, and the balls rolled and scattered everywhere.

Just then the lordly boar from Bimlow, and the pedigreed sow from Appin, waddled in to see what was doing, and if there might be anything to eat. They were followed by the whole herd, grunting, squealing and quarrelling. They investigated the broken box and the other litter. These they tossed aside contemptuously. They smelt the yellow balls and decided they could be eaten.

They ate.

It was nearly dark now, and Davie and Brid went inside to have tea. They were very tired and went to bed early.

. Next morning they were much impressed by the eerie silence of the place. No squealing under the house, no grunting at the back door, no aimless bickering at the troughs.

Davie looked out, and his eyes goggled. Many excited moments passed in convincing himself that he was really seeing what he saw. Then at last he yelled, "Brid! Brid! Come and look!"

Brid came. What they gazed upon left them too terror-stricken to gather the joy that the sight should have brought them. Everywhere were pigs. Dead pigs. Unmistakably dead. The lordly boar lay beneath the very window, looking twice as large in death. Near by was the Appin sow, if possible more hideous in her mortality. Scattered to left and right were pigs. All the pigs, and all dead.

Davie could only speak in whispers now. He felt that the hand of the Lord had smitten them. A miracle of some sort. Only the fear of Hawkins made him sorry it had happened. But how had it happened? Why this sudden visitation?

Still, he and Brid felt that in some way they had caused it all — that they had been the humble instruments of Fate.

Recovering from the first shock, he and Brid visited the corpses. They *were* corpses all right. But a certain inner conviction was gained by poking the dead pigs in their distended tummies with sticks. They visited the lot — hundreds of them. Then they sat down and smoked some of Hawkins's tobacco that they had found on the kitchen shelf. Hawkins had left it there to dry after its accidental immersion in a bucket of skim milk. This nearly dry tobacco they wrapped in newspaper as containers.

"Heh, Brid!" Davie was suddenly inspired, "Do you remember those yellowish balls yesterday?"

Brid remembered.

"They done it! They was poison of some sort!"

"Gosh!" said Brid. "We are in for it now."

"Well, how was we to know? We did what he said."

"Won't make any difference," said Brid, gloomily.

Brid was right. It didn't.

Hawkins unexpectedly turned up that afternoon. He was red-eyed, bleared and un-
steady. He seemed to be seeing things. He saw the pigs, and didn't believe — at
first. Then he saw the Appin sow, and did believe. Davie and Brid disappeared, as
much out of respect for Hawkins's feelings as for their own safety. But they could
hear from their coign of vantage in the hay-stack the sound of low moaning. It was
very distressing — very harrowing. Then the boar was discovered. The low moaning
gave way to the sounds of a strong man in his wrath.

"You fools!" roared the voice, "come here at once, wherever you are!" The alternative to non-appearance was too horrible to mention.

Davie and Brid came forth. But though they tried to comfort they could give no
explanation of the tragedy.

"You did it! And you are going to be sorry you were ever born." The boys started
to retreat hurriedly, but there was nowhere to go — only Hawkins's place and the
Brush Farm. From a distance they watched Hawkins in his agony. He, too, visited
every corpse, from the Bimlow boar to the youngest piglet, and he, too, poked each
one in the tummy with a stick.

There was no tea that night — Hawkins had no appetite, and the boys were afraid
to enter the house. They slept in the dray shed. In the morning a dazed and sobered
Hawkins called them. His very grief had made him mild, and he spoke not unkindly.
Davie and Brid instinctively felt that it was a very bad sign. "Surely, you boys must
know something about it — how the pigs came to die like that?"

The boys knew nothing; of course they did not mention the yellow-grey balls. They
milked the cows and separated, but there were no pigs to feed on the skim milk.
They just left this, feeling it unwise to question Hawkins as to its disposal. Then
they ate an uneasy breakfast. Hawkins ate nothing.

The long day passed, the boys watching Hawkins warily. He visited each pig again and again, and poked each one solemnly. But they were dead — even deader than they were yesterday. There were alternations of low lament and fiercely profane railings against Fate.

So the next day passed, and the next. But the live-long heat of mid-summer made it imperative that something be done about it. On the fourth day Hawkins said, "Give a hand! Catch Toby, and put the plough harness on him, and bring a spare-chain and swingle bar."

Toby was brought. He was a sensitive and temperamental Clydesdale. He viewed the pigs with considerable emotion. Hawkins took him in hand and led him to the mortal remains of the lordly boar. Toby was backed, with difficulty to the spare-chain that had been hitched round the boar's hind legs. The plan was to drag the pigs to a ragged hole in the sidling facing the main road. This hole was once a quarry or a place for digging road metal. Davie didn't quite know.

The burial plans had not been made clear to Toby. He seesawed and fidgeted. In a sudden accession of rage Hawkins kicked Toby in the ribs as a kind of hint that he was to move. Toby moved. In an inspired flash it came to him that he was dragging PIG. He moved faster, and soon, out of all control, he was galloping wildly with a huge black mound bouncing incongruously after him. There was something ludicrous about the sight, but Davie and Brid had to enjoy it inwardly. With terrible red-rimmed eyes Hawkins watched Toby gallop around the paddock three times. Even Hector must have been somewhat worn after a similar experience around the walls of Troy. Certainly the boar was worn. There was not really too much of him left after his rocky journey around the sidling. Toby stopped, trembling violently and snorting in an exaggerated ecstasy of indignity. Hawkins rewarded him with a blow on the ear that nearly felled him, and then almost pulled his head off. For good measure he kicked Toby in the stomach, great, grunt producing kicks. Toby apologised by standing subdued. Then Hawkins yelled, "You idiots, don't stand gaping like — like —", he nearly said "stuck pigs", but restrained himself in time, out of respect for the dead. "Put Tim in the dray!"

Tim and the dray appeared in good time. Toby was dismissed and disgraced. Tim was not a horse to dispute legitimate orders.

There followed a horrible job. The Appin sow went first. The dray was backed to her, released and tipped; the sow was rolled against the inclined bottom, fastened in with ropes, and then the shafts were pulled down over Tim. The sow was deposited in the hole. Then the senior wives; then the lordly boar — what was left of him; then the big barrows; then the juniors; then the small barrows; and last the piglets and sowlets — tons and tons and tons of pig. All in the common grave of the ragged quarry. Long hours of sweating, nauseating toil it was.

Hawkins stood on the lip of that old-time excavation, and gazed upon the dead. His dead. The boys almost felt sorry for him. Almost — but not quite. Somewhere in that black mass was the boar, and Davie could feel that compensation didn't matter now. His thigh felt pleasant to the touch.

Hawkins would have preferred cremation for his dead, but there was not firewood enough within many miles sufficient for such a job. It had to be burial.

Picks, shovels and mattocks were brought. But that hole was in a rocky place, and the thin overlay of soil was too scant for proper burial. Proper burial seemed very necessary. Hawkins decided on making a quick job of it by blowing in with gelignite the top bank with its slight overhang. From somewhere he conjured up a lot of explosive — a kerosene tin full of it. Hawkins certainly did seem to have some strange hoards. There were coils of fuse and numberless bright caps. With an old auger he bored long holes between the rocks and low down to get the full strength of the explosion. The boys watched from the bank. There followed an endless placing of charges and tamping of holes and cutting of fuses.

"Set!" said Hawkins at last. "Shift, you two! Behind the cowshed!"

They heard the splutter of fuses, and ran for the cowshed. Hawkins soon followed. It seemed an age before anything happened. But it was worth waiting for. From their vantage point they saw a dusty, irregular volcano rise from the sidling, and then, in the instant, their ears were shattered by the crash and roar of the explosions. The ground shook violently, and the rafters and iron of the cowshed rattled. A momentary vision was vouchsafed them, in the spew of dust and rock and grass tussock, of the dark forms of many pigs. Everything in that hole went towards the high zenith of the heavens. The distant ridges of black-butt and ironbark reverberated in a rumbling thunder, punctuated by the nearer sounds of falling pigs. There was a crater on that hillside, clean, purified and rocky, while all the land around for many a rood was strewn with rocks and blown earth — and pigs. There they all were, every one of them, on the hillside, a little worse for wear, perhaps, but scattered under the blue sky, mourned but unburied.

Hawkins surveyed them in silence. Then convulsive fists were raised to Heaven — and Job's recorded efforts were made to seem quite feeble.

Davie and Brid just vanished. That was their last vision of Hawkins. How they managed to escape is not too clear, but they next appeared in the tall timber, with Hawkins a pleasant memory, and the thigh gash well avenged.

getting your teeth into
Hawkins's Pigs

how well did you understand the story?

1. Davie felt that pigs were Hawkins's main interest because
   (a) Hawkins just happened to have more of them than any other animal;
   (b) they were the most profitable animal to raise;
   (c) Hawkins felt a kind of relationship to pigs;
   (d) Hawkins was fond of bacon.
2. When Davie found the box of yellow-grey balls he
   (a) was very interested in them;
   (b) had a premonition there was something wrong with them;
   (c) thought they were just more rubbish to throw away;
   (d) had a feeling they might be valuable.
3. In the morning Davie and Brid were first struck by
   (a) the strange quietness around the house;
   (b) the sight of all the dead pigs;
   (c) a feeling that God had killed all the pigs;
   (d) fear at how Hawkins would react when he found the dead pigs.
4. How did Hawkins first react when he saw the dead pigs?
   (a) He lost his temper and called for the boys.
   (b) He moaned in anguish.
   (c) He refused to believe his eyes.
   (d) He let out a string of curses.
5. When the dazed Hawkins called the boys in on the second morning, he spoke mildly. The boys felt that
   (a) this was a dangerous sign and would probably mean bad things were to follow;
   (b) this was a great relief as they had expected him to be really nasty;
   (c) his mind had been affected by the loss of the pigs;
   (d) he had forgiven them.
6. They had to bury the pigs finally because
   (a) then they would be out of sight and so out of mind;
   (b) the heat of the sun was making them smell;
   (c) the flies were getting to them;
   (d) it would give them something to do and take their minds off the tragedy.
7. As they stood by the burial place of the pigs, Davie's scarred thigh felt pleasant to the touch because
   (a) it was warm from all the exertion;
   (b) his wounds had long since healed;
   (c) it somehow sensed that it was being avenged;
   (d) there was a chance that one day some compensation would be paid.
8. Hawkins drilled the holes for the explosive deep into the rock
   (a) so that the full strength of the explosion would go into breaking up the rock and soil;
   (b) because he was a perfectionist;
   (c) because he got a kick out of doing things like that;
   (d) so that he could fit sufficient explosive into it.

9. In the momentary vision they had following the explosion they saw
   (a) black-butt and ironbark trees being smashed;
   (b) horses running for their lives;
   (c) rocks, dust, tussocks of grass and pigs being flung into the air;
   (d) the rafters and iron of the cowshed starting to buckle.

straighten out this trough-full

You've probably heard of the well-known newspaper the *Mullengudgery Meanderer*. Since the district around Mullengudgery has nothing to do with pigs, the newspaper was very interested in the whole business of Hawkins's pigs. They sent ace reporter Henry Pootles to cover the story and get all the facts. Unfortunately, Henry, with his remarkable propensity for foul-ups, got all the facts confused. Here is the report he sent back to his office.

Your job

Straighten out any incorrect details and put the incidents into the order in which they happened in the story.

Young Davie and his mate, Bird, were brought up on Broom Farm before they started working for Hawkins. Though Hawkins had pigs and horses on his farm, he had more cows than anything else. But it was the pigs that Davie and Bird hated. Davie had been bitten by the saddleback sow from Appin one time, and he'd had to spend two weeks in hospital.

Anyway, it seems that on this occasion Hawkins had been going away to Parramatta, so he left the boys with instructions to clean out the dairy. The pigs were snuffling around and they got hold of some poison somehow and ate it. Davie and Bird didn't know so they just went ahead chucking out grey, ball-type things and other junk for the cows to eat.

Next morning the pigs were real crook, and died shortly after. Davie and Bird had a swig of Hawkins's beer and waited for their boss to come back. He was shocked by the tragedy but got straight into cleaning up the mess. First they dragged all the carcases over to the haystack. Then Bird had this great idea about blowing a hole in the ground and burying all the bodies. Hawkins got a hand grenade and tried to use that, and surprisingly it worked OK. Soon the horses were all buried, and Davie felt kind of glad, especially about the Berkshire Boar from Bargo. Davie and Bird plan to work for Hoskins for quite a while yet.

short sentences

One of the interesting features of style used in the original story is the short sentence. A sentence tends to be traditionally defined as a group of words that makes sense on its own, or a group of words containing a finite verb, that is, a verb that has a subject. There are several two-word sentences in the story that come under this definition and a couple of two-word non-sentences. The non-sentences still make sense to us because of the meaning that is implicit in them, even though it is not actually stated.

example of a two-word sentence

"Hawkins left."

Your job

Find another four examples of two-word sentences from the story.

example of a two-word non-sentence

"Dead pigs."

Your job

Find another two examples from the story of two-word non-sentences.

figurative language — "a fair cow"?

There is a remarkable amount of figurative language in English that is derived from reference to animals. If we say that something or someone is "a fair cow" we mean that it, or the person, is a real nuisance. Figurative language conveys in a different, usually interesting, way some meaning that is fairly commonly understood.

1. The following are metaphors, similes, or common sayings referring to pigs, which convey some meaning that is fairly generally understood. Write out the meaning of each phrase in your workbook.
   going the whole hog
   squealing like a stuck pig
   a pig of a man
   a road hog
   a pig-headed person
   bring home the bacon
   you can't make a silk purse out of a sow's ear
2. Use animals or birds to complete the following similes. You could use the ones that spring most readily to mind but, as they are likely to have lost a certain amount of freshness through frequent use, try your hand at thinking of new, interesting ones.
   as clumsy as ....
   as cunning as ....
   as wise as ....
   as slow as ....
   as nervous as ....
   as sleepy as ....
   as dumb as ....
   as happy as ....
   as sure-footed as ....

jumbled word meanings

Write down the words in the left-hand column. These words have been taken from the story. Then look at the right-hand column, select the correct meanings and place them next to the words in the left-hand column.

intimated	scornfully
withered	passionate expression of grief
intuition	made known
contemptuously	highest point
ludicrous	a place giving a good view of something
distended	shrivelled
warily	swollen out like a balloon
coign	immediate insight
lament	ridiculous
zenith	cautiously

spelling

See whether you can complete the following words by filling in the missing letters. They are all taken from the story.

comp–ns–tion	s–l–m–ly
phil–s–ph–c–lly	acce–s–on
r––t–ne	t–mp–ram–nt–l
–nv–st–g–te	s–o–a–h
v–s–t–on	leg–t–m–te
–rap–ed	cr–m–ti–n

Fasten your seat-belts and get ready for a rather frightening look at the world of tomorrow through the eyes of Bruce Dawe.

In the New Landscape

In the new landscape there will be only cars
and drivers of cars and signs saying
FREE SWAP CARDS HERE
and exhaust-fumes drifting over the countryside
and sounds of acceleration instead of birdsong

In the new landscape there will be no more streets
begging for hopscotch squares, only roads
the full width between buildings and a packed mob
of hoods surging between stop-lights
— so dense a sheep-dog with asbestos pads
could safely trot across
(Streets will be underground and pedestrians pale.
Motorists on the other hand will be tanned.)

In the new landscape there will be no trees
unless as exotica for parking-lots
— and weeds,
weeds, too, will be no more

And we will construct in keeping with these times
a concrete god with streamlined attributes
not likely to go soft at the sight or sound of
little children under the front wheels
or lovers who have wilfully forgotten
to keep their eyes on the road,
while by a ceremonial honking of motor-horns
we'll raise a daily anthem of praise
to him in whose stone lap are laid
the morning sacrifices, freshly-garlanded, death's rictus carved
on each face with the sharp obsidian blade
of fortuitousness (steam-hoses will be used
to cleanse the altar . . .)

And in the new landscape after a century or so
of costly research it will be found
that even the irreplaceable parts
will be replaceable, after which
there will be only cars

Bruce Dawe

what's in the new landscape?

Cars! Cars everywhere! Only cars! Or are there also other things in the new landscape? Look at the following list of things that you might, or might not, find in the new landscape. Put two headings in your workbook, ''In the New Landscape'' and ''Not in the New Landscape'', and assign each item to its correct column. Check the poem when you're not sure.

   streets begging for hopscotch squares, exhaust-fumes, stop-lights, sounds of acceleration, trees, birdsong, drivers of cars, signs, parking-lots, cars, weeds, roads

what does it mean?

In the left-hand column of this list are words taken from *In the New Landscape*, and in the right-hand column are their meanings. The only problem is that the two lists are not matched. Write down the words in your workbook and beside each write the correct meaning.

exotica	deliberately
asbestos	wreathed
attributes	consisting of ritual
wilfully	open jaws
ceremonial	chance
garlanded	dark volcanic stone
rictus	a fibrous material that does not burn
obsidian	qualities
fortuitousness	extravagant foreign things

analysis

The fourth stanza, which begins ''And we will construct . . .'', has a serious, deliberately grandiose tone, and calls on the images of religion to describe the new landscape.
1. Choose one line from this stanza that suggests that the new landscape will be approved by the people of the future.
2. What is the ''altar'' referred to in the last line of this stanza, and what does
   ''. . . (steam-hoses will be used
   to cleanse the altar . . .)''
   mean?
3. What effect does the serious, approving tone have on the reader?
4. What is meant by the fifth stanza, beginning ''And in the new landscape after a century or so''?

creative writing

Now that you've looked briefly at Bruce Dawe's poem, try your hand at writing your own, using the same title. Instead of cars you may like to make one of the following the horrifying centre of your vision of the future:
   drink cans   cigarette packets   blocks of home units   TV sets
   Pay particular attention to the tone you set for your poem. Be aware of what you are trying to achieve through it.
   On completion of the poems, read your efforts around the class and allow time for commendation and criticism.

In *Small Town* the poet is offhandedly piecing together some personal impressions of a small town. If the pieces seem somewhat loosely connected and incomplete, don't worry. That's how the human mind often works.

Small Town

Down here the starlings sit
on our television aerials (tall
for city reception) and yesterday a woman drank Dettol.

Next door the forty-year-old
child is a collector of junk:
bits of old motorbikes, picture
frames, toilet seats, Singer

stands and old chairs. His father
died last week and the son
lives now in a Home. Their old
house sinks further into

itself each day. There are three
policemen, three hotels
and two schools. The woman who
drank Dettol died, and

Councillor P. might run
for Mayor again this
year and they're finally
building conveniences, for tourists.

Oh, and I forgot to put
the rubbish out last night.
Another visit to the Tip. I
always bring back something.

B. A. Breen

Imagine that the small town depicted in the poem has a newspaper. Here are headings of the news items appearing on page one:

Toilets For Visitors
Town Statistics
Pests Interfere With Media
Stop Press: Latest on Poisons Case
A Hoarder and His Hoard
Town Dump Is Important
Local Government News

plan a layout for the front page

1. Think of a name for your newspaper. Put it at the top of the page and letter it in a distinctive way.
2. Choose a headline from the seven headings listed above. "Splash" it under the paper's name.
3. Plan spaces for the other six headings.
4. Write a brief report under each heading. Write it in your own words but base it on the information given in the poem.

Example

questions

1. To what extent does *Small Town* provide a cross-section of life as it is lived by humans in the Western world?
2. Why do you think the poet allows the items of information in the various stanzas to overlap?
3. Which of the following words would you use to describe the small town in this poem?
   pathetic, exotic, contented, frustrating, petty, timeless, tedious
   Justify your choice.
4. Why is the forty-year-old called a "child"?
5. Can you see any comparison between the old house sinking "further into itself" and those who used to live in it?
6. Can you suggest why, of all things, the poet chooses to finish off the poem with rubbish and the tip?

associations

Think of a small town, any small town that you may have visited, or simply imagine one. Next, think of some of the physical features of the town, for example, a dusty seat in the centre of the local park. Then, dream up some local person, for example, an old woman in an old-fashioned black dress. Next, imagine some habit, hobby or possession belonging to the person — for example, the old lady loves cats and is said to have a houseful. Finally, put together all three images in a stanza like those in *Small Town*.

Let's put it all down like this:

Physical features of the town	The local person	Habit, hobby, possession	Stanza
A dusty seat in the centre of the local park	An old lady in an old-fashioned black dress	She loves cats and is said to have a houseful	On a dusty park bench sits* the old lady with the house- ful of cats that she loves like children and feeds* for hours . . .

* Note clipped lines and the flow-over to the following stanza.

Can you build up, say, four more stanzas, to complete your own small-town poem?

discussion

Would you enjoy living in a small town? Discuss the plus and minus features. Consider what you would like most about it and what would drive you up the wall.

Do you ever feel you've been got at but don't quite know how? This poem is about the sly kind of commercial that hits hard when you least expect it.

Testimonials

(A Ballad for the Subliminal Age)

A man lay in a car-smash down in George Street,
As I passed by his voice rose rather high,
He was lighting a cigarette with a tow-truck blow-torch
And in between deep puffs I heard him cry:

It's the special filter-tip that makes the difference,
It's the menthol blend that soothes the sorest throat,
It's the fine gold pack for which you pay no extra,
It's the smoke top men prefer on plane or boat!

As I walked down a back street that same evening
I saw a house on fire, a crowd looked on,
A fireman staggered from the blazing wreckage,
An old lady in his arms then sang this song:

It's the special filter-tip that makes the difference,
It's the menthol blend that soothes the sorest throat,
It's the fine gold pack for which you pay no extra,
It's the smoke top men prefer on plane or boat!

The Amoco oil-refineries were exploding,
As I approached a man flew through the air,
And a guard on duty at the main gate murmured:
"There goes one full-time smoker who will swear

It's the special filter-tip that makes the difference,
It's the menthol blend that soothes the sorest throat,
It's the fine gold pack for which you pay no extra,
It's the smoke top men prefer on plane or boat!"

Bruce Dawe

The poem's title, including the subtitle in brackets, indicates that we are going to come across something quite unusual as we read the poem. So let's define the two important words in the title that you might not be familiar with.

testimonial: a declaration of good character or quality, a strong recommendation based on personal acquaintance with, or knowledge of, somebody or something.

subliminal: below the level of conscious thought. When applied to advertising this refers to messages (usually reminders) inserted as flashes on the television or movie screen in between other programme material. However, they come and go so quickly that the viewer's conscious mind does not pick them up but the subconscious mind does. In this way they are implanted in the mind without the viewer's awareness.

Now that we've dealt with "testimonial" and "subliminal", see if you can work out how they occur in the poem.

exercise

Look back through the poem and answer these questions.
1. Who are delivering the testimonials?
2. What are the testimonials about?
3. Under what circumstances are the testimonials being given?
4. Can you suggest *why* they are giving them?
5. What is there about the form (shape or construction) of the poem that resembles subliminal advertising?
6. Write a paragraph in which you use the word "macabre" (meaning gruesome or ghastly) to describe aspects of the poem.
7. Why does Bruce Dawe depict our present civilisation as "The Subliminal Age"?

tough techniques

Since this poem is about advertising and brainwashing, let's look at some of the techniques used.

Here are seven techniques commonly used in advertising to persuade the public to buy:

1. An appeal is made to *science*, perhaps by tossing around some scientific terminology.
2. Words are used that have wonderful *associations* for the buyer, for example, creamy, soft, lustrous, smooth, milky white and so on.
3. The idea is put across that you, the buyer, are getting *something for nothing*.
4. A link is made with great and famous people. You the consumer are about to join that vast crowd of *successful* people who also use this product, the implication being that perhaps you can be great and successful too.
5. The lure of the *jet set* and its associated glamour.
6. The product has *some kind of edge* over similar products: this is the brand that gives you more.
7. The use of *alliteration* (words with the same first letters or sounds) so that a phrase or phrases from the commercial stick in your memory.

exercise 1

Write down the jingle in the poem and, using circles, underlining or stars, indicate each of the seven techniques being used. An example has been done from line 1 of the jingle to help you.

The appeal to science: *"It's the special filter-tip that makes the difference."*

exercise 2

Draw an exotic full-page cigarette ad. Supply language — the language of *persuasion*. Incorporate in either your sketch or your language the "tough techniques" you wish to use. On your fully completed ad, use arrows to indicate which of the seven "tough techniques" are used.

discussion

Point out the uses and abuses of advertising. Do you think Bruce Dawe's poem offers a fair comment on advertising in our time — or is it ridiculously far-fetched?

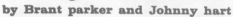

ORBIT

Each day, the old lady
from the home for the aged
walks to the park
carefully treading
a spinning world.

She chooses a corner seat,
exchanges the pasts of old women
for the protest
of present traffic.
The lights
flash their authority;
a time to stay, to go.
But she is fixed
among dead moons.

She stirs.
To overstay would be a *sign*
and perhaps there is a little time
before her universe
shudders to a halt.

Audrey Longbottom

getting into "orbit"

1. Why has the poem been given the title *Orbit*?
2. The phrases "carefully treading" and "a spinning world" both seem to have two levels of meaning. See if you can explain the two meanings for each phrase.
3. What is meant by the following lines?
   "exchanges the pasts of old women
   for the protest
   of present traffic."
   What *is* the "protest" of present traffic?
4. What is meant by
   ". . . she is fixed
   among dead moons"?
5. "She stirs." What is the effect of this very brief statement on the poem?
6. "To overstay would be a *sign*" — a sign of what?
7. Write a short evaluation of this poem. Comment on the features you like, or any aspects that you feel detract from its achievement.

creative writing

Try your hand at writing your own poem focusing on old age, but perhaps on a slightly different aspect of old age. Use the following situation as a stimulus for your writing.

Scene: From home to a cricket ground and back.
Character: An old cricket umpire.
Subject: Once he was a fine player himself, but now he's just an old man. Each Saturday afternoon he dresses in his tired umpire's clothes, leaves home, catches a bus to the park and umpires a game. Sometimes things go well and he enjoys himself. Sometimes he makes bad decisions because of his failing eyesight, and the afternoon is ruined because he can feel the resentment of the players.
Theme: Old age.

Try to capture the atmosphere and feelings as sensitively as you can. Share your efforts with the class.

News About the News

Here's what one city daily puts into every issue.

Let's investigate just a few of the fifty-two features.

headlines

Their function is to make an impact on the reader, such as shock, dismay, scandal, elation, sensation. Why? Impact increases readership and makes newspaper sales soar.

Look at this headline and its supporting news story.

LATE CITY

DIAL-A-DISEASE!
7 OUT OF 10 PUBLIC PHONES FILTHY

SYDNEY'S PUBLIC telephones could make you sick . . . very sick.

By PAT MALONE

They could give you broncho-pneumonia, scarlet fever, tonsilitis or skin infections.

Seven out of 10 tested carried the harmful bacteria known as golden staph.

These startling results were revealed by a special Sun survey, which proved that the mouthpiece of every public telephone harbours thousands of germs.

Laboratory tests on 10 City telephones discovered potentially dangerous organisms in all but two cases.

Three phones provided homes for what is defined as "large" concentrations of bacteria — hundreds of thousands of germs in each mouthpiece.

Only one contained a "light" concentration — but even then, there were many thousands of organisms in the mouthpiece.

Six phones revealed concentrations of Group A streptococcus, an active organism which can cause scarlet fever, tonsilitis, and many skin infections.

This organism can live for months outside the body.

Seven of the ten phones contained staphylococcus aureus, better known as golden staph, which can be a cause of broncho-pneumonia, and is normally associated with boils, styes and wound infections.

Swabs from each phone were taken by a laboratory analyst and cultivated at Micro Scientific Laboratories in Chatswood.

Of the six separate strains of bacteria found, only two were potentially dangerous — but the harmful organisms were found in eight of the 10 samples.

The public telephones tested were at the corner of Eddy Avenue and Pitt Street, outside Central Railway, corner Wentworth Avenue and Elizabeth Street, corner Wentworth Avenue and Campbell Street, corner Bridge and Pitt Streets, two in Harrington Street, one in Carrington Street, and one inside and one outside the post-office on King and York Streets.

Telecom Australia claim all City telephones are disinfected at least once a week — and those outside post-offices are treated every day.

Commission employees do some of the cleaning work — the rest is given to sub-contractors.

A Telecom spokesman would say only, "We use a disinfectant solution which is considered suitable by the Commission."

Common disinfectant would kill all but the harmless bacilli found in the samples.

But samples taken from two phones outside a post-office — which Telecom claim are cleaned daily — showed the presence of staphylococcus aureus, and one contained streptococcus.

Sydney bacteriologist Dr Richard Benn said of the results:

"It would be too much to hope to have every public telephone absolutely sterile, but with use of disinfectant a relatively safe standard can be maintained.

"The Group A streptococcus

is carried in the throat of about 5 per cent of the population, while staphylococcus aureus is present in the noses of three people in 10," Dr Benn said.

"There is a possibility that these germs could find their way from the telephone to the user, but as yet there is no evidence to show this.

"Each germ is electrostatically charged and once it gets somewhere like a phone mouthpiece, it tends to stay there until it dies.

"It would take a pretty strong breath to blow it free."
● How the phones were tested — and what the results look like — see centre spread.

what do you think?

1. A headline and news story like this are likely to make an impact on a lot of people. Why?
2. How are the headline and news story designed to get through to you personally?
3. In what way was the paper itself involved in exposing this telephone scandal?
4. What element of the news story horrifies you most?
5. Name the organisation on which the newspaper is trying to bring pressure to bear.
6. What motives might a newspaper have in raising an issue like this?

the political cartoon

People often get a kick out of seeing serious issues ridiculed. To cater for this taste, newspapers offer the political cartoon.

This Berto cartoon goes a step further by inserting a little reminder to show what the cartoonist is having a go at!

I hate being 41st out of the depot!

debate topic

There's nothing that can't be laughed at.

editorial (Notice the word "editor" in there?)

The purpose of a newspaper editorial is to put forward the newspaper's view on important matters, such as pollution.

In "The Sun Says" (the *Sun*'s editorial comment) that follows, the newspaper attacks an ugly display of beer-can throwing and littering that took place at a Test Cricket match.

OCKER SHOCKER

THE YOBS, louts and fools on The Hill at the Sydney Cricket Ground have supplied only a tiny part of the steady rubbishing this city gives itself.

But it was a great weekend for the Ugly Australian.

He belched his way through a Test match, getting arrested and throwing beer cans at anyone in sight.

The rubbish he left behind would have shamed an old-fashioned piggery.

It would be easy to dismiss the cricketing loudmouths as a minority if it weren't for similar evidence of littering and selfishness on our beaches, harbour and parks.

A city which prides itself on so many natural beauties seems to be going out of its way to destroy them.

A run-in yesterday between picnickers and conservationists at a Woronora River picnic spot illustrates the Sydney madness.

Some Friends of the Earth got together to clean up the area and made two big piles of rubbish.

Picnickers flung cans and bottles back into the bush.

Many schemes have been proposed to cope with our litter, among them a tax on disposable containers or even an outright ban on them.

None will work while otherwise decent people who pay their bills and remember Mother's Day show no consideration for others or their own surroundings.

See how skilfully the editorial shifts from an ugly happening at the Sydney Cricket Ground to the problem of pollution in the city itself. Then it generalises about a serious failing in the way Australians act towards one another.

try your own editorial

1. Choose a controversial issue that you know something about, for example, schooling, poverty, Aborigines, drugs, sexism, cruelty to animals, pollution.
2. Model your editorial on "The Sun Says" example by beginning with a definite incident and then going on to consider the Australian character in general.
3. Length: make it about half the length of "The Sun Says" item — say, five or six short paragraphs.

news item

"The owner of a chocolate factory was prosecuted for employing school students to wrap chocolates."

Here's a letter on this subject.

YOUR SAY
Sydney's liveliest letters

ANGRY

I WAS angered to read of the fine imposed on Mr W. Pulkownik for employing some children after hours in his factory (The Sun, February 24).

Here is a self-confessed lover of children, whom the children obviously admire and respect, doing a good job teaching kids the dignity of labour and keeping them off the streets, and what happens?

Some interfering busy-body from the Department of Labour and Industry shrieks "exploitation."

What utter nonsense!

No wonder Australia is in the mess it is.

No wonder there are so many bludgers about when, from school age, people are educated not to work, but to hold out their hands for someone to put something into them.

The Government's inspectors would be better employed in cracking down on people who leave good jobs to get the dole.

(Mrs) MARIE J. MUNRO
Beverly Hills

discussion

1. Give arguments for and against the employment of school students as factory workers.
2. Is a newspaper just wasting valuable space when it publishes letters from readers? What are some of the reasons for giving readers a chance to express their views?

Briefly read again the fifty-two good reasons for reading the *Sun*. Notice how many of them probably want to guide or advise you on something, for example, your health, fishing, racing, your legal problems and, not least of all, "Your Dog".

YOUR DOG

A SUN GUIDE BY GARRY SOMERVILLE

DOGS PREFER BUSY LIFE

A DOG is happiest when he leads the way of life for which he has been bred.

This knowledge is born with him and doesn't have to be learned. It is instinctive.

Like us, he is happiest when actively occupied.

This is especially so for working dogs like sheep and cattle dogs and hunting breeds.

Confining a natural field dog to a residential section of the city without adequate exercise borders on cruelty and prospective owners should consider this before obtaining these breeds.

If a dog is following the scent of a bunny and suddenly sights it, all his senses are ignited and instincts aroused to a peak. He would then be happy.

A greyhound may have three lame legs but as soon as he sees a hare move, he forgets his sorrows and becomes "turned on."

Give a dog something useful to do which he understands and he will be delighted.

Sheep dogs love herding and mustering, hounds are delighted to chase, gundogs are excited when searching and retrieving.

They seem to know and demonstrate why they have been bred.

From a behavioural point of view, a dog shows contentment when it rolls on its back, yawns or sighs.

Children attract dogs to schools and playgrounds.

Dogs' fantastic sense of scent puts them in paradise when using their "thinking" noses. We view a scene, they breathe it.

They quickly become impregnated with their master's scent and enjoy being near him because of this.

They also love the sound of the human voice. If the tone is pleasant they will react accordingly. This is one of the many reasons why dogs are referred to as companions.

Being a pack animal and fond of company, dogs thrive best with constant human companionship.

From a purely scientific point of view dogs only need food, water and shelter to be happy.

But that doesn't mean they are the happiest!

The unhappiest canines are the over-indulged, pampered pets which are forced to live in luxurious idleness.

There is no happier animal than a dog which lives the life of a dog.

People lap up good advice and guidance. Let's see just how guided you were.

1. Write down any points about dog care in this item that were new to you.
2. The test of a fascinating feature series is that you can't wait to buy tomorrow's paper to read the next article. Is this the way "Your Dog" affects you? If "yes", why? If "no", why not?
3. The whole article is written around a contrast. What is that contrast?
4. Make a 200-word summary of the article under these three headings:
    Different Dogs, Different Lives
    Understanding and Contentment
    A Dog and Its Senses

the comic strips or the funnies

These are worth their weight in gold to jaded readers of gloomy news stories. Here's an Andy Capp cartoon to prove it.

the columnist

A witty newspaper columnist like Mike Gibson faces the *daily* task of writing about some familiar topic or object — in this case, spray cans.

He has to come up with both the funny angle and the personal angle every time. Why?

Readers like a columnist they can relate to and identify with. They like to read about and chuckle over the funny kind of experience that could very possibly come their way as well. After all, who hasn't been hazed by sprays — but it takes a Mike Gibson to make us laugh about it.

Read and enjoy "Happy Sprays Are Here Again".

MIKE GIBSON

HAPPY SPRAYS ARE HERE AGAIN

AND lo and behold, so it came to pass, as the last Rugby League ball of the year was kicked, that the Aerosol season was upon us again.

Once more, when the bathroom door is left ajar, shall we hear the tell-tale sound of two "sssts" as the worry is taken out of being close.

Once more, as we enter the kitchen, shall we gag upon the atmosphere, as spray-can warfare is joined against summer's beasties that creep and crawl and fly.

Once more, to make sure we avagoodweegend, shall we spray our faces and arms with that magic compound that drives mosquitoes and bush flies, in a glass cage with a hairy arm, into a frenzy.

It seems there is little today that you can't get in a spray.

From the time you first squirt that shaving lather on your fizzgig in the morning to the time you get home at night and your wife is still spraying the starch on the last of the day's ironing it's a push-button society all the way.

"Will you tell the kids to stop jumping on that patch on the loungeroom carpet in there . . . I've sprayed it three times today to try to get that wine stain out of it," my wife bellows.

I can see the little lady has had a rough day.

Her hair is all over the place. She hasn't even had enough time to run a spray through it.

She is spraying the frying pan before pouring in the Chinese omelette.

"Sorry about the roast dinner I said we'd have," she explains, "but the oven was so dirty, I had to give it a clean . . ."

"And now you can't get the smell of the spray-cleaner out of it . . ." I nod, knowingly.

From the bathroom down the hall comes the sound of the flush, as Dangerous Dan emerges in his pyjamas, having concluded the final stage of his evening's ablutions.

"And if you've finished in there, give it a spray with the air-freshener!" my wife yells.

"That boy's getting worse," she says, shaking her head.

"I mean, he's only four . . . if he doesn't improve, we'll have to take him to the doctor . . ."

One of the great certainties of the upcoming aerosol season is that we will find something new added to the realms of spray-can products.

Perhaps tomato sauce. How much easier at the cricket if you could buy your pie, confident in the knowledge that you had a spray-can of rich, red Fountain brand right there in your kick.

Or maybe tobacco smoke. For those trying to cut down on the dreaded fags, for those who find leaving bumpers around a dirty habit, why not a can from which they can have a discreet spray of nicotine fumes when they can no longer control the urge?

As the spray-can society balloons, we read that one of humanity's greatest dangers is the gases emitted along with the spray, gases which scientists claim are endangering our future living prospects.

And we know this is true. We know that if God had meant us to go around spraying all day, he would have told us to follow Samuel Taylor to the promised land of non-fat coffee whitener and honey.

But we spray on, confident in the knowledge that modern-day brainpower will save the day.

As the spray-cans of today destroy the earth's ozone supplies, so tomorrow we will have cans full of artificial ozone that we can carry around with us.

Ah yes. As they say in church, folks, let us spray.

Now press on with answers to the following questions.
1. Why would you think "Happy Sprays Are Here Again" is aimed only at Australian readers?
2. Mike Gibson's language is pretty colloquial (homely) isn't it? See if you can find words in the article that correspond with the following: insects, stubble, pocket, cigarettes, knowledge.
3. There's a mention of commercials. Can you name the products?
4. What serious issue does Mike Gibson briefly refer to?
5. There's a little bit of poetry in there somewhere. Can you spot it?
6. Mike Gibson goes in for a little speculation about what might ultimately come in spray cans. What is this?
7. Who is Samuel Taylor? (If you don't know, have a guess.)
8. "The promised land of non-fat coffee whitener and honey." This is a misquote. Which book is it based on? Can you give the correct quote?

THE CALAMANDER CHEST

Joseph Payne Brennan

"From the Indies, sir!" said the secondhand dealer, pressing his palms together. "Genuine calamander wood — a rare good buy, sir!"

"Well — I'll take it," replied Ernest Maax somewhat hesitantly.

He had been strolling idly through the antique and secondhand shop when the chest caught his attention. It had a rich, exotic look which pleased him. In appearance the dark brown, black-striped wood resembled ebony. And the chest was quite capacious. It was at least two feet wide and five feet long, with a depth of nearly three feet. When Maax learned that the dealer was willing to dispose of it for only twelve dollars, he could not resist buying it.

What made him hesitate a little was the dealer's initial low price and quite obvious pleasure upon completing the transaction. Was that fine-grained wood only an inlay or did the chest contain some hidden defect?

When it was delivered to his room the next day, he could find nothing wrong with it. The calamander wood was solid and sound and the entire chest appeared to be in fine condition. The lid clicked smoothly into place when lowered, and the big iron key turned readily enough.

Feeling quite satisfied with himself, Maax carefully polished the dark wood and then slid the chest into an empty corner of his room. The next time he changed his lodgings, the chest would prove invaluable. Meanwhile it added just the right exotic touch to his rather drab chamber.

Several weeks passed, and although he still cast occasional admiring glances at his new possession, it gradually began to recede from his mind.

Then one evening his attention was returned to it in a very startling manner. He was sitting up, reading, late in the evening, when for some reason his eyes lifted from his book and he looked across the room toward the corner where he had placed the chest.

A long white finger protruded from under its lid.

He sat motionless, overwhelmed with sudden horror, his eyes riveted on this appalling object.

It just hung there unmoving, a long pale finger with a heavy knuckle bone and a black nail.

After his first shock, Maax felt a slow rage kindling within him. The finger had no right to be there; it was unreasonable — and idiotic. He resented it bitterly, much as he would have resented the sudden intrusion of an unsavoury roomer from down the hall. His peaceful, comfortable evening was ruined by this outrageous manifestation.

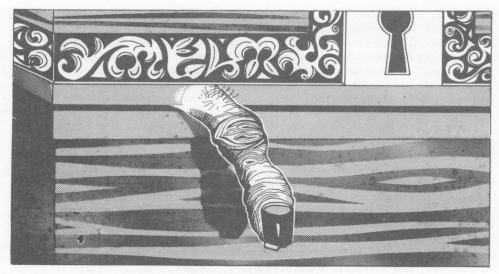

With an oath, he hurled his book straight at the finger.

It disappeared. At least he could no longer see it. Tilting his reading light so that its beams shot across the room, he strode to the chest and flung open the lid.

There was nothing inside.

Dropping the lid, he picked up his book and returned to the chair. Perhaps, he reflected, he had been reading too much lately. His eyes, in protest, might be playing tricks on him.

For some time longer he pretended to read, but at frequent intervals he lifted his eyes and looked across the room toward the calamander chest. The finger did not reappear and eventually he went to bed.

A week passed and he began to forget about the finger. He stayed out more during the evening, and read less, and by the end of a week he was quite convinced that he had been the victim of nothing more than an odd hallucination brought on by simple eye strain.

At length, at the beginning of the second week, deciding that his eyes had had a good rest, he bought some current magazines and made up his mind to spend the evening in his room.

Some time after he took up the first magazine, he glanced over at the chest and saw that all was as it should be. Settling comfortably in his chair, he became absorbed in the magazine and did not put it aside for over an hour. As he finally laid it down and prepared to pick up another, his eyes strayed in the direction of the chest — and there was the finger.

It hung there as before, motionless, with its thick knuckle and repulsive black nail.

Crowding down an impulse to rush across the room, Maax slowly reached over to a small table which stood near his chair and felt for a heavy metal ash tray. As his hand closed on the tray, his eyes never left the finger.

Rising very slowly, he began to inch across the room. He was certain that the ash tray, if wielded with force, would effectively crush anything less substantial than itself which it descended on. It was made of solid metal, and it possessed a sharp edge.

When he was a scant yard away from the chest, the finger disappeared. When he lifted the lid, the chest, as he had expected, was empty.

Feeling considerably shaken, he returned to his chair and sat down. Although the finger did not reappear, he could not drive its hideous image out of his mind. Before going to bed, he reluctantly decided that he would get rid of the chest.

He was in sound health and his eyes had had a week's rest. Therefore, he reasoned, whatever flaw in nature permitted the ugly manifestation rested not with him but with the chest itself.

Looking back, he recalled the secondhand dealer's eagerness to sell the chest at a ridiculously low price. The thing must already have had an evil reputation when the antique dealer acquired it. Knowing it, the unscrupulous merchant had readily consented to part with it for a small sum.

Maax, a practical young man, admitted the possibility of a non-physical explanation only with reluctance, but felt that he was not in a position to debate the matter. The preservation of stable nerves came first. All other considerations were secondary.

Accordingly, on the following day, before leaving for work, he arranged with his landlady to have the chest picked up and carted off to the city dump. He included specific directions that upon arrival it was to be burned.

When he arrived back at his room that evening, however, the first thing that met his gaze was the calamander chest. Furious, he hurried down the hall to his landlady's apartment and demanded an explanation. Why had his orders been ignored?

When she was able to get a word in, the patient woman explained that the chest actually had been picked up and carted off to the dump. Upon arrival, however, the man in charge of the dump had assured the men who lugged in the chest that there must be some mistake. Nobody in his right mind, he asserted, would destroy such a beautiful and expensive article. The men must have picked up the wrong one; surely there must be another left behind, he said, which was the worthless one the owner wanted discarded.

The two men who had taken the chest to the dump, not feeling secure in their own minds about the matter, and not wishing to make a costly mistake, had returned the chest later in the day.

Completely nonplussed by this information, Maax muttered an apology to the landlady and went back to his room, where he plopped into a chair and sat staring at the chest. He would, he finally decided, give it one more chance. If nothing further happened, he would keep it; otherwise he would take immediate and drastic measures to get rid of it once and for all.

Although he had planned to attend a concert that evening, it began to rain shortly after six o'clock and he resigned himself to an evening in his room.

Before starting to read, he locked the chest with the iron key and put the key in his pocket. It was absurd that he had not thought of doing so before. This would, he felt, be the decisive test.

While he read, he maintained a keen watch on the chest, but nothing happened until well after eleven, when he put aside his book for the evening. As he closed the book and started to rise, he looked at the chest — and there was the finger.

In appearance it was unchanged. Instead of hanging slack and motionless, however, it now seemed to be imbued with faint life. It quivered slightly and it appeared to be making weak attempts to scratch the side of the chest with its long black nail.

When he finally summoned up sufficient courage, Maax took up the metal ash tray as before and crept across the room. This time he actually had the tray raised to strike before the finger vanished. It seemed to whisk back into the chest.

With a wildly thumping heart, Maax lifted the lid. Again the box was empty. But then he remembered the iron key in his pocket and a new thrill of horror coursed down his spine. The hideous digital apparition had unlocked the chest! Either that, or he was rapidly losing his sanity.

Completely unnerved, he locked the chest for a second time and then sat in a chair and watched it until two o'clock in the morning. At length, exhausted and deeply shaken, he sought his bed. Before putting out the light, he ascertained that the chest was still locked.

As soon as he fell asleep, he experienced a hideous nightmare. He dreamed that a persistent scratching sound woke him up, that he arose, lit a candle, and looked at the chest. The protruding finger showed just under the lid and this time it was galvanised with an excess of life. It twisted and turned, drummed with its thick knuckle, scratched frantically with its flat black nail. At length, as if it suddenly became aware of his presence, it became perfectly still — and then very deliberately beckoned for him to approach. Flooded with horror, he nevertheless found himself unable to disobey. Setting down the candle, he slowly crossed the room like an automaton. The monstrous beckoning finger drew him on like some infernal magnet which attracted human flesh instead of metal.

As he reached the chest, the finger darted inside and the lid immediately lifted. Overwhelmed with terror and yet utterly unable to stop himself, he stepped into the chest, sat down, drew his knees up to his chin and turned onto his side. A second later the lid slammed shut and he heard the iron key turn in the lock.

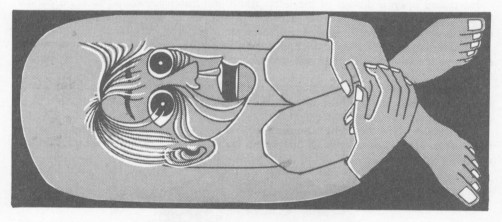

At this point in the nightmare he awoke with a ringing scream. He sat up in bed and felt the sweat of fear running down his face. In spite of the nightmare — or because of it — he dared not get up and switch on the light. Instead, he burrowed under the bedclothes and lay wide awake till morning.

After he had regained some measure of self-composure, he went out for black coffee and then, instead of reporting to his job, rode across town to the modest home of a truck driver and mover whom he had hired at various times in the past. After some quite detailed and specific plans had been agreed upon, he paid the mover ten dollars and departed with a promise to pay him an equal amount when the job was done. After lunch, considerably relieved, he went to work.

He entered his room that evening with a confident air, but as soon as he looked around, his heart sank. Contrary to instructions, the mover had not picked up the chest. It remained in the corner, just where it had been.

This time Maax was more depressed than angry. He sought out a telephone and called up the mover. The man was profusely apologetic. His truck had broken down, he explained, just as he was starting out to pick up the chest. The repairs were nearly completed, however, and he would absolutely be out to carry off the chest the first thing in the morning.

Since there was nothing else he could do, Maax thanked him and hung up. Finding himself unusually reluctant to return to his room, he ate a leisurely dinner at a nearby restaurant and later attended a movie. After the movie he stopped and had a hot chocolate. It was nearly midnight before he got back to his room.

In spite of his nightmare of the previous evening, he found himself looking forward to bed. He had lost almost an entire night's sleep and he was beginning to feel the strain.

After assuring himself that the calamander chest was securely locked, he slipped the iron key under his pillow and got into bed. In spite of his uneasiness he soon fell asleep.

Some hours later he awoke suddenly and sat up. His heart was pounding. For a moment he was not aware of what had awakened him — then he heard it. A furious scratching, tapping, thumping sound came from one corner of the room.

Trembling violently, he got out of bed, crossed the room and pressed the button on his reading lamp. Nothing happened. Either the electricity was shut off, or the light bulb had burned out.

He pulled open a drawer of the lamp stand and frantically searched for a candle. By the time he found one and applied a match to its wick the scratching sound had redoubled in intensity. The entire room seemed filled with it.

Shuddering, he lifted the candle and started across the room toward the calamander chest. As the wavering light of the candle flickered into the far corner, he saw the finger.

It protruded far out of the chest and it was writhing with furious life. It thrummed and twisted, dug at the chest with its horrible black nail, tapped and turned in an absolute frenzy of movement.

Suddenly, as he advanced, it became absolutely still. It hung down limp. Engulfed with terror, Maax was convinced that it had become aware of his approach and was now watching him.

When he was halfway across the room, the finger slowly lifted and deliberately beckoned to him. With a rush of renewed horror Maax remembered the ghastly events of his dream. Yet — as in the nightmare — he found himself utterly unable to disobey that diabolical summons. He went on like a man in a trance.

Early the next morning the mover and his assistant were let into Maax's room by the landlady. Maax had apparently already left for work, but there was no need of his presence since he had already given the housekeeper detailed instructions in regard to the disposal of the chest.

The chest, locked but without a key, stood in one corner of the room. The melted wax remains of a candle, burned to the end of its wick, lay nearby.

The landlady shook her head. "A good way to burn the house down," she complained. "I'll have to speak to Mr Maax. Not like him to be so careless."

The movers, burdened with the chest, paid no attention to her. The assistant growled as they started down the stairs. "Must be lined with lead. Never knew a chest so heavy before!"

"Heavy wood," his companion commented shortly, not wishing to waste his breath.

"Wonder why he's dumpin' such a good chest?" the assistant asked later as the truck approached an abandoned quarry near the edge of town.

The chief mover glanced at him slyly. "I guess I know," he said. "He bought it off Jason Kinkle. And Kinkle never told him the story on it. But he found out later, I figure — and that's why he's ditchin' it."

The assistant's interest picked up. "What's the story?" he asked.

They drove into the quarry grounds and got out of the truck.

"Kinkle bought it dirt cheap at an auction," the mover explained as they lifted out the chest. "Auction of old Henry Stubberton's furniture."

The assistant's eyes widened as they started up a steep slope with the chest. "You mean the Stubberton they found murdered in a . . ."

"In a chest!" the mover finished for him. *"This chest!"*

Neither spoke again until they set down the chest at the edge of a steep quarry shaft.

Glancing down at the deep water which filled the bottom of the shaft, the mover wiped the sweat from his face. "A pretty sight they say he was. All doubled up an' turnin' black. Seems he wasn't dead when they shut him in, though. They say he must have tried to claw his way out! When they opened the chest, they found one of his fingers jammed up under the lid, near the lock! Tried to pick the lock with his fingernail, it looked like!"

The assistant shuddered. "Let's be rid of it, then. It's bad luck sure!"

The mover nodded. "Take hold and shove."

They strained together and in another second the calamander chest slipped over the edge of the quarry and hurtled toward the pool of black water far below. There was one terrific splash and then it sank from sight like a stone.

"That's good riddance and another tenner for me," the mover commented.

Oddly enough, however, he never collected the tenner, for after that day Mr Ernest Maax dropped completely out of sight. He was never seen or heard of again. The disgruntled mover, never on the best of terms with the police, shrugged off the loss of the tenner and neglected to report the disposal of the chest. And since the landlady had never learned the mover's name, nor where he intended taking the chest, her sparse information was of no help in the search.

The police concluded that Maax had got into some scrape, changed his name, and effected a permanent change of locale.

getting the facts straight

Here is a factual outline of the story. Unfortunately, all kinds of errors have crept in. See if you can get the facts straight.

Rewrite the outline, and correct the errors, which are in *italic* type for your convenience. Those followed by an asterisk should be corrected by quoting directly from the story.

PLOT OUTLINE
Title: The *Salamander* Chest
Author: Joseph Payne *Brenan*
Outline: *Max* is offered a genuine *sandalwood* chest that is supposed to come from *Malacca*. He buys it *without hesitation*. In appearance the wood was *ivory-coloured*. At first everything is normal, then, *two days* after the purchase, *a stubby black thumb** protrudes from under its lid. It is *slender-boned with a polished nail**.

Even when *Max* hurls a *shoe* at the finger *it will not disappear*. However, when he looks he finds the chest is empty. When the finger next appears he flings a *reading lamp* at it. He decides to get rid of the chest, reasoning that *whatever flaw in nature permitted the beautiful apparition rested not with it but with himself**.

He arranges to have the chest carried off to a *charity*. Later on, however, he is *overjoyed* to find that the chest has not been destroyed after all. He decides to give the chest one more chance. If nothing further happened he would keep it, otherwise he would take *protracted and thoughtful moves** to get rid of it.

Although he had planned to go to the wrestling, he is forced to stay home *by lack of funds,* and is *playing a game of patience* when the finger reappears. Once again, he is just about to strike it when it disappears. Again the chest is empty when he looks inside. Then *Max* remembers he locked the chest and has the *aluminium* key in his *desk. The terrible phantom finger had unlocked the chest!**

He experiences a nightmare in which *the finger crosses the room and taps him on the forehead.* He decides he must get rid of the chest! He negotiates for its removal with a truck driver. However, the truck driver *cannot find his address* and so the chest remains with him.

That night the finger beckons and *Max cannot obey.*

The removalist returns and the chest is taken away. The removalist's assistant growls: *"Must be made of cardboard. Never knew a chest could be so light!"**

As they drive the chest to the city *scrap heap,* the removalist tells his assistant about the chest. Its original owner, a *Mr Bubbleton,* was *once trapped inside.* However, *he managed to recover.* Nevertheless, he left his finger behind, which accounts for the legend of the finger. The removalists dragged the chest *to the top of the scrap heap, collected their tenner,* and *reported Max's disappearance to the police.*

lifting the lid on participles

Every now and then, the author of *The Calamander Chest* starts one of his sentences with a participle. (A participle is part of a verb. Most verbs have both a present participle and a past participle — for example, verb: to send; present participle: sending; past participle: sent.)

Example

"Dropping the lid, he picked up his book and returned to the chair."

The author could have simply written: "He dropped the lid, picked up his book and returned to his chair." Why didn't he? For two reasons:
1. to give more variety to his writing, and
2. to really stress the action of dropping the lid.

exercise

The following sentences have been taken from the story, but they have been changed so that they no longer begin with present or past participles. Rewrite the sentences so that each one begins with a present or past participle.
1. He rose very slowly and began to inch across the room.
2. Maax crowded down an impulse to rush across the room, slowly reached over to a small table which stood near his chair and felt for a heavy metal ash tray.
3. The unscrupulous merchant knew it and had readily consented to part with it for a small sum.
4. He was trembling violently as he got out of bed and crossed the room to press the button on his reading lamp.
5. He was flooded with horror, but nevertheless found himself unable to disobey.
6. The mover glanced down at the deep water that filled the bottom of the shaft and wiped the sweat from his face.
7. Maax was engulfed with terror and was convinced that it had become aware of his approach and was now watching him.
8. He was overwhelmed with terror and yet utterly unable to stop himself, so he stepped into the chest, sat down, drew his knees up to his chin and turned onto his side.
9. Maax felt quite satisfied with himself as he carefully polished the dark wood and then slid the chest into an empty corner of the room.

When you have finished this exercise, look up the sentences in the story. Remember, they all begin with participles.

common mistakes you can make with participles

1. Don't forget that phrases beginning with participles (called participial phrases) should definitely refer to someone or something in the sentence. For example, consider this sentence:

    "Shutting the lid of the chest, the lock clicked into place."

In this sentence, who or what is shutting the lid? It's not the lock! The sentence should read:

    "Shutting the lid, *Maax* heard the lock click into place."

Here we are left in no doubt about *who* is shutting the lid.

2. Also, don't forget that participial phrases should be put as close as possible to the person or thing to which they refer. For example, consider:
Maax saw the terrible finger creeping across the room.''
It is doubtful that the finger crept across the room since it mainly stayed close to the chest. *Maax* does the creeping, so the sentence must be changed to:
"*Creeping across the room, Maax* saw the terrible finger.''
OR
"*Maax, creeping across the room,* saw the terrible finger.''

exercise

Rewrite the following sentences, keeping an eye open for participial phrases that refer to the wrong person or thing. If there is no possible reference, supply your own.
1. Peering out of the window, the trees looked ghostly in the moonlight.
2. The black shadows swayed in the wind twisting in grotesque shapes.
3. The old door had a broken knob slammed by the storm.
4. Tormented by the dreadful sight, there was nothing to do but shrink into a corner.
5. Maax rose from his bed shaking with apprehension.
6. Hurling the heavy ash tray, it hit the chest and caused the finger to vanish.
7. The awful digit eventually destroyed him gnarled by suffering.
8. Keeping to the wall, the old chest could be viewed in secret.
9. Attracted fatally by the dreadful apparition, there was no escape.
10. Setting down the candle, there was the rest of the room to cross before the chest could be reached.

split words — spelling

The following twenty-five words have been chosen from the story because they are often mis-spelt.
Note that each word has been divided into two parts at the point where the syllable is usually accented in pronunciation. The parts have been rearranged so that they no longer correspond.
Try re-forming the words like this:
care / ulous *becomes* careless
If you are in any doubt, find the word in the story and check it there.

gen	less	explana	ital
exot	ion	specif	ion
care	ulous	non	cient
capa	ic	deci	trary
mo	ually	suffi	aurant
transac	less	dig	sity
possess	uine	appari	ic
manifesta	tial	con	manent
grad	cious	ab	sive
repul	antly	rest	tion
substan	tion	inten	solutely
reluct	sive	per	plussed
unscrup	tion		

split words — meanings

When you have finished re-assembling the words, line them up against their meanings. The first one is given as an example.

Once again, if you are in doubt, check out the word in its context in the story (the sentence and passage in which the word is to be found). If you are still doubtful, look it up in your dictionary.

As these are long exercises, you might like to spread them over several periods.

Word	Meaning
careless	without care
_____	loathsome
_____	definite
_____	ghostly appearance
_____	lasting
_____	strength
_____	roomy
_____	ownership
_____	enough, adequate
_____	still
_____	the real thing
_____	big, solid
_____	concerning fingers or toes

Word	Meaning
_____	positively
_____	little by little
_____	when something is made clear
_____	opposite
_____	eating place
_____	unwillingly
_____	without a conscience
_____	sudden and mysterious appearance
_____	perplexed and bewildered
_____	rare, colourful and foreign
_____	getting something settled once and for all
_____	the performing of some business

creative horror

One of the most dramatic and chilling parts of *The Calamander Chest* is the description of the nightmare on page 165. It begins with the words "As soon as he fell asleep . . ." and ends with "Instead, he burrowed under the bedclothes and lay wide awake till morning."

exercise 1

Read again Brennan's description of the nightmare. Note how he describes different sounds, colours, shapes and feelings, and makes comparisons in order to achieve an impression of overwhelming, unavoidable horror. Then supply answers to the following questions, quoting directly from the nightmare.
1. What were the two different kinds of scratching made by the finger?
2. Name one other kind of noise made by the finger.
3. Name a colour and a shape mentioned together in the story.
4. Find two similes in the story. (Remember that a simile is a comparison using the words "like" or "as".)
5. Quote the two phrases that tell us
   (a) that Maax was completely horrified, and
   (b) that Maax was absolutely terrified.

exercise 2

Write a paragraph of your own, weaving together strands of colour, shape, comparison and feeling that describe one of the following events.
   In a nightmare, the eye sockets of a skull hypnotise you and draw you towards a slowly opening door.
   OR
   In a nightmare, a trapdoor in your bedroom floor opens and an arm extends towards you.

Like many inventors, Anton Leeuwenhoek was at first ridiculed. Nobody really understood his purpose in constructing an odd contraption of lenses.

THE MICROSCOPE

Anton Leeuwenhoek was Dutch.
He sold pincushions, cloth, and such.
The waiting townsfolk fumed and fussed
As Anton's dry goods gathered dust.

He worked, instead of tending store,
At grinding special lenses for
A microscope. Some of the things
He looked at were:

        mosquitoes' wings,
the hairs of sheep, the legs of lice,
the skin of people, dogs, and mice;
ox eyes, spiders' spinning gear,
fishes' scales, a little smear
of his own blood,

        and best of all,
the unknown, busy, very small
bugs that swim and bump and hop
inside a simple water drop.

Impossible! Most Dutchmen said.
This Anton's crazy in the head.
We ought to ship him off to Spain.
He says he's seen a housefly's brain.
He says the water that we drink
Is full of bugs. He's mad, we think!

They called him dumkopf, which means dope.
That's how we got the microscope.

Maxine Kumin

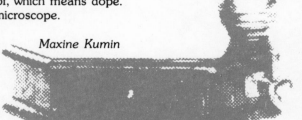

Although it doesn't actually happen in the poem, it would come as no surprise to learn that Leeuwenhoek was eventually hauled up before a judge by the townsfolk and charged with telling a string of unbelievable lies. It is even possible that the judge — who hadn't quite grasped it all himself — said something like this:

"Anton Leeuwenhoek, you are charged by these good townsfolk with the neglect of your dry goods business occasioned by malicious falsehoods resultant upon your having claimed to view through an utterly impossible contraption of lenses the following unbelievable sights — a housefly's blood, a water drop full of lice's legs, a little smear of your own scales, spider's blood, mosquitoes' hairs, sheep's spinning gear, ox skin, the eyes of people, dogs and mice, and bug's wings.

"As far as your own personal character is concerned, the townsfolk have called you a dopekopf, which means a drug taker, and, because perhaps you are crazy in the eyeballs and have gone and invented this contraption called a telescope, they have threatened to ship you off to England, where I believe you were born. Have you anything to say in your own defence?"

It's easy to imagine Leeuwenhoek shouting out angrily that all the facts about his invention and his character have been twisted.

exercise

Untwist the facts. Rewrite the judge's charge correctly, referring to the poem for the true facts about Leeuwenhoek's character and what he viewed under his microscope.

inventor's corner

Try combining a couple of stanzas of inventive poetry with a little inventive artwork. First, look at the poetry.

All through the poem, the end words of every pair of lines rhyme. This rhyme scheme is called "rhyming couplets".

poetry exercise

Using the first stanza of *The Microscope* as your model, try writing a stanza of your own about a wonderful new invention which is half astronomical telescope and half microscope. By directing this invention at stars and planets, the viewer is able to do to space what Leeuwenhoek did to commonplace objects — that is, look at them in startling detail.

Here's an example using the first stanza of *The Microscope* as a model:

Reginald worked alone,
He even ordered meals by phone.
By working his brain at a furious pace,
He built a microscope for viewing space.

Get the idea? Now try your own stanza, explaining very briefly the invention of a space microscope. Make sure your stanza contains two pairs of rhyming couplets and pay some attention to beat. Try to have roughly the same number of beats per line as the original.

When you have completed your stanza, attach this verse to it:

> Some of the things
> He looked at were . . .

Put in some of the space objects Reginald might have seen. Invent your own names for these, for example:

> Some of the things
> He looked at were Martian Krings,
> the rooms of Kreeps, the lopes of Ploques . . . .

artwork exercise

The ovals above represent areas viewed by Reginald's space microscope. You might decide on circles, squares or other shapes to accompany your poetry. Within whatever shapes you choose, draw the space objects viewed by your space microscope. When you have finished, your artwork interpretation of objects from space will make a vivid contribution to your poem.

Finally, refer to the last stanza of *The Microscope* and the concluding couplet. Read what most Dutchmen said about "this Anton" and what they thought they ought to do with him. Note the dry-as-dust statement of fact at the end.

exercise

Make up a stanza of your own about what ought to happen to Reginald (or whatever other "space microscope hero" you have chosen), based on the last stanza in *The Microscope*. Finish off with a statement of fact and make it, too, as dry as dust.

discussion topic

The townsfolk hide their fear of Leeuwenhoek's microscope behind a show of anger.

Do you think this statement is correct or incorrect? Give reasons for or against, based on facts given in the poem.

Do you think we would be reading too much into the poem if we said that the townsfolk, seeing new knowledge as a threat, acted as most human beings still do today?

If humans were in galactic space, would they be any more human than they were back on planet Earth? For a rather pessimistic opinion, read the following poem.

Space Poem

We stopped at a large asteroid
during our transgalactic run.
The crew, all bored and bloody-minded,
got off determined for some fun.

Some F-type alienoids were hanging
from rocks by their pink sucker-pads.
They soon let go. Those who resisted
took a fair beating from my lads.

Then from the cliff above a shower
of pebbles struck the ground like hail—
an M-type on a ledge stood swinging
a great stone in his functional tail.

He killed a man before I got him
in the disintegrator ray.
The crew retreated to the airlock.
The F-types screamed and climbed away.

I've called the medic-bank in Theta
on my molecular stenophone.
We must have got a bug, or virus.
The crew are sickening one by one.

The specimen we caged is thriving,
watching me as I close this file.
My God, I'd swear the thing was smiling
if I thought things like that could smile.

T. F. Kline

There's a distinct resemblance between this poem and a log book recording the events of a voyage — a voyage of disaster.

Let's imagine that many questioning signals were transmitted from various departments in Space Centre Earth across the immense gulf of light years to a missing spaceship. However, the only answer that was ever received back on Earth was in the form of a poem.

From the body of this poem, scientific experts from the various space departments managed to piece together all the answers (except one) to their signals. See how you manage.

exercise

Find the answers by referring to the poem. Sometimes you'll need to quote a few lines from the poem. At other times a word or phrase will do. The answer to the first signal is supplied as an example. Record the answers in your workbook.

Space Centre Earth Department	Outward signal	Answer (from the poem)
Navigation	Where was your last port of call and on what run?	"We stopped at a large asteroid during our transgalactic run."
Space anthropology	State the types of alienoids encountered. Describe their physical appearance and habits. Were they hostile or friendly? Were any specimens taken? If so, how many? How were they stored? What was the specimen's main feature? Is the specimen doing well? How do you know?	
Space weapons	Were any weapons used on the voyage? If so, which ones?	
Space medicine	Have you noticed any sign of disease on board? If so, what is its possible cause? Is there any possibility that the disease will spread? How do you know? Have you called any medical centre? Which one? How did you contact them?	
Mass media	Relay one special message for the benefit of humankind.	(There is no answer to this question in the poem. Use your imagination.)

the transgalactic moral of *Space Poem*

The poem contains a moral (or lesson to be learnt) that is neatly summed up in a couple of the proverbs that follow:

A bird in the hand is worth two in the bush.
Whatsoever a man soweth that shall he also reap.
Don't count your chickens before they're hatched.
Those who live in glass houses should not throw stones.
Crime does not pay.
As you make your bed so you must lie in it.
There is no rose without a thorn.

exercise

See if you can spot the relevant (particularly applicable) proverbs.
Discuss their relevance and the irrelevance of the other proverbs.
Start your answer in this way.

The truth of the proverb .... is shown in *Space Poem* because ....

the theme of *Space Poem*

The theme of any piece of creative work such as a painting, a piece of music, a story or a poem is the central idea that pervades every aspect of the work.

exercise

Try finding the theme of *Space Poem* by choosing two phrases from the following list to complete this statement of theme.

Statement of theme

Human beings sometimes .... whatever is strange and unfamiliar to them because they ....

are often mean
are basically shy
react very oddly to
are out for a cheap thrill
like owning unusual things
confront and claim for themselves
sample and scientifically examine
have scientific reasons for doing so
create difficulties for
deliberately destroy

Test your theme by producing evidence from the poem to show that it pervades every aspect of the poem.

THE OTHER FOOT

Story by Ray Bradbury
Dramatised by Martin Walsh

CAST: Hattie Johnson
Grant Johnson
Alice Johnson
Ronald Johnson
Willie Johnson
Elizabeth Brown
Ralph Brown
First Man
Second Man
First Woman
Second Woman
Kid
Mayor
White Man
Crowd

SCENE ONE

The scene is the planet Mars, sometime in the future. Hattie Johnson is working in her kitchen. She hears her three children shouting outside.

GRANT: Come on, Ma! Hey, Ma, come on! You'll miss it!

ALICE: Hey, Ma!

HATTIE: I'm coming. *(She goes outside)* Where did you hear this rumour?

GRANT: Up at Jones'. They say a rocket's coming, the first one in twenty years, and a white man is in it!

RONALD: What's a white man?

HATTIE: You'll find out. Yes, indeed, you'll find out.

RONALD: Tell us about one, Ma.

HATTIE: Well, it's been a long time. I was a little girl, you see. That was back in 1975.

RONALD: Tell us what happened.

HATTIE: Well, first of all, they got white hands.

ALICE *(laughing)*: White hands!

HATTIE: And they got white arms.

ALICE *(laughing harder)*: White arms!

HATTIE: And white faces.

GRANT: White like this, Ma? *(He throws some dust on his face)*

HATTIE: Whiter than that. *(She looks at the sky)* Maybe you better go inside.

GRANT: Oh, Ma! We got to watch! Nothing's going to happen, is it?

HATTIE: I don't know. I got a feeling, is all.

ALICE: We just want to see the ship and maybe see that white man. What's he like, Ma?

HATTIE *(shaking her head):* I don't know.

ALICE: Tell us some more!

HATTIE: Well, the white people live on Earth. That's where we all came from, twenty years ago. We just up and came to Mars. We built towns, and here we are. And no men have come up in all that time.

GRANT: Why didn't they come up?

HATTIE: Right after we got up here, Earth got in an atom war. They blew each other up. They forgot us. When they finished fighting, they didn't have any rockets. Took them until recently to build more. So here they come now, twenty years later, to visit. *(She begins to walk away)* You wait here. I'm going down to Elizabeth Brown's house.

SCENE TWO

The home of Ralph and Elizabeth Brown. The Brown family is getting ready to leave in the family car. Hattie appears.

ELIZABETH: Hey, there, Hattie! Come on along!

HATTIE: Where you going?

ELIZABETH: To see the white man!

RALPH: These children never seen one.

HATTIE: What are you going to do with that white man?

RALPH: Do? Just look at him, is all.

HATTIE: You sure?

RALPH: What else can we do?

HATTIE: I don't know. I just thought there might be trouble.

ELIZABETH: Trouble?

HATTIE: You know. *(She pauses)* You ain't going to lynch him?

RALPH *(laughing):* Bless you, child, no! We're going to shake his hand.

(A car pulls up. It's Willie, Hattie's husband)

HATTIE: Willie!

WILLIE *(angry):* What are you doing here? *(He looks at the others)* You going like a bunch of fools to see that man come in?

RALPH *(smiling):* That appears to be right.

WILLIE: Well, take your guns along. I'm on my way home for mine right now!

HATTIE: Willie!

WILLIE: What right have they got coming up here this late? Why don't they leave us in peace? Why didn't they blow themselves up on that old world?

HATTIE: Willie, that's no Christian way to talk.

WILLIE: I'm not feeling Christian. I'm just feeling mean. After all them years of doing what they did to our folks. My mom and dad, and your mom and dad ... you remember? You remember what Greenwater, Alabama, was like? You remember how they hanged my father on Knockwood Hill and shot my mother? Or have you got a short memory?

HATTIE *(sadly):* I remember.

WILLIE: You remember Dr Phillips and Mr Burton and their big houses? My mother washed their clothes. Dad worked for them until he was old. The thanks he got was being hung by Dr Phillips and Mr Burton. Well, the shoe's on the other foot now. We'll see who gets lynched, who rides the back of streetcars, who gets segregated in shows.

HATTIE: Oh, Willie, you're talking trouble.

WILLIE: Everybody's thought on this day, thinking it would never be. Well, here's the day, and we can't run away.

HATTIE: Ain't you going to let the white people live up here?

WILLIE *(smiling):* Sure. They can come up and work here. All they got to do is live in their own part of town, shine our shoes, and mop up our floors. That's all we ask. And once a week, we hang one or two of them.

HATTIE: You don't sound human, and I don't like it.

WILLIE: You'll have to get used to it. Let's go find my guns and some rope.

HATTIE: Oh, Willie! Oh, Willie!

SCENE THREE

The centre of town. Willie Johnson is on the steps of City Hall. Hattie is there, too. Willie has gathered guns and ammunition. A large crowd is around him.

HATTIE: Willie! What are you doing? Those people, they all have guns.

WILLIE: I stopped at every house. I told them to get their guns, some paint, and some rope. And here we all are, the welcoming committee! Yes, sir!
(The crowd shouts to Willie. They hold up guns and ropes. Willie holds up a rope tied in the shape of a hangman's noose. The crowd cheers).

HATTIE: Willie! Willie! Have you thought about what you're doing?

WILLIE: That's all I have thought about for twenty years. I was sixteen when I left Earth, and I was glad to leave. There wasn't anything there for me or you or anybody like us. We've had peace here, the first time we ever drew a solid breath. Now, come on.

FIRST MAN: Willie, what are we going to do?

WILLIE: Here's a gun. Here's another. *(He starts passing out guns to the crowd)* Here's a shotgun. Here's a pistol.

SECOND MAN: What's the paint for, Willie?

WILLIE *(smiles):* I'll show you. *(He picks up a can of yellow paint and a brush. Then he walks through the crowd to a bus on the side of the street. He climbs inside and paints a sign that says: "For Whites — Rear Section." Part of the crowd cheers as Willie walks back up the City Hall steps)*

SECOND MAN: Let's paint all the buses with signs like that!

WILLIE: Any volunteers? *(Hands go up)* Get going! *(A group leaves)* Now who's going to rope off theatre seats, leaving the last two rows for whites? *(Hands go up)* Go on! *(Another group leaves)* Let's see now. Oh yes. We got to pass a law this afternoon. There will be no marriages between races!

FIRST WOMAN: That's right!

WILLIE: All shoeshine boys quit their jobs today!

KID: I'm quitting right now!

WILLIE: Got to pass a minimum wage law, don't we?

FIRST MAN: Sure!

WILLIE: Pay them white folks at least 10 cents an hour.

SECOND WOMAN: That's right! That's right!

MAYOR *(pushing through the crowd):* Now look here, Willie Johnson. Get down off these steps. You're making a mob.

WILLIE: That's the idea, Mayor.

MAYOR: The same thing you always hated when you were a kid. You're no better than some of those white men you yell about!

WILLIE: This is the other shoe, Mayor, and the other foot. *(Willie looks at the faces around him. Some are smiling. Some look unsure. Some are drawing away)*

MAYOR: You'll be sorry.

WILLIE: We'll have an election and get a new mayor!

KID *(pointing to sky):* Here it comes! Here it comes!

SCENE FOUR

A rocket sweeps across the sky. It circles over a nearby field and lands. The crowd, led by Willie, rushes over. The rocket is still. Then a door slides open, and an old man steps out.

KID: A white man! It's a white man!

(The White Man is tall and very thin. He looks old and tired. He has to lean against the side of the ship because he is so weak. He smiles weakly. The crowd is silent)

WHITE MAN: It doesn't matter who I am. I'd just be a name to you, anyhow. *(He pauses)* It was twenty years ago that you left Earth. That's a long, long time. After you left, the War came. The Third War. It went on for a long time. Until last year. We bombed all the cities of the world. We ruined them all. And when we finished with the big cities, we went to the little cities. We bombed and buried them too. *(He pauses)* We bombed Natchez, Mississippi.

CROWD: Oh!

WHITE MAN: And Columbus, Georgia.

CROWD: Oh, no!

WHITE MAN: We bombed Greenwater, Alabama.

CROWD: No! No!

(Willie Johnson's head jerks up. Hattie sees an odd look come into his eyes)

FIRST MAN: Memphis! Did they burn Memphis?

WHITE MAN: Memphis was blown up.

FIRST MAN: Fourth Street in Memphis?

WHITE MAN: All of it.

FIRST WOMAN: Detroit?

WHITE MAN: Gone.

(The crowd is remembering now. After twenty years, they are remembering the places they thought they had forgotten)

SECOND MAN: Philadelphia?

SECOND WOMAN: I remember Philadelphia.

ELIZABETH: New York City?

RALPH: I had a store in Harlem!

WHITE MAN: Harlem was bombed out. And all over, everything is radioactive. Farms, roads, food — radioactive. Everything.

WILLIE *(softly):* Greenwater, Alabama. That's where I was born.

HATTIE *(to Willie):* Gone. All of it gone. The man said so.

WHITE MAN: We ruined everything, like fools. We killed millions. I don't think there are more than 500 000 people left in the world — all kinds and types. And out of all the ruin, we found enough metal to build this one rocket. And we came to Mars to seek your help.

WILLIE *(half aloud):* Knockwood Hill in Greenwater. I remember. *(He grips the hangman's noose. Hattie puts a hand on his arm)*

WHITE MAN: We've been fools. We've brought the Earth down about our heads. You have rockets here which you haven't tried to use in twenty years. I've come to ask you to use them. To come to Earth and bring the survivors to Mars. We've been stupid and evil. All the Chinese and the Indians and the Russians and the British and the Americans. We're asking to be taken in. There's room for everyone. I've seen your fields from above. Your soil is good. We'll come and work it for you. *(He pauses. There is silence)* If you want, I'll get into my ship and go back. We won't bother you again. Or we could come here and work for you and do the things you did for us. Clean your houses. Cook your meals.

Shine your shoes. Humble ourselves in the sight of God for the things we have done to ourselves, to others, to you.
(There is a long silence in the crowd. They stare at the White Man. Willie holds his rope. Those around him watch to see what he will do. Hattie suddenly steps forward)

HATTIE: Mister! Do you know Knockwood Hill in Greenwater, Alabama?

WHITE MAN: Just a minute. *(He speaks to someone inside the rocket. A moment later, he is handed a photographic map)*

HATTIE: You know the big oak on top of the hill, mister?

WHITE MAN: Yes.

HATTIE: Is the oak tree still there?

WHITE MAN: It's gone. Blown up. The hill's gone and the oak tree, too. You see? *(He hands the map to Hattie. Willie steps forward and grabs the map)*

WILLIE: That's where my father was shot and hanged.

HATTIE *(to White Man)*: Tell me about Greenwater.

WHITE MAN: What do you want to know?

HATTIE: Dr Phillips. Is he still alive?
(The White Man again speaks to someone inside the rocket ship. He is handed the answer)

WHITE MAN: Killed in the war.

HATTIE: And his son?

WHITE MAN: Dead.

HATTIE: What about their house?

WHITE MAN: Burned. Like all the other houses.

HATTIE: What about the other big tree on Knockwood Hill?

WHITE MAN: All the trees burned.

WILLIE: What about Mr Burton and his house?

WHITE MAN: No houses at all left, no people.

WILLIE: You know Mrs Johnson's washing shack? My mother's shack? That's where my mother was shot.

WHITE MAN: That's gone, too. Everything's gone. You can see for yourself. *(He holds out the pictures)*

WILLIE: No. You don't have to show me. *(He slowly drops his rope on the ground)*

SCENE FIVE

Willie and Hattie have driven home. They are now getting out of their car.

HATTIE: It's a new start for everyone.

WILLIE: Yes.

HATTIE: They are taking down the new signs and cutting down the ropes in the theatres.

WILLIE: What happens next is up to all of us. The time for being fools is over. I knew that when he talked. Now the white man is as lonely as we have always been. He's got no home now, just like we didn't have one for so long. Now everything is even. We can start all over again — on the same level.
(The children run out of the house and over to the car)

ALICE: Daddy, you see the white man?

GRANT: You get a good look at him?

RONALD: What did he look like, Daddy?

WILLIE: Seems like for the first time today I really seen the white man. I really seen him clear.

drama card

Draw up the following drama card in your workbook and supply answers under each of the headings.

Setting (Where does the play take place? What kind of scenery would you need?):...
....
....

Plot (What is the story about?):..
....
....

Climax (Describe the point in the play where the highest point of emotional conflict is reached):..
....
....

Characters (How would you play the part of the following characters?):

Willie Johnson:...
....
....

White Man:...
....
....

Mayor:..
....
....

Hattie:..
....
....

Title (Explain why the play is called *The Other Foot*): ....
....
....
....

Conclusion (Do you think the ending of the play is good or bad? Give reasons for your judgment): ....
....
....

theme

The theme of a play is the underlying idea that runs through it. Very often the theme makes important comments on human behaviour. The theme of *The Other Foot* revolves around the relationship between black people and white people. It deals especially with prejudice. This is bias against certain people or ideas and is a form of discrimination.

1. Write down examples from the play of prejudice against black people in America.
2. Write down examples of prejudice against the white people coming to Mars.

Another theme that the writer of the play concentrates on is the evil of warfare.

3. Explain how the writer strives to show us that warfare is both stupid and evil.

The final message of the play is that all men should live as brothers, not enemies.

4. Explain how the writer strives to show that people should live happily together.

actions and reactions

Explain how each of the following characters reacts to the coming of the white man.

emotions and feelings

Select appropriate lines from the play to illustrate each of the entries in this table.

Emotions and feelings	Dialogue
sadness hatred fear joy curiosity regret excitement revenge	

characterisation

What do you learn about each of the following characters from their speech? Copy this table into your workbook and fill in the column "Your evaluation".

Characters	Dialogue	Your evaluation
Hattie	"I don't know. I just thought there might be trouble."	
Willie	"Well, take your guns along. I'm on my way home for mine right now!"	
Second Man	"Let's paint all the buses with signs like that!"	
White Man	"We've been fools. We've brought the Earth down about our heads.	
Mayor	"Now look here, Willie Johnson. Get down off these steps. You're making a mob."	

Here's a poem that takes you right to the heart of the alternative culture movement. It's a far cry from the great consumer society.

Barney

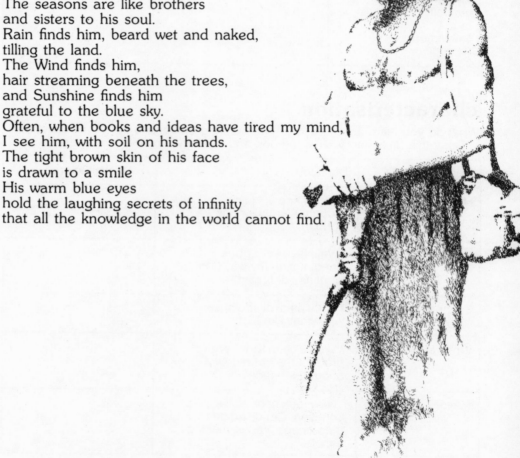

Nature is a mantle
he wears around his shoulders.
The seasons are like brothers
and sisters to his soul.
Rain finds him, beard wet and naked,
tilling the land.
The Wind finds him,
hair streaming beneath the trees,
and Sunshine finds him
grateful to the blue sky.
Often, when books and ideas have tired my mind,
I see him, with soil on his hands.
The tight brown skin of his face
is drawn to a smile
His warm blue eyes
hold the laughing secrets of infinity
that all the knowledge in the world cannot find.

looking into *Barney*

This poem describes a simple life, one that is in harmony with nature. Barney seems to be a markedly different person from us. Perhaps he is someone we find ourselves envying in some measure. And, although *our* lifestyle is hardly mentioned in this poem, it somehow seems to be under scrutiny, and we can see that we're missing out on something.

1. What is meant by
   "Nature is a mantle
   he wears around his shoulders"?
2. What is the effect of the repetition
   "Rain finds him . . ."
   "The Wind finds him . . ."
   "and Sunshine finds him . . ."?
3. Why are capital letters used for Rain, Wind and Sunshine?
4. Why does the poet refer to the "*laughing* secrets of infinity"?
5. To which society does "knowledge" belong and to which society do the "laughing secrets of infinity" belong? What is the difference between the two societies?
6. Write a paragraph evaluating this poem. Comment on the qualities that impress you or any aspects that you feel detract from its effectiveness.

write-a-lifestyle

Write a poem describing a lifestyle that differs from your own. Concentrate basically on description, but try to build in some emotional reaction as well, showing how you feel about this different lifestyle — whether it is to be pitied, laughed at, astounded, envied or some other reaction.

When you have finished doing this, exchange poems with other students and evaluate the effectiveness of their efforts.

Have you ever been on the road — you know, thumbing your way, hitching, hoping for a lift from some sympathetic motorist? If so, you'll probably have no trouble identifying with this poem.

The Hitch Hiker

I have waited days
Beside roads in Queensland,
Got to know their ways.

I am familiar with
Their bric-à-brac, pierced
Beer cans, combs, old hats,

Salvage of picnics, breakdowns,
Love affairs, scraps
Of women's weeklies, used perhaps
For sandwiches, or worse.

The Townsville Times, September 10,
Carried an item on Floyd Paterson.

What year would that be?
Things seem to last indefinitely
Under the bone-dry dust
Of a thousand travelling salesmen.

Roadsides are desert islands. There
You are cast up like driftwood,
Dependent on the tides and moods
of motorists, and there you stay,
Flotsam and jetsam of the highway.

Hugo Williams

looking beneath the surface

1. What two meanings does the phrase "Got to know their ways" have in this poem?
2. What is "bric-à-brac"? Consult a dictionary if necessary.
3. What do you think the poet means by "or worse" in this phrase?
   ". . . used perhaps
   For sandwiches, or worse."
4. The poet refers to a particular incident he remembers reading in a scrap of the *Townsville Times*. What effect does the poet achieve by referring to a specific incident such as this? Would it detract from the poem if you had never heard of Floyd Paterson before?
5. "September 10" and "Paterson" are imperfect or half-rhymes. Find another pair of half-rhymes in this poem.
6. What does the poet mean by "roadsides are desert islands"?
7. The poet mentions the "tides" and "moods" of motorists. What does he mean by these? How do the "tides" of motorists differ from the "moods" of motorists?
8. What image has this poet chosen to summarise the life of a hitch hiker?

"And His Soul Goes Marching On."

The Universal Soldier is an anti-war song that doubles as a poem with a grim core of truth.

*The Universal Soldier**

He's five foot two and he's six feet four.
He fights with missiles and with spears.
He's all of thirty-one and he's only seventeen.
He's been a soldier for a thousand years.

He's a Catholic, a Hindu, an atheist, a Jain,
A Buddhist and a Baptist and a Jew,
And he knows he shouldn't kill and he knows he always will,
Kill you for me, my friend, and me for you.

And he's fighting for Canada, he's fighting for France,
He's fighting for the U.S.A.
And he's fighting for the Russians and he's fighting for Japan,
And he thinks we'll put an end to war this way.

And he's fighting for democracy, he's fighting for the Reds,
He said it's for the peace of all.
He's the one who must decide who's to live and who's to die,
And he never sees the writing on the wall.

But without him how would Hitler have condemned him at Dachau?
Without him Caesar would have stood alone.
He's the one who gives his body as a weapon of the war,
And without him all this killin' can't go on.

He's the Universal Soldier and he really is to blame,
His orders come from far away no more —
They come from here and there and you and me, and, brothers,
*   can't you see*
This is not the way we put an end to war?

                                   Buffy Sainte-Marie

There is no single person who could be called *the* Universal Soldier. The idea of such a person is an abstract one, that is, it is a general idea formed from a number of examples.

Let's visualise the Universal Soldier surrounded by his attributes (main characteristics or qualities). Each one corresponds to a stanza in the poem. Note that each attribute has an *italicised* word or words that provide a focal point.

he is *loyal* to his leaders and dies for them, thus ensuring that there will always be war

each of us *commands* him and so each of us bears a share of the guilt for his existence

THE UNIVERSAL SOLDIER

he subscribes to every *religious* and other belief, yet he kills — anyone

he's been *every kind of soldier in every kind of age*

in every *political* system he is given the power to pass sentence of death — on himself

he's fighting for *peace everywhere* — so there'll be no more fighting

exercise

List the focal word or words in numerical order to correspond with the order of the six stanzas in the poem.

Example
Stanza 1: every kind of soldier in every kind of age.

Over to you!

Here are some other very familiar war slogans and expressions.
Cannon fodder
He made the supreme sacrifice
Your Country Needs You
The war to end wars
Making this country safe for democracy
God's on our side
Quote a line from the poem that would apply to each of these expressions.

questions

1. This poem deals in contrasts and contradictions. For example, in the first line the Universal Solider is *both* five feet two *and* six feet four. Quote the contradiction that you think is the most blatant and shocking.
2. Find the word or phrase in the poem that fits each of the following definitions:
   (a) a German town and later a notorious concentration camp in World War II;
   (b) a Roman general;
   (c) One who denies or disbelieves the existence of any God;
   (d) sentenced to death;
   (e) a warning of disaster to come;
   (f) a form of government in which political power resides in all the people and is exercised by them directly or by elected representatives;
   (g) to be held responsible, to accuse.
3. In the second-last line of the poem we are all held responsible for the actions of the universal soldier. How can this be possible?
   Do you agree or disagree with this sweeping statement? Explain the point of view you adopt.

debate topic

Look at the question at the end of the poem.
   How *can* we put an end to war? Perhaps you think war is a necessary evil. Divide your class into two groups, work out your arguments for or against, and discuss this topic.

The Most Dangerous Game

Richard Connell

"Off there to the right — somewhere — is a large island," said Whitney. "It's rather a mystery —"

"What island is it?" Rainsford asked.

"The old charts call it 'Ship-Trap Island,'" Whitney replied. "A suggestive name, isn't it? Sailors have a curious dread of the place. I don't know why. Some super-stition —"

"Can't see it," Rainsford remarked, trying to peer through the dank tropical night that was palpable as it pressed its thick warm blackness in upon the yacht.

"You've good eyes," said Whitney with a laugh, "and I've seen you pick off a moose moving in the brown fall brush at four hundred yards, but you can't see four miles or so through a moonless Caribbean night."

"Nor four yards," admitted Rainsford. "Ugh! It's like moist velvet."

"It will be light enough in Rio," promised Whitney. "We should make it in a few days. I hope the jaguar guns have come from Purdey's. We should have some good hunting up the Amazon. Great sport, hunting."

"The best sport in the world," agreed Rainsford.

"For the hunter," amended Whitney. "Not for the jaguar."

"Don't talk rot, Whitney," said Rainsford. "You're a big-game hunter, not a philosopher. Who cares how a jaguar feels?"

"Perhaps the jaguar does," observed Whitney.

"Bah! They've no understanding."

"Even so, I rather think they understand one thing at least — fear. The fear of pain and the fear of death."

"Nonsense," laughed Rainsford. "This hot weather is making you soft, Whitney. Be a realist. The world is made up of two classes — the hunters and the hunted. Luckily, you and I are hunters. Do you think we've passed that island yet?"

"I can't tell in the dark. I hope so."

"Why?" asked Rainsford.

"The place has a reputation — a bad one."

"Cannibals?" suggested Rainsford.

"Hardly. Even cannibals wouldn't live in such a God-forsaken place. But it's got into sailor lore, somehow. Didn't you notice that the crew's nerves seem a bit jumpy today?"

"They were a bit strange, now you mention it. Even Captain Nielsen —"

"Yes, even that tough-minded old Swede, who'd go up to the devil himself and ask him for a light. Those fishy blue eyes held a look I never saw there before. All I could get out of him was: 'This place has an evil name among seafaring men, sir.' Then he said to me, very gravely: 'Don't you feel anything?' — as if the air about us was actually poisonous. Now, you mustn't laugh when I tell you this — I did feel something like a sudden chill.

"There was no breeze. The sea was as flat as a plateglass window. We were drawing near the island then. What I felt was a — a mental chill — a sort of sudden dread."

"Pure imagination," said Rainsford. "One superstitious sailor can taint the whole ship's company with his fear."

"Maybe. But sometimes I think sailors have an extra sense that tells them when they are in danger. Sometimes I think evil is a tangible thing — with wave-lengths, just as sound and light have. An evil place can, so to speak, broadcast vibrations of evil. Anyhow, I'm glad we're getting out of this zone. Well, I think I'll turn in now, Rainsford."

"I'm not sleepy," said Rainsford. "I'm going to smoke another pipe up on the after-deck."

"Good night, then, Rainsford. See you at breakfast."

"Right. Good night, Whitney."

There was no sound in the night as Rainsford sat there but the muffled throb of the engine that drove the yacht swiftly through the darkness, and the swish and ripple of the wash of the propeller.

Rainsford, reclining in a steamer chair, indolently puffed on his favourite brier. The sensuous drowsiness of the night was on him. "It's so dark," he thought, "that I could sleep without closing my eyes; the night would be my eyelids —"

An abrupt sound startled him. Off to the right he heard it, and his ears, expert in such matters, could not be mistaken. Again he heard the sound, and again. Somewhere, off in the blackness, someone had fired a gun three times.

Rainsford sprang up and moved quickly to the rail, mystified. He strained his eyes in the direction from which the reports had come, but it was like trying to see through a blanket. He leaped upon the rail and balanced himself there, to get greater elevation; his pipe, striking a rope, was knocked from his mouth. He lunged for it; a short, hoarse cry came from his lips as he realised he had reached too far and had lost his balance. The cry was pinched off short as the blood-warm waters of the Caribbean Sea closed over his head.

He struggled up to the surface and tried to cry out, but the wash from the speeding yacht slapped him in the face and the salt water in his open mouth made him gag and strangle. Desperately he struck out with strong strokes after the receding lights of the yacht, but he stopped before he had swum fifty feet. A certain coolheadedness had come to him; it was not the first time he had been in a tight place. There was a chance that his cries could be heard by someone aboard the yacht, but that chance was slender, and grew more slender as the yacht raced on. He wrestled himself out of his clothes, and shouted with all his power. The lights of the yacht became faint and ever-vanishing fireflies; then they were blotted entirely by the night.

Rainsford remembered the shots. They had come from the right, and doggedly he swam in that direction, swimming with slow, deliberate strokes, conserving his strength. For a seemingly endless time he fought the sea. He began to count his strokes desperately; he could do possibly a hundred more, and then —

Rainsford heard a sound. It came out of the darkness, a high, screaming sound, the sound of an animal in an extremity of anguish and terror.

He did not recognise the animal that made the sound; he did not try to; with fresh vitality he swam toward the sound. He heard it again; then it was cut short by another noise, crisp, staccato.

"Pistol shot," muttered Rainsford swimming on.

Ten minutes of determined effort brought another sound to his ears — the most welcome he had ever heard — the muttering and growling of the sea breaking on a rocky shore. He was almost on the rocks before he saw them; on a night less calm he would have been shattered against them. With his remaining strength he dragged himself from the swirling waters. Jagged crags appeared to jut up into the opaqueness; he forced himself upward, hand over hand. Gasping, his hands raw, he reached a flat place at the top. Dense jungle came down to the very edge of the cliffs. What perils that tangle of trees and underbrush might hold for him did not concern Rainsford just then. All he knew was that he was safe from his enemy, the sea, and that utter weariness was on him. He flung himself down at the jungle edge and tumbled headlong into the deepest sleep of his life.

When he opened his eyes he knew from the position of the sun that it was late in the afternoon. Sleep had given him new vigour; a sharp hunger was picking at him. He looked about him, almost cheerfully.

"Where there are pistol shots, there are men. Where there are men, there is food," he thought. "But what kind of men?" he wondered, "in so forbidding a place?" An unbroken front of snarled and jagged jungle fringed the shore.

He saw no sign of a trail through the closely knit web of weeds and trees; it was easier to go along the shore, and Rainsford floundered along by the water. Not far from where he had landed, he stopped.

Some wounded thing, by the evidence a large animal, had thrashed about in the underbrush; the jungle weeds were crushed down and the moss was lacerated; one patch of weeds was stained crimson. A small, glittering object not far away caught Rainsford's eye and he picked it up. It was an empty cartridge.

"A twenty-two," he remarked. "That's odd. It must have been a fairly large animal, too. The hunter had his nerve to tackle it with a light gun. It's clear that the brute put up a fight. I suppose the first three shots I heard was when the hunter flushed his quarry and wounded it. The last shot was when he trailed it here and finished it."

He examined the ground closely and found what he had hoped to find — the print of hunting boots. They pointed along the cliff in the direction he had been going. Eagerly he hurried along, now slipping on a rotten log or a loose stone, but making headway; night was beginning to settle down on the island.

Bleak darkness was blacking out the sea and jungle when Rainsford sighted the lights. He came upon them as he turned a crook in the coast line, and his first thought was that he had come upon a village, for there were so many lights. But as he forged along he saw to his great astonishment that all the lights were in one enormous building — a lofty structure with pointed towers plunging upward into the gloom. His eyes made out the shadowy outlines of a palatial chateau; it was set on a high bluff, and on three sides of it cliffs dived down to where the sea licked greedy lips in the shadows.

"Mirage," thought Rainsford. But it was no mirage, he found, when he opened the tall spiked gate. The stone steps were real enough; the massive door with a leering gargoyle for a knocker was real enough; yet about it all hung an air of unreality.

He lifted the knocker, and it creaked up stiffly, as if it had never before been used. He let it fall, and it startled him with its booming loudness. He thought he heard footsteps within; the door remained closed. Again Rainsford lifted the heavy knocker, and let it fall. The door opened then, opened as suddenly as if it were on a spring, and Rainsford stood blinking in the river of glaring gold light that poured out. The first thing Rainsford's eyes discerned was the largest man he had ever seen — a gigantic creature, solidly made and black-bearded to the waist. In his hand the man held a long-barrel-revolver, and he was pointing it straight at Rainsford's heart.

Out of the snarl of beard two small eyes regarded Rainsford.

"Don't be alarmed," said Rainsford, with a smile which he hoped was disarming. "I'm no robber. I fell off a yacht. My name is Sanger Rainsford of New York City."

The menacing look in the eyes did not change. The revolver pointed as rigidly as if the giant were a statue. He gave no sign that he understood Rainsford's words, or that he had even heard them. He was dressed in uniform, a black uniform trimmed with grey astrakhan.

"I'm Sanger Rainsford of New York," Rainsford began again. "I fell off a yacht. I am hungry."

The man's only answer was to raise with his thumb the hammer of his revolver. Then Rainsford saw the man's free hand go to his forehead in a military salute, and he saw him click his heels together and stand at attention. Another man was coming down the broad marble steps, an erect, slender man in evening clothes. He advanced to Rainsford and held out his hand.

In a cultivated voice marked by a slight accent that gave it added precision and deliberateness, he said: "It is a very great pleasure and honour to welcome Mr Sanger Rainsford, the celebrated hunter, to my home."

Automatically Rainsford shook the man's hand.

"I've read your book about hunting snow leopards in Tibet, you see," explained the man. "I am General Zaroff."

Rainsford's first impression was that the man was singularly handsome; his second was that there was an original, almost bizarre quality about the general's face. He was a tall man past middle age, for his hair was a vivid white; but his thick eyebrows and pointed military moustache were as black as the night from which Rainsford had come. His eyes, too, were black and very bright. He had high cheek bones, a sharp-cut nose, a spare, dark face, the face of a man used to giving orders, the face of an aristocrat. Turning to the giant in uniform, the general made a sign. The giant put away his pistol, saluted, withdrew.

"Ivan is an incredibly strong fellow," remarked the general, "but he has the misfortune to be deaf and dumb. A simple fellow, but, I'm afraid, like all his race, a bit savage."

"Is he Russian?"

"He is a Cossack," said the general, and his smile showed red lips and pointed teeth. "So am I. . . . Come," he said, "we shouldn't be chatting here. We can talk later. Now you want clothes, food, rest. You shall have them. This is a most restful spot."

Ivan had reappeared, and the general spoke to him with lips that moved but gave forth no sound.

"Follow Ivan, if you please, Mr Rainsford," said the general. "I was about to have my dinner when you came. I'll wait for you. You'll find that my clothes will fit you, I think."

It was to a huge, beam-ceilinged bedroom with a canopied bed big enough for six men that Rainsford followed the silent giant. Ivan laid out an evening suit, and Rainsford, as he put it on, noticed that it came from a London tailor who ordinarily cut and sewed for none below the rank of duke.

The dining-room to which Ivan conducted him was in many ways remarkable. There was a mediaeval magnificence about it; it suggested a baronial hall of feudal times with its oaken panels, its high ceiling, its vast refectory table where two-score men could sit down to eat. About the hall were the mounted heads of many animals — lions, tigers, elephants, moose, bears; larger or more perfect specimens Rainsford had never seen. At the great table the general was sitting, alone.

"You'll have a cocktail, Mr Rainsford," he suggested. The cocktail was surpassingly good; and Rainsford noted, the table appointments were of the finest — the linen, the crystal, the silver, the china.

They were eating borsch, the rich, red soup with whipped cream so dear to Russian palates. Half apologetically General Zaroff said: "We do our best to preserve the amenities of civilisation here. Please forgive any lapses. We are well off the beaten track, you know. Do you think the champagne has suffered from its long ocean trip?"

"Not in the least," declared Rainsford. He was finding the general a most thoughtful and affable host, a true cosmopolite. But there was one small trait of the general's that made Rainsford uncomfortable. Whenever he looked up from his plate he found the general studying him, appraising him narrowly.

"Perhaps," said General Zaroff, "you were surprised that I recognised your name. You see, I read all books on hunting, published in English, French, and Russian. I have but one passion in my life, Mr Rainsford, and it is the hunt."

"You have some wonderful heads here," said Rainsford as he ate a particularly well cooked filet mignon. "That Cape buffalo is the largest I ever saw."

"Oh, that fellow. Yes, he was a monster."

"Did he charge you?"

"Hurled me against a tree," said the general. "Fractured my skull. But I got the brute."

"I've always thought," said Rainsford, "that the Cape buffalo is the most dangerous of all big game."

For a moment the general did not reply; he was smiling his curious red-lipped smile. Then he said slowly: "No. You are wrong, sir. The Cape buffalo is not the most dangerous big game." He sipped his wine. "Here in my preserve on this island," he said in the same slow tone, "I hunt more dangerous game."

Rainsford expressed his surprise. "Is there big game on this island?"

The general nodded. "The biggest."

"Really?"

"Oh, it isn't here naturally, of course. I have to stock the island."

"What have you imported, general?" Rainsford asked. "Tigers?"

The general smiled. "No," he said. "Hunting tigers ceased to interest me some years ago. I exhausted their possibilities, you see. No thrill left in tigers, no real danger. I live for danger, Mr Rainsford."

The general took from his pocket a gold cigarette case and offered his guest a long black cigarette with a silver tip; it was perfumed and gave off a smell like incense.

"We will have some capital hunting, you and I," said the general. "I shall be most glad to have your society."

"But what game —" began Rainsford.

"I'll tell you," said the general. "You will be amused, I know. I think I may say, in all modesty, that I have done a rare thing. I have invented a new sensation. May I .pour you another glass of port, Mr Rainsford?"

"Thank you, General."

The general filled both glasses, and said: "God makes some men poets. Some He makes kings, some beggars. Me He made a hunter. My hand was made for the trigger, my father said. He was a very rich man with a quarter of a million acres in the Crimea, and he was an ardent sportsman. When I was only five years old he gave me a little gun, specially made in Moscow for me, to shoot sparrows with. When I shot some of his prize turkeys with it, he did not punish me; he complimented me on my marksmanship. I killed my first bear in the Caucasus when I was ten. My whole life has been one prolonged hunt. I went into the army — it was expected of noblemen's sons — and for a time commanded a division of Cossack cavalry, but my real interest was always the hunt. I have hunted every kind of game in every land. It would be impossible for me to tell you how many animals I have killed."

The general puffed at his cigarette.

"After the debacle in Russia I left the country, for it was imprudent for an officer of the Czar to stay there. Many noble Russians lost everything. I, luckily, had invested heavily in American securities, so I shall never have to open a tea-room in Monte Carlo or drive a taxi in Paris. Naturally, I continued to hunt — grizzlies in your Rockies, crocodiles in the Ganges, rhinoceroses in East Africa. It was in Africa that the Cape buffalo hit me and laid me up for six months. As soon as I recovered I started for the Amazon to hunt jaguars, for I had heard they were unusually cunning. They weren't." The Cossack sighed. "They were no match at all for a hunter with his wits about him, and a high-powered rifle. I was bitterly disappointed. I was lying in my tent with a splitting headache one night when a terrible thought pushed its way into my mind. Hunting was beginning to bore me. And hunting, remember, had been my life. I have heard that in America business men often go to pieces when they give up the business that has been their life."

"Yes, that's so," said Rainsford.

The general smiled. "I had no wish to go to pieces," he said. "I must do something. Now, mine is an analytical mind, Mr Rainsford. Doubtless that is why I enjoy the problems of the chase."

"No doubt, General Zaroff."

"So," continued the general, "I asked myself why the hunt no longer fascinated me. You are much younger than I am, Mr Rainsford, and have not hunted as much, but you perhaps can guess the answer."

"What was it?"

"Simply this: hunting had ceased to be what you call 'a sporting proposition'. It had become too easy. I always got my quarry. Always. There is no greater bore than perfection."

The general lit a fresh cigarette.

"No animal had a chance with me any more. That is no boast; it is a mathematical certainty. The animal had nothing but his legs and his instinct. Instinct is no match for reason. When I thought of this it was a tragic moment for me, I can tell you."

Rainsford leaned across the table, absorbed in what his host was saying.

"It came to me as an inspiration what I must do," the general went on.

"And that was?"

The general smiled the quiet smile of one who has faced an obstacle and surmounted it with success. "I had to invent a new animal to hunt," he said.

"A new animal? You are joking."

"Not at all," said the general. "I never joke about hunting. I needed a new animal. I found one. So I bought this island, built this house, and here I do my hunting. The island is perfect for my purposes — there are jungles with a maze of trails in them, hills, swamps —"

"But the animal, General Zaroff?"

"Oh," said the general, "it supplies me with the most exciting hunting in the world. No other hunting compares with it for an instant. Every day I hunt, and I never grow bored now, for I have a quarry with which I can match my wits."

Rainsford's bewilderment showed in his face.

"I wanted the ideal animal to hunt," explained the general. "So I said: 'What are the attributes of an ideal quarry?' And the answer was, of course: 'It must have courage, cunning, and, above all, it must be able to reason.'"

"But no animal can reason," objected Rainsford.

"My dear fellow," said the general, "there is one that can."

"But you can't mean —" gasped Rainsford.

"And why not?"

"I can't believe you are serious, General Zaroff. This is a grisly joke."

"Why should I not be serious? I am speaking of hunting."

"Hunting? Good heavens, General Zaroff, what you speak of is murder."

The general laughed with entire good nature. He regarded Rainsford quizzically. "I refuse to believe that so modern and civilised a young man as you seem to be harbours romantic ideas about the values of human life. Surely your experiences in the war —" He stopped.

"Did not make me condone cold-blooded murder," finished Rainsford stiffly.

Laughter shook the general. "How extraordinarily droll you are!" he said. "One does not expect nowadays to find a young man of the educated class, even in America, with such a naive, and, if I may say so, mid-Victorian point of view. It's like finding a snuff-box in a limousine. Ah, well, doubtless you had Puritan ancestors. So many Americans appear to have had. I'll wager you'll forget your notions when you go hunting with me. You've a genuine new thrill in store for you, Mr Rainsford."

"Thank you, I'm a hunter, not a murderer."

"Dear me," said the general, quite unruffled, "again that unpleasant word. But I think I can show you that your scruples are quite ill-founded."

"Yes?"

"Life is for the strong, to be lived by the strong, and, if need be, taken by the strong. The weak of the world were put here to give the strong pleasure. I am strong. Why should I not use my gift? If I wish to hunt, why should I not? I hunt the scum of the earth — sailors from tramp ships — lascars, blacks, Chinese, whites, mongrels — a thoroughbred horse or hound is worth more than a score of them."

"But they are men," said Rainsford hotly.

"Precisely," said the general. "That is why I use them. It gives me pleasure. They can reason, after a fashion. So they are dangerous."

"But where do you get them?"

The general's left eyelid fluttered down in a wink. "This island is called Ship-Trap," he answered. "Sometimes an angry god of the high seas sends them to me. Sometimes, when Providence is not so kind, I help Providence a bit. Come to the window with me."

Rainsford went to the window, and looked out toward the sea.

"Watch! Out there!" exclaimed the general, pointing into the night. Rainsford's eyes saw only blackness, and then, as the general pressed a button, far out to sea Rainsford saw the flash of lights.

The general chuckled. "They indicate a channel," he said, "where there's none: giant rocks with razor edges crouch like a sea monster with wide-open jaws. They can crush a ship as easily as I crush this nut." He dropped a walnut on the hardwood floor and brought his heel grinding down on it. "Oh, yes," he said casually, as if in answer to a question, "I have electricity. We try to be civilised here."

"Civilised? And you shoot down men?"

A trace of anger was in the general's black eyes, but it was there for but a second, and he said, in his most pleasant manner: "Dear me, what a righteous young man you are! I assure you I do not do the thing you suggest. That would be barbarous. I treat these visitors with every consideration. They get plenty of good food and exercise. They get into splendid physical condition. You shall see for yourself tomorrow."

"What do you mean?"

"We'll visit my training school," smiled the general. "It's in the cellar. I have about a dozen pupils down there now. They're from the Spanish bark *San Lucar,* that had the bad luck to go on the rocks out there. A very inferior lot, I regret to say. Poor specimens, and more accustomed to the deck than to the jungle."

He raised his hand and Ivan, who served as waiter, brought thick Turkish coffee. Rainsford, with an effort, held his tongue in check.

"It's a game, you see," pursued the general blandly. "I suggest to one of them that we go hunting. I give him a supply of food and an excellent hunting knife. I give him three hours' start. I am to follow, armed only with a pistol of the smallest calibre and range. If my quarry eludes me for three whole days, he wins the game. If I find him" — the general smiled — "he loses."

"Suppose he refuses to be hunted?"

"Oh," said the general, "I give him his option, of course. He need not play that game if he doesn't wish to. If he does not wish to hunt, I turn him over to Ivan. Ivan once had the honour of serving as official knouter to the Great White Czar, and he has his own ideas of sport. Invariably, Mr Rainsford, invariably they choose the hunt."

"And if they win?"

The smile on the general's face widened. "To date I have not lost," he said.

Then he added, hastily, "I don't wish you to think me a braggart, Mr Rainsford. Many of them afford only the most elementary sort of problem. Occasionally I strike a tartar. One almost did win. I eventually had to use the dogs."

"The dogs?"

"This way, please. I'll show you."

The general steered Rainsford to a window. The lights from the windows sent a flickering illumination that made grotesque patterns on the courtyard below, and Rainsford could see moving about there a dozen or so huge black shapes; as they turned toward him, their eyes glittered greenly.

"A rather good lot, I think," observed the general. "They are let out at seven every night. If anyone should try to get into my house — or out of it — something extremely regrettable would occur to him." He hummed a snatch of song from the *Folies-Bergères.*

"And now," said the general, "I want to show you my new collection of heads. Will you come with me to the library?"

"I hope," said Rainsford, "that you will excuse me tonight, General Zaroff. I'm really not feeling at all well."

"Ah, indeed?" the general inquired solicitously. "Well, I suppose that's only natural, after your long swim. You need a good, restful night's sleep. Tomorrow you'll feel like a new man, I'll wager. Then we'll hunt, eh? I've one rather promising prospect —"

Rainsford was hurrying from the room.

"Sorry you can't go with me tonight," called the general. "I expect rather fair sport — a big, strong black. He looks resourceful — Well, good night, Mr Rainsford; I hope that you have a good night's rest."

The bed was good and the pyjamas of the softest silk, and he was tired in every fibre of his being, but nevertheless Rainsford could not quiet his brain with the opiate of sleep. He lay, eyes wide open. Once he thought he heard stealthy steps outside his room. He sought to throw open the door; it would not open. He went to the window and looked out. His room was high up on one of the towers. The lights of the chateau were out now, and it was dark and silent, but there was a fragment of sallow moon, and by its wan light he could see, dimly, the courtyard; there, weaving in and out in the pattern of shadow, were black, noiseless forms; the hounds heard him at the window and looked up, expectantly, with their green eyes. Rainsford went back to the bed and lay down. By many methods he tried to put himself to sleep. He had achieved a doze when, just as morning began to come, he heard, far off in the jungle, the faint report of a pistol.

General Zaroff did not appear until luncheon. He was dressed faultlessly in the tweeds of a country squire. He was solicitous about the state of Rainsford's health.

"As for me," sighed the general, "I do not feel so well. I am worried, Mr Rainsford. Last night I detected traces of my old complaint."

To Rainsford's questioning glance the general said: "Ennui. Boredom."

Then, taking a second helping of crepes suzette, the general explained: "The hunting was not good last night. The fellow lost his head. He made a straight trail that offered no problems at all. That's the trouble with these sailors; they have dull brains to begin with, and they do not know how to get about in the woods. They do excessively stupid and obvious things. It's most annoying. Will you have another glass of Chablis, Mr Rainsford?"

"General," said Rainsford firmly, "I wish to leave this island at once."

The general raised his thickets of eyebrows; he seemed hurt. "But, my dear fellow," the general protested, "you've only just come. You've had no hunting —"

"I wish to go today," said Rainsford. He saw the dead black eyes of the general on him, studying him. General Zaroff's face suddenly brightened.

He filled Rainsford's glass with venerable Chablis from a dusty bottle.

"Tonight," said the general, "we will hunt — you and I."

Rainsford shook his head. "No, General," he said. "I will not hunt."

The general shrugged his shoulders and delicately ate a hothouse grape. "As you wish, my friend," he said. "The choice rests entirely with you. But may I not venture to suggest that you will find my idea of sport more diverting than Ivan's?"

He nodded toward the corner to where the giant stood, scowling, his thick arms crossed on his hogshead of chest.

"You don't mean —" cried Rainsford.

"My dear fellow," said the general, "have I not told you I always mean what I say about hunting? This is really an inspiration. I drink to a foeman worthy of my steel — at last."

The general raised his glass, but Rainsford sat staring at him.

"You'll find this game worth playing," the general said enthusiastically. "Your brain against mine. Your woodcraft against mine. Outdoor chess! And the stake is not without value, eh?"

"And if I win —" began Rainsford huskily.

"I'll cheerfully acknowledge myself defeated if I do not find you by midnight of the third day," said General Zaroff. "My sloop will place you on the mainland near a town."

The general read what Rainsford was thinking.

"Oh, you can trust me," said the Cossack. "I will give you my word as a gentleman and a sportsman. Of course you, in turn, must agree to say nothing of your visit here."

"I'll agree to nothing of the kind," said Rainsford.

"Oh," said the general, "in that case — But why discuss it now? Three days hence we can discuss it over a bottle of Veuve Cliquot, unless —"

The general sipped his wine.

Then a businesslike air animated him. "Ivan," he said to Rainsford, "will supply you with hunting clothes, food, a knife. I suggest you wear moccasins; they leave a poorer trail. I suggest too that you avoid the big swamp in the south-east corner of the island. We call it Death Swamp. There's quicksand there. One foolish fellow tried it. The deplorable part of it was that Lazarus followed him. You can imagine my feelings, Mr Rainsford. I loved Lazarus; he was the finest hound in my pack. Well, I must beg you to excuse me now. I always take a siesta after lunch. You'll want to start, no doubt. I shall not follow till dusk. Hunting at night is so much more exciting than by day, don't you think? Au revoir, Mr Rainsford, au revoir."

General Zaroff, with a deep courtly bow, strolled from the room.

From another room came Ivan. Under one arm he carried khaki hunting clothes, a haversack of food, a leather sheath containing a long-bladed hunting knife; his right hand rested on a cocked revolver thrust in the crimson sash about his waist.

Rainsford had fought his way through the bush for two hours. "I must keep my nerve. I must keep my nerve," he said through tight teeth.

He had not been entirely clear-headed when the chateau gates snapped shut behind him. His whole idea at first was to put distance between himself and General Zaroff, and, to this end, he had plunged along, spurred on by the sharp rowels of something very like panic. Now he had got a grip on himself, had stopped, and was taking stock of himself and the situation.

He saw that straight flight was futile; inevitably it would bring him face to face with the sea. He was in a picture with a frame of water, and his operations, clearly, must take place within that frame.

"I'll give him a trail to follow," muttered Rainsford, and he struck off from the rude path he had been following into the trackless wilderness. He executed a series of intricate loops; he doubled on his trail again and again, recalling all the lore of the fox hunt, and all the dodges of the fox. Night found him leg-weary, with hands and face lashed by the branches, on a thickly wooded ridge. He knew it would be insane to blunder on through the dark, even if he had the strength. His need for rest was imperative and he thought: "I have played the fox, now I must play the cat of the fable." A big tree with a thick trunk and outspread branches was near by, and, taking care to leave not the slightest mark, he climbed up into the crotch, and stretching out on one of the broad limbs, after a fashion, rested. Rest brought him new confidence and almost a feeling of security. Even so zealous a hunter as General Zaroff could not trace him there, he told himself; only the devil himself could follow that complicated trail through the jungle after dark. But, perhaps, the general was a devil —

An apprehensive night crawled slowly by like a wounded snake, and sleep did not visit Rainsford, although the silence of a dead world was on the jungle. Toward morning when a dingy grey was varnishing the sky, the cry of some startled bird focused Rainsford's attention in that direction. Something was coming through the bush, coming slowly, carefully, coming by the same winding way Rainsford had come. He flattened himself down on the limb, and through a screen of leaves almost as thick as tapesfry, he watched. The thing that was approaching him was a man.

It was General Zaroff. He made his way along with his eyes fixed in utmost concentration on the ground before him. He paused, almost beneath the tree, dropped to his knees and studied the ground. Rainsford's impulse was to hurl himself down like a panther, but he saw that the general's right hand held something small and metallic — an automatic pistol.

The hunter shook his head several times, as if he were puzzled. Then he straightened up and took from his case one of his black cigarettes; its pungent incense-like smoke floated up to Rainsford's nostrils. Rainsford held his breath. The general's eyes had left the ground and were travelling inch by inch up the tree. Rainsford froze there, every muscle tensed for a spring. But the sharp eyes of the hunter stopped before they reached the limb where Rainsford lay; a smile spread over his brown face. Very deliberately he blew a smoke ring into the air; then he turned his back on the tree and walked carelessly away, back along the trail he had come. The swish of the underbrush against his hunting boots grew fainter and fainter.

The pent-up air burst hotly from Rainsford's lungs. His first thought made him feel sick and numb. The general could follow a trail through the woods at night; he could follow an extremely difficult trail; he must have uncanny powers; only by the merest chance had the Cossack failed to see his quarry.

Rainsford's second thought was even more terrible. It sent a shudder of cold horror through his whole being. Why had the general smiled? Why had he turned back?

Rainsford did not want to believe what his reason told him was true, but the truth was as evident as the sun that had by now pushed through the morning mists. The general was playing with him! The general was saving him for another day's sport! The Cossack was the cat; he was the mouse. Then it was that Rainsford knew the full meaning of terror.

"I will not lose my nerve. I will not."

He slid down from the tree, and struck off again into the woods. His face was set and he forced the machinery of his mind to function. Three hundred yards from his hiding place he stopped where a huge dead tree leaned precariously on a smaller, living one. Throwing off his sack of food, Rainsford took his knife from its sheath and began to work with all his energy.

The job was finished at last, and he threw himself down behind a fallen log a hundred feet away. He did not have to wait long. The cat was coming again to play with the mouse.

Following the trail with the sureness of a bloodhound, came General Zaroff. Nothing escaped those searching black eyes, no crushed blade of grass, no bent twig, no mark, no matter how faint, in the moss. So intent was the Cossack on his stalking that he was upon the thing Rainsford had made before he saw it. His foot touched the protruding bough that was the trigger. Even as he touched it, the general sensed his danger and leaped back with the agility of an ape. But he was not quite quick enough; the dead tree, delicately adjusted to rest on the cut living one, crashed down and struck the general a glancing blow on the shoulder as it fell; but for his alertness, he must have been smashed beneath it. He staggered, but he did not fall; nor did he drop his revolver. He stood there, rubbing his injured shoulder, and Rainsford, with fear again gripping his heart, heard the general's mocking laugh ring through the jungle.

"Rainsford," called the general, "if you are within sound of my voice, as I suppose you are, let me congratulate you. Not many men know how to make a Malay man-catcher. Luckily for me, I too have hunted in Malacca. You are proving interesting, Mr Rainsford. I am going now to have my wound dressed; it's only a slight one. But I shall be back. I shall be back."

When the general, nursing his bruised shoulder, had gone, Rainsford took up his flight again. It was flight now, a desperate, hopeless flight, that carried him on for some hours. Dusk came, then darkness, and still he pressed on. The ground grew softer under his moccasins; the vegetation grew ranker, denser; insects bit him savagely. Then, as he stepped forward, his foot sank into the ooze. He tried to wrench it back, but the muck sucked viciously at his foot as if it were a giant leech. With a violent effort, he tore his foot loose. He knew where he was now. Death Swamp and its quicksand.

His hands were tight closed as if his nerve were something tangible that someone in the darkness was trying to tear from his grip. The softness of the earth had given him an idea. He stepped back from the quicksand a dozen feet or so and, like some huge prehistoric beaver, he began to dig.

Rainsford had dug himself in in France when a second's delay meant death. That had been a placid pastime compared to his digging now. The pit grew deeper; when it was above his shoulders, he climbed out and from some hard saplings cut stakes and sharpened them to a fine point. These stakes he planted in the bottom of the pit with the point sticking up. With flying fingers he wove a rough carpet of weeds and branches and with it he covered the mouth of the pit. Then, wet with sweat and aching with tiredness, he crouched behind the stump of a lightning-charred tree.

He knew his pursuer was coming; he heard the padding sound of feet on the soft earth, and the night breeze brought him the perfume of the general's cigarette. It seemed to Rainsford that the general was coming with unusual swiftness; he was not feeling his way along, foot by foot. Rainsford, crouching there, could not see the general, nor could he see the pit. He lived a year in a minute. Then he felt an impulse to cry aloud with joy, for he heard the sharp crackle of the breaking branches as the cover of the pit gave way; he heard the sharp scream of pain as the pointed stakes found their mark. He leaped up from his place of concealment. Then he cowered back. Three feet from the pit a man was standing, with an electric torch in his hand.

"You've done well, Rainsford," the voice of the general called. "Your Burmese tiger pit has claimed one of my best dogs. Again you score. Again you score. I think, Mr Rainsford, I'll see what you can do against my whole pack. I'm going home for a rest now. Thank you for a most amusing evening."

At daybreak Rainsford, lying near the swamp, was awakened by a sound that made him know that he had new things to learn about fear. It was a distant sound, faint and wavering, but he knew it. It was the baying of a pack of hounds.

Rainsford knew he could do one of two things. He could stay where he was and wait. That was suicide. He could flee. That was postponing the inevitable. For a moment he stood there, thinking. An idea that held a wild chance came to him, and tightening his belt, he headed from the swamp.

The baying of the hounds drew nearer, then still nearer, even nearer. On a ridge Rainsford climbed a tree. Down a watercourse, not a quarter of a mile away, he could see the bush moving. Straining his eyes, he saw the lean figure of General Zaroff; just ahead of him Rainsford made out another figure whose wide shoulders surged through the tall jungle weeds; it was the giant Ivan, and he seemed pulled forward by some unseen force; Rainsford knew that Ivan must be holding the pack in leash.

They would be on him any minute now. His mind worked frantically. He thought of a native trick he had learned in Uganda. He slid down the tree. He caught hold of a springy young sapling and to it he fastened his hunting knife, with the blade pointing down the trail; with a bit of wild grapevine he tied back the sapling. Then he ran for his life. The hounds raised their voices as they hit the fresh scent. Rainsford knew now how an animal at bay feels.

He had to stop to get his breath. The baying of the hounds stopped abruptly, and Rainsford's heart stopped too. They must have reached the knife.

He shinned excitedly up a tree and looked back. His pursuers had stopped. But the hope that was in Rainsford's brain when he climbed died, for he saw in the shallow valley that General Zaroff was still on his feet. But Ivan was not. The knife, driven by the recoil of the springing tree, had not wholly failed.

Rainsford had hardly tumbled to the ground when the pack took up the cry again.

"Nerve, nerve, nerve!" he panted as he dashed along. A blue gap showed between the trees dead ahead. Even nearer drew the hounds. Rainsford forced himself on toward the gap. He reached it. It was the shore of the sea. Across a cove he could see the gloomy grey stone of the chateau. Twenty feet below him the sea rumbled and hissed. Rainford hesitated. He heard the hounds. Then he leaped far out into the sea ...

When the general and his pack reached the place by the sea, the Cossack stopped. For some minutes he stood regarding the blue-green expanse of water. He shrugged his shoulders. Then he sat down, took a drink of brandy from a silver flask, lit a perfumed cigarette, and hummed a bit from *Madame Butterfly*.

General Zaroff had an exceedingly good dinner in his great panelled dining-hall that evening. With it he had a bottle of Pol Roger and half a bottle of Chambertin. Two slight annoyances kept him from perfect enjoyment. One was the thought that it would be difficult to replace Ivan; the other was that his quarry had escaped him; of course the American hadn't played the game — so thought the general as he tasted his after-dinner liqueur. In his library he read, to soothe himself, from the works of Marcus Aurelius. At ten he went up to his bedroom. He was deliciously tired, he said to himself, as he locked himself in. There was a little moonlight, so, before turning on his light, he went to the window and looked down at the courtyard. He could see the great hounds, and he called "Better luck another time" to them. He switched on the light.

A man, who had been hiding in the curtains of the bed, was standing there.

"Rainsford!" screamed the general. "How in heaven's name did you get here?"

"Swam," said Rainsford. "I found it quicker than walking through the jungle."

The general sucked in his breath and smiled. "I congratulate you," he said. "You have won the game."

Rainsford did not smile. "I am still a beast at bay," he said in a low, hoarse voice. "Get ready, General Zaroff."

The general made one of his deepest bows. "I see," he said. "Splendid! One of us is to furnish a repast for the hounds. The other will sleep in this very excellent bed. On guard, Rainsford." ...

He had never slept in a better bed, Rainsford decided.

hounding down the answers

Test yourself for accuracy in your recall of the story's details by giving concise answers to these questions.

1. What causes Rainsford to fall from the yacht?
2. What is Rainsford's first name?
3. Where is his home town?
4. Rainsford has written a book. What is it about? (Be specific.)
5. Give the name and race of Zaroff's servant.
6. What affliction does he have?
7. "I have played the fox, now I must play the cat of the fable." So what does Rainsford do?
8. "Then it was that Rainsford knew the full meaning of terror." What has just happened?
9. Describe a Malay man-catcher and the effect it had on the general.
10. "He thought of a native trick he had learned in Uganda." What is this trick?
11. See if you can name eight different kinds of drink (including a soup) mentioned in the story.
12. All these exotically named drinks tell us something about the general's way of life. What is it?
13. How does the general react to Rainsford's sudden reappearance in the chateau at the end of the story?

getting deeply enmeshed in the story

Note: you may have to discuss these questions with your teacher.

1. Dramatic irony is a device used in writing. It occurs when a character makes a remark that he or she thinks is trivial or unimportant, but the reader or viewer knows otherwise. The remark is important, prophetic and fateful for the character concerned.

In the light of this definition, and from your knowledge of the story, explain why the following remarks can be called ironic.

"Great sport, hunting."
"The best sport in the world," agreed Rainsford.
"For the hunter," amended Whitney, "not for the jaguar."
"Don't talk rot, Whitney," said Rainsford. "You're a big game hunter, not a philosopher. Who cares how a jaguar feels?"
"Perhaps the jaguar does," observed Whitney.
"Bah! They've no understanding."
"Even so, I rather think they understand one thing at least — fear. The fear of pain and the fear of death."
"Nonsense," laughed Rainsford. "This hot weather is making you soft, Whitney. Be a realist. The world is made up of two classes — the hunters and the hunted. Luckily, you and I are hunters. Do you think we've passed that island yet?"

2. Richard Connell builds an evil atmosphere around the name "Ship-Trap Island" by making Whitney and Nielsen comment on their strange feelings towards it. Sum up what they say in your own words.

3. By using suspense, a reader's or viewer's curiosity is built up but is deliberately not satisfied until later in the plot. Note the expression "the suspense is killing me". In other words, a reader or viewer is lured on to read more or watch more by the absolute need to find out what happens next. There is an ideal example of suspense in this story that starts with General Zaroff's pronouncement, "I had to invent a new animal to hunt." Of course, we can guess what the "new animal" is, but we are not allowed to know for sure until some paragraphs later.
   Quote some examples from this section of the story to show how the high level of suspense is maintained.

4. "And now," said the general, "I want to show you my new collection of heads. Will you come with me to the library?" What is macabre and horrifying about this offer?

5. When the general suggests "outdoor chess", what does he really mean?

6. "Life is for the strong, to be lived by the strong, and, if need be, taken by the strong. The weak of the world were put here to give the strong pleasure. I am strong. Why should I not use my gift?" So says General Zaroff.
   Discuss this view of life. Does it have any moral justification?

hunting up the right verb

Action in a piece of writing is much more credible (believable) if a writer has used verbs that exactly fit the circumstances about which he is writing. Richard Connell is expert at selecting the right verb for the right occasion.

exercise

Relate each of the strong verbs in the left-hand column to the particular circumstance it suits best in the right-hand column.

Example

"The pent-up air burst hotly from Rainsford's lungs" relates to "Rainsford had been holding his breath while the general stood below the very tree he was hiding in."

   Note: check your answers by looking up the strong verb in the story. (Page numbers are given in brackets.)

Action-packed verbs	Circumstances
He *strained* his eyes (page 199)	Rainsford had been holding his breath while the general stood below the very tree he was hiding in
Rainsford's impulse was to *hurl* himself down (page 210)	The sea water closed over his head
He tried to *wrench* it back (page 212)	He was moving on sand
Rainsford *sprang* up and moved (page 199)	The tropical night surrounded the yacht
They were *blotted* entirely (page 200)	Getting up a tree
Rainsford *floundered* along (page 200)	His foot was stuck in the quicksand
It *pressed* its thick warm blackness (page 198)	The unsuspecting general was below Rainsford's tree
He *shinned* excitedly (page 213)	A distant view
The cry was *pinched off* short (page 199)	The lights of the yacht sailed off into the night
The pent-up air *burst* hotly from Rainsford's lungs (page 211)	An abrupt sound startled him

   Use each of the words in *italic* type in the left-hand column as a verb in a sentence, making sure that it is appropriate to the circumstance you create in your sentence.

figure it out!

Most written and spoken language is figurative to some extent. Figures of speech such as the metaphor and simile clarify and colour ideas. A simile is a comparison of two things using "like" or "as". A metaphor likens one thing to another without using "like" or "as". In fact, one thing is treated as if it were the other.

Let's look at some of the metaphors and similes in *The Most Dangerous Game*.

similes

In the following similes the comparisons have been separated and mixed so that they no longer correspond. Match the comparisons and then check your answers against the story.

the sea was (page 199)	like a panther
a moonless Caribbean night (page 198)	as if it were a giant leech
his thick eyebrows and pointed military moustache were (page 201)	like a sea monster with wide-open jaws
an apprehensive night crawled slowly by (page 210)	like some huge prehistoric beaver, he began to dig
Rainsford's impulse was to hurl himself down (page 210)	like moist velvet
he stepped back from the quicksand a dozen feet or so and (page 212)	as black as the night
giant rocks with razor edges crouch (page 207)	as flat as a plate glass window
the muck sucked viciously at his foot (page 212)	like a wounded snake

metaphors

The metaphor is more subtle than the simile.

Explain in your own words what is meant by each of the following metaphors.

"The lights of the yacht became faint and ever-vanishing fireflies . . ."
"Rainsford stood blinking in the river of glaring gold light that poured out."
". . . he had plunged along, spurred on by the sharp rowels of something very like panic."
"Toward morning when a dingy grey was varnishing the sky . . ."
". . . a sharp hunger was picking at him."
". . . the sea licked greedy lips in the shadows."
". . . he forced the machinery of his mind to function."
"With flying fingers he wove a rough carpet of weeds and branches . . ."

See if you can also find an example of personification in these metaphors. Personification is the name given to the figure of speech in which things are given human characteristics.

trap a word

Here are twenty words from the story that are associated with hunting. Write the words in your workbook, and underline them as you trap them in the grid.

Words:

sport	fear	flushed	quarry
hunter	wounded	shot	cunning
instinct	jaguar	moose	grizzlies
trail	fox	panther	bloodhound
stalking	pit	baying	beast

```
g r i s t a f g b l o j r s
b l o o d h o u n d b e o t
g r t r a t x z z l t f o a
g f l u s h e d c n s h x l
r w q u a t e t u f s p o k
i o j b e s r h n o u i d i
z u a l o q u a n w o u n n
z n g o o p j a i z z l t g
l d m y f e a a n l h i x d
i e u b a y i n g s p o r t
e d a o x b w m t u g b s o
s a w f e a r o o h a a l i
j q u a r r y t u o e r k n
p i n s t i n c t b s r n g
```

lights, verbs, action!

"The pent-up air *burst* hotly from Rainsford's lungs."

Now, you might ask, why in heaven's name did Richard Connell choose the word "burst"? Well, Rainsford is up a tree and has just escaped detection by the murderous General Zaroff. The verb *burst* — a strong one — aptly describes the sudden release of breath from Rainsford's lungs after Zaroff's departure. There are a number of ways of describing how air goes in and out of the lungs. Just remember that the word you choose must *fit* the circumstances. For example, it's no use talking or writing about air bursting hotly from your lungs if you're simply floating round a pool on your li-lo.

exercise 1 (to be completed in your workbook)

Here are a number of words describing how air goes in and out of the lungs: snuffle, snort, sigh, sob, respire, burst, breathe, puff, sniffle, exhale, inhale, gasp, belch, rasp, gulp.

Grade them so that the words get stronger and stronger as they rise along a line, like this (some clues are given to help you):

!* * *!
_____ **BURST** __ **A harsh sound**
_____ **From the stomach**
_____ **–––– in air**
_____ **I've got the –––––––s**
_____ **In alarm**
_____ **A –––– of wind**
_____ **. . . and this!**
_____ **A pig does this . . .**
_____ **A cold sound**
_____ **A weary sound**
_____ **A sad sound**
_____ **To breathe in and out**
_____ **Air out**
_____ **Air in**
__**BREATHE**_____

exercise 2

The words in exercise 1 are synonyms. They are all words dealing with various ways in which air goes in and out of the lungs, and so they all have *approximately* the same meaning.

(a) Think of as many synonyms as you can for the following five words from the story: sprang, terrible, wrestled, desperately, abrupt.

(b) Grade each set of words according to scale of strength, just as you did for "breathe" and "burst".

words that enrich

Words that enrich by adding description and explanation to basic ideas are to be found in every piece of written and spoken language. Remove such words and groups of words and any piece of communication becomes stark and uninteresting.

Enriching words and groups of words (indicated by numbered spaces) have been removed from the following passages. Clues have been supplied to help you re-enrich the passages. The missing words or word groups are set out below.

Rewrite each of the passages, inserting the relevant missing words or phrases as you go. Keep testing what you have written for coherence (sense). As you complete each passage, find it in the story and check your effort with the Connell original.

passage 1

"He struggled up to the surface and tried to cry out, but the wash ....(1).... slapped him.....(2).... and the ....(3).... water in his ....(4).... mouth made him gag and strangle. ....(5).... he struck out ....(6).... after the ....(7).... lights of the yacht, but he stopped before he had swum ....(8)...."

(1) caused by something
(2) where?
(3) kind of
(4) shape

(5) tells how
(6) tells how
(7) describes what they were doing
(8) how far?

Missing words and word groups

salt
fifty feet
from the speeding yacht
desperately

open
in the face
receding
with strong strokes

passage 2

"Following the trail ....(1).... came General Zaroff. Nothing escaped those ....(2).... eyes, no ....(3).... blade of grass, no ....(4).... twig, no mark, no matter how faint, ...(5)...."

(2) how?
(2) describes movement and colour
(3) condition

(4) shape
(5) where?

Missing words and word groups

crushed
in the moss
with the sureness of a bloodhound

bent
searching black

passage 3

"He knew his pursuer was coming; he heard the ....(1).... sound of feet ....(2)...., and the ....(3).... breeze brought him the perfume ....(4)...."

(1) kind of
(2) where?

(3) kind of
(4) belonging to

Missing words and word groups

night
of the general's cigarette

on the soft earth
padding

plot, setting, characters all rolled up in one

Did you notice that
1. the story is set within the confines of Ship-Trap Island and its surrounding waters?
2. the story line or plot reads like an extended tour around the island?
3. the characters are closely involved with the scenery?

If you did notice these three things about *The Most Dangerous Game*, you will realise that in this story the plot, setting and characters are inseparable.

Let's work an exercise around this idea of togetherness.

Map outline

Look at the outline map of Ship-Trap Island. The dotted line shows the route Rainsford followed from the time he fell off the yacht. The numbers indicate places or objects on or near the island where critical happenings occurred.

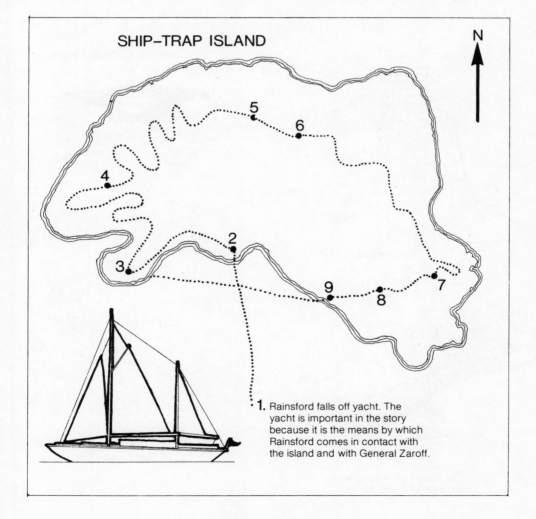

SHIP–TRAP ISLAND

N

1. Rainsford falls off yacht. The yacht is important in the story because it is the means by which Rainsford comes in contact with the island and with General Zaroff.

Places

Also, look at the nine sketches depicting the places and objects on the island seen or visited by Rainsford. These sketches are not arranged in any particular order.

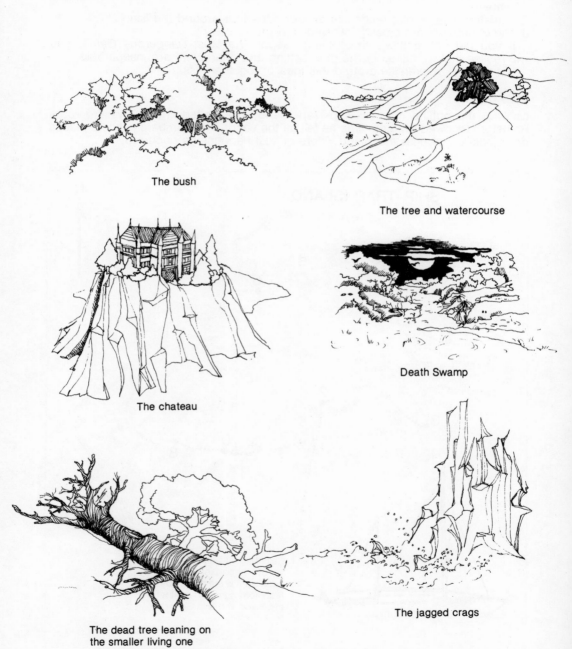

The bush

The tree and watercourse

The chateau

Death Swamp

The dead tree leaning on
the smaller living one

The jagged crags

Rainsford's last effort on the shore of the sea

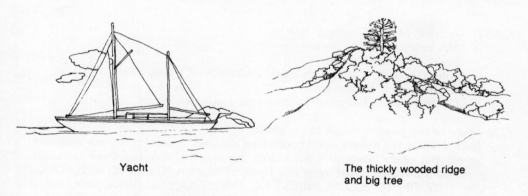

Yacht

The thickly wooded ridge
and big tree

exercise

1. Draw a large outline map of Ship-Trap Island in your workbook. Leave out the numbers and dotted route.
2. Work out where the nine places and objects are on the island. Put in your own sketches on your outline.

Example

The yacht will be the first object to sketch. It is Number 1 on the outline map.

Rainsford goes from the yacht to Number 2. What is this place? Select it from among the other eight sketches and sketch it in in your own style.

3. Join up all the sketches with a dotted line showing the route followed by Rainsford around the island.
4. Arrow each of the nine places or objects on your map. Write a few lines explaining the importance of that place or object in the story.

Finally, remember that the plot, characters and setting are all rolled up in one to make a story.

The Curse of Kali

CAST: A priest of the Temple of Kali
Mrs Foley, the housekeeper
Pringle, the manservant
John Goodwin, a strong, ex-Commando type of young man
Helen Carroll, his fiancee
Colonel Harley Galloway, an aristocrat and a gentleman

(The figure of the priest appears like a ghost)

PRIEST *(softly):* There is a twilight world beyond the shadows. A world only dimly explored for all your brave lamps of science. Into this world of shadows there came an accursed disbeliever *(voice rising to a frenzy of rage),* A MAN WHO WAS FOOL- ISH ENOUGH TO KILL A PRIEST OF THE GODDESS! *(Voice taking on a silky, deadly note)* He brought down upon his head the wrath of our Goddess — Kali, the Great Destroyer.

But, let us hear about the night that Kali came to claim her victim. *(The priest fades)*

MRS FOLEY: One evening not so long ago, I received a telephone call from Mr Goodwin to say that he and his fiancee were on their way.

The Colonel, I knew, was expecting them and I was pleased they would be arriving that evening for dinner. The Colonel had not been himself lately and I thought the young couple might cheer him up.

From what Mr Goodwin later told me, I can picture their drive through the countryside to the Colonel's house ... The two-seater car purring along the Southampton Road that passes through some of the loveliest country in England. The driver, John Goodwin, was a stocky young man in his late twenties. His fiancee, sitting beside him, was Helen Carroll, a pretty girl some years younger.

After rounding a series of bends, they caught sight of the house — the only house they had seen for the last hour. It was a great big building, and it stood out in the falling dusk like a beacon, because every window in the house was a blaze of light.

The strangeness of this brilliantly-lit mansion in its solitary setting held both young people silent. It was Helen Carroll who spoke first.

HELEN: So that's your uncle's house, John?

GOODWIN *(grimly):* That's it right enough. Mr Archerfield — he's that solicitor chap who got in touch with me — he told me to look out for the lighted house.

HELEN: John . . .

GOODWIN: Yes?

HELEN *(quietly):* You're worried about all this, aren't you?

GOODWIN: Well, Helen, it is odd! You spoke of Colonel Galloway being my uncle. Actually, he's not. Just some relative of my father's by marriage.

HELEN: What's he like?

GOODWIN: I've never set eyes on him.

HELEN *(surprised):* John . . .?

GOODWIN: Dad used to talk about him before he died and this solicitor chap told me a few things. It seems that Colonel Galloway's getting on — he's over sixty now. He retired about twelve months ago because of a bad heart.

HELEN: Yes?

GOODWIN: But he's one of these chaps who has always lived dangerously. He's been through two wars but even that wasn't excitement enough. Some time ago he took an expedition through India . . . to Nepal on the borders of Tibet. But apparently the strain of that was too much for even his iron constitution so he bought that house over there and retired.

HELEN: And, after all these years, he wants to see you?

GOODWIN: So Mr Archerfield said. First of all, the old boy wanted to know my war record.

HELEN: Why?

GOODWIN: Who knows? But when he heard I was an ex-Commando and was lucky enough to pull off a D.S.O. for that Calais job, then everything was, apparently, all right. So here we are, asked out to dine with a rich relative whom I've never even seen.

HELEN: But does he live in that big place all alone?

GOODWIN: I gather he does. He does have a housekeeper and a manservant who look after him — a Mrs Foley and a chap named Pringle. Ah, this must be the entrance to the drive.

HELEN: The gates are open. He must be expecting us ... *(She breaks off as from some distance away there comes the fierce yapping and howling of dogs)*

HELEN: John ... listen!

GOODWIN *(frowning)*: I didn't know the Colonel went in for kennels!

HELEN: But they're not hunting dogs. I know that deep baying cry. It's more like a mastiff ...

GOODWIN: Oh, surely not!

HELEN *(slowly)*: A distant relative whom you've never seen suddenly asks you for help ... a relative who is terrified of the darkness ... and lives in wide grounds policed by savage dogs ... John ... what does all this mean?

GOODWIN: We'll soon find out, darling. *(He slows down the car and stops)*

GOODWIN: Here we are. Now ... out you get. *(They knock on the door of the house. It is opened by a manservant)*

PRINGLE *(Cockney type)*: Would you be Mr Goodwin, sir?

GOODWIN: Yes, and this is my fiancee, Miss Carroll.

PRINGLE: I'm Pringle, sir, and this is Mrs Foley.

MRS FOLEY: Glad to meet you *(nodding)*, Mr Goodwin — Miss Carroll. I hope your stay here will be pleasant.

PRINGLE: The Colonel's expecting you. Will you come inside?

GOODWIN: Thank you. *(They enter. Pringle closes the door behind them)*

PRINGLE: The Colonel's in the reception room.

MRS FOLEY: But first, Miss, I'll take your hat, if you don't mind.

HELEN: But I do mind. I want to wear my hat ...

MRS FOLEY *(seriously)*: The Colonel mightn't like it, miss. It's that ornament in it — the dagger!

GOODWIN *(surprised)*: You mean Colonel Galloway might object to the ornament in Miss Carroll's hat?

MRS FOLEY: I'm afraid that's right, sir.

PRINGLE: He doesn't like anything like that, sir. No weapons at all. Funny old chap, he is ...

GOODWIN: And he lives in very peculiar surroundings! What's the reason for it, Pringle? All the blazing lights — with extra bulbs lying beside them.

PRINGLE: If one bulb fails, it's a matter of seconds to slip in the spare one, Mr Goodwin. The master doesn't like the darkness. He thinks IT might strike out of the shadows and ...

GOODWIN: IT?

COLONEL *(calling in an elderly aristocratic voice)*: Pringle! Pringle, have they arrived?

PRINGLE: Yes, sir.

COLONEL *(entering)*: Well ... ? So you're young Goodwin, eh?

GOODWIN: Yes, sir.

COLONEL: Commando, eh! Thought so, by the cut of you! So this is your fiancee? Got a cool head, young woman?

HELEN *(calmly):* I think so, Colonel.

COLONEL: Good! All right, Pringle. Show them upstairs. After dinner we'll get down to business ...

(The scene changes. It is after dinner. They are sitting in the lounge)

COLONEL: Cigar, my boy?

GOODWIN: No thank you, Colonel.

COLONEL: Cigarette then — you Miss Carroll?

HELEN: Thank you.

COLONEL: How about you, my boy?

GOODWIN: Thanks.

COLONEL: Now to business. Perhaps you noticed some very odd things at dinner tonight? No metal cutlery — you probably wondered why we use this new plastic stuff?

GOODWIN: Well, yes, we did ...

COLONEL: Then, I'm going to tell you a story. If you want to laugh at it, well and good! That's what I want!

GOODWIN: Something that happened to you, sir?

COLONEL: Yes, it was twelve months ago tonight. Know anything about Nepal?

HELEN *(frowning):* Nepal? Isn't that in India — on the borders of Tibet?

COLONEL: You know your geography, young woman! That's where it is — tucked away under the Himalayas — a tiny, remote country that holds all the secrets in the world! Well, twelve months ago, a party of mountain climbers decided they'd have a shot at Everest. I met 'em at Katmandu and they asked me to come part of the way with 'em ...

HELEN: You're keen on mountain climbing, Colonel?

COLONEL: Not really. Big game shooting is more my line and it happened I'd heard some peculiar stories about the great white bear — big as a man — that's supposed to haunt the lower slopes of Everest. I was determined I was going to try to bring back a specimen — the first the world had ever seen.

GOODWIN: But what's all this got to do with ...?

COLONEL: Just a minute my boy ... I'm coming to it! Everything went well until about the tenth day. We were climbing pretty steadily and it looked like we might be successful. It was late afternoon when we reached the lamaserie. Know anything about the Tibetan lamas?

GOODWIN: Very little.

COLONEL *(grunting):* You're lucky! This place — it was little more than a mud hut, with the usual pile of prayer stones outside it right in our path. But more to the point, a wizened old man with a shaven head also barred our way. He started yabbering and waving his arms about and when we called on our interpreter we had our first shock.

HELEN: What was that?

COLONEL: It seemed that this lamaserie was a shrine to Dordjelatru, the Great God of the Mountain. We were intruders and this greasy old sinner refused to let us pass. Now what with being tired, the altitude and this disappointment, I suppose I lost my temper. I was carrying an icepick and I made a threatening gesture with it. To my horror, the blessed thing slipped out of my hand and the blade clove the old boy's skull almost in half.

HELEN *(horrified):* How awful!

GOODWIN: What did you do?

COLONEL: Naturally, I ran and picked the old chap up. But it was too late. He glared up at me with the most malignant pair of eyes I'd ever seen ... muttered something that sent our Nepalese bearers flying for their lives and then died in my arms. When the boys came back I learned that the old blighter had pronounced a pretty black curse on me ... the curse of Kali, the Destroyer.

GOODWIN: What kind of curse?

COLONEL *(slowly):* He said that, twelve months from then to the minute, I'd be dead. Killed by a destroyer that came out of nowhere — invisible, yet all-powerful!! That I'd go out of this world as I came into it! Naked, alone ... and that no power on this earth could halt my end ... *(he pauses)* Well, what do you think?

GOODWIN *(quietly):* Do you honestly believe this crazy curse?

COLONEL *(slowly):* I didn't ... not at first ...

HELEN: What do you mean?

COLONEL: A month after the ... the accident, I was in Bombay, staying at the Taj Mahal hotel. I'd gone to bed early and at about three in the morning I was woken up by the sound of a gong. A tinkling, silver gong being struck eleven times ... and when I sat up, there at the foot of my bed stood that dirty lama. He had a tiny gong in his hand — he was striking it. After the eleventh chime, he paused, smiled and said: "One month is gone." I jumped up and switched on the light. The room was empty.

HELEN: It must have been a dream.

COLONEL: Then why do I have it *every* month? The same thing happens. But each time, the silver chimes ... grow less. Last month he beat on the gong only once. Towards the end, I've been afraid to sleep! Afraid even of the dark ... in case ... it should be lurking there ... waiting for me.

GOODWIN: So that's the reason you live in this glare of electric light, surrounded by dogs ... forbidding anything like a weapon in the house?

COLONEL: Exactly. *(Suddenly harsh)* I'm no coward! But when you don't sleep your nerves go! And when they go, you do things ... foolish things ... perhaps in the hope of finding comfort ... and protection.

HELEN: So you asked John down here.

COLONEL: I did. I'm a fighter! I'll tackle anything I can see. But this ... this wears away a man's courage, slowly, treacherously. I had to have someone with me ... tonight of all nights.

GOODWIN: You mean ...

COLONEL *(in a trembling voice)*: Tonight is the night it's supposed to happen. *(In a strangled voice)* Kali the Destroyer is supposed to come for me tonight.

GOODWIN *(after a slight pause)*: Colonel?

COLONEL *(still trembling)*: Yes, my boy.

GOODWIN: If nothing happens tonight?

COLONEL: If nothing happens within the next two hours, then I'll know it's all my imagination! The appearance of that lama ... that single chiming ... it was all a dream. And I'll go back to living a normal life ... if nothing happens within the next two hours ...

GOODWIN: Nothing will! Do you play chess, sir?

COLONEL: Yes, I do.

GOODWIN: There's nothing like a game of chess to steady the nerves. I suggest we get out the board ... and before we know it, the next two hours will be gone ... and your nightmare with them ...

(Some hours later the guests are taken to their rooms)

MRS FOLEY *(opening the door):* Here's your bedroom, miss.

HELEN: Thank you, Mrs Foley.

PRINGLE: Your room's along this way, sir.

GOODWIN: Right. *(Turning to Helen)* Goodnight, darling. Sleep well. I'll see you at breakfast.

HELEN: Goodnight, John. *(She closes the door)*

GOODWIN: Where's my room, Pringle?

PRINGLE: Around here, sir. Y'know, sir ... it is a good night. I've never seen the Colonel look younger. He came into the bathroom as I was drawing his bath. "Pringle, me boy", he says, just like his old self, "I'm going to sleep tonight," he says. "We've broken the curse!"

GOODWIN *(dryly):* You never really believed in it, did you, Pringle?

PRINGLE: I don't know, sir. You see, I couldn't help overhearing the story the Colonel told you tonight. It wasn't quite right ...

GOODWIN *(puzzled):* I ... I don't understand.

PRINGLE: I was with him when it happened — up there on that mountain. And it wasn't an accident. That priest might have infuriated the Colonel, but he should have controlled himself better. It's a vile temper he's got.

GOODWIN: You mean — he struck deliberately?

PRINGLE: Only in blind rage, mind you.

GOODWIN: But even so, you surely don't believe in this invisible power that can strike out of the air and ... *(Interrupting him clear as crystal comes the single stroke of a silver gong)*

PRINGLE *(startled):* Great heavens, sir! Did you hear that? *(Muffled — a sudden terrified scream is heard)*

PRINGLE: That's the Colonel! In the bathroom. Come on, sir ... this way. *(They dash down the passage)*

PRINGLE: Here we are ...

GOODWIN *(calling):* Colonel! Colonel Galloway — are you all right? *(He rattles the handle of the door)*

GOODWIN: The door's locked!

PRINGLE: And there's no light in there! See ... under the door ... it's pitch black.

GOODWIN: Get your shoulders against the door. We've got to open it! Now ... when I say ready ... Now! *(Grunt of effort ... splintering of woodwork)*

PRINGLE *(cry of alarm):* Look, sir! There he is ... lying on the floor ... still wet from his bath.

GOODWIN: What's that in his hand?

PRINGLE: It's the spare electric globe ... and the socket ... it's empty, sir ... look! But is he dead? *(Goodwin kneels beside the Colonel and feels for his pulse)*

GOODWIN *(slowly):* Electrocuted.

PRINGLE: You mean ...

GOODWIN: The globe in the socket must have failed. In his terror of being alone in the dark, he tried to replace it with a spare. The current was still on ... he was sopping wet from the bath ...

PRINGLE *(slowly in awe):* Killed by a destroyer that came from nowhere ... invisible but all-powerful. That priest said he'd go out like this ... that's what he said, sir.

GOODWIN *(sharply):* Nonsense, Pringle. Colonel Galloway electrocuted himself! It's nothing more than a tragic accident. Tragic, but perfectly natural.

PRINGLE *(slowly):* And what about that sound, sir? That stroke of the gong we heard? How would you explain that?

GOODWIN *(staring at him ... slowly):* I don't know, Pringle ... I don't know ...

(The figure of the priest makes a ghostly appearance)

PRIEST *(slowly):* A strange, weird and uncanny revenge came to the Colonel from that twilight world beyond the shadows. *(Fades again with a spine-chilling crackle of laughter)* Ha Ahha — Ahaha ...

calling all editors!

Imagine that you have the task of editing this play so that it will fit into a certain time-slot for a radio programme. In looking for places to make any cuts, it is important to remember that no essential information should be lost, and that the flow of the action should not be disrupted. Cuts may be brief (one exchange of dialogue) or reasonably long (several exchanges).

Here is an example of a fairly long cut that could be made successfully.

Example
Cut from:
Goodwin: ". . . Just some relative of my father's by marriage."
  to
Goodwin: ". . . he bought that house over there and retired."

exercise

1. Read through the play carefully again and find two other places where cuts might be made. Use the example above to guide you in the type of cuts you suggest.
2. Divide the class into editorial panels, each with four or five students. Each panel should discuss their members' suggested cuts and arrive at a group decision on the best two suggestions.

Getting across background information

There are two main methods of getting across essential background information in a play. The first is to use an announcer, narrator, stage manager, chorus, or some other person or persons to relate the relevant information to the audience before the action really begins. This technique is fairly easy to use and is generally quite acceptable.

The second method is usually a little more complicated and more difficult to use. It involves letting the essential background information emerge from an interchange of dialogue between the characters.

Look at *The Curse of Kali.* The writer has chosen to use two characters as narrator/information-givers at the start of the play. They are the priest and Mrs Foley and they serve as an example of the first method of getting information across. Actually the priest's main function is to create suspense and give the play a tense, expectant atmosphere right from the beginning. Mrs Foley is more directly an information-giver. Her lengthy introductory speech could be replaced by an interchange of dialogue between characters (method two). Two scenes would be needed — a phone conversation between John Goodwin and Mrs Foley, and dialogue between John and Helen Carroll as they drive towards the Colonel's house.

exercise

Try your hand at changing Mrs Foley's introductory speech into the two brief scenes just outlined. Be sure to convey all the important information contained in Mrs Foley's speech. Try to keep the individual speeches fairly brief, so that there are plenty of interchanges between characters. Use the following beginnings for each scene.

Suggested beginning for Scene 1
  (*A phone rings*)
  MRS FOLEY: Hullo. Colonel Galloway's residence . . .
Now continue!

Suggested beginning for Scene 2
  (*Sound of a car engine purring in the background*)
  HELEN: John, I'm still not clear why we're going to your uncle's house.
Now continue to Helen's speech, "So that's your uncle's house, John?"

edited dialogue

In a script of this kind where suspense and an expectant atmosphere are wanted, it is important that dialogue is brief and fast-moving. Unnecessary words will tend to slow down the action and "kill" any atmosphere.

Imagine that the original script for this play submitted by budding playwright Henry Pootles was very wordy and slow-moving. The present play represents Henry Pootles's script with the language quite drastically reshaped by an editor who has managed to make the dialogue briefer and punchier.

Here is one extract from the original script, and the line that the editor used to replace it in the present script.

Example

Henry's original script:
> HELEN: What sort of a person is your aristocratic relative, John?

Editorial rewrite:
> HELEN: What's he like?

Got the idea? Look at the following lines from Pootles's original script. Then read through the play and find the line the editor has used to replace each of them.

1. GOODWIN: As a matter of fact you are quite right. We were wondering about that.
2. GOODWIN: I'm not quite sure that I understand exactly what you're driving at.
3. PRINGLE: It seems to me that you are implying that . . .
4. GOODWIN: I find it rather hard to believe that the sound we can hear is made by such a creature.
5. COLONEL: As a matter of fact that is one of the games that I'm quite partial to, my boy.
6. GOODWIN: Could you please elaborate a little more on exactly what sort of a curse he had pronounced on you?
7. HELEN: I want you to know that I'm very appreciative to you for your kindness in directing me.
8. MRS FOLEY: Your description of the situation is exceptionally accurate, sir.
9. GOODWIN: Is the story you're about to relate one that involved yourself, sir?

sound effects

1. Look right through the script and make a list of all the sound effects needed to present this play. The first one is given to help you: *(the sound of a car engine purring).*
2. Get together a sound effects team to record the required sounds. A lot of fun can be had by making up any sounds for which you can't easily get the real sound. For example, one student may be able to make a good imitation of a hound baying.
3. Discuss the effect of sound effects on the play. Do they improve it? You may have to have a dry run without the sound effects, and then a second reading with the sound effects, in order to judge the difference.

The school holidays are almost over and teachers everywhere are getting themselves ready to resume teaching. This short, interesting poem gives you a chance
to look at a part of school life from the other side — through the eyes of a teacher.
It's built around his thoughts as he gets ready for the coming term. Read it through
and then tackle the questions.

School in the Holidays

A week of holiday reconciling me to work
I go up to school for the necessary books
And find the cleaning ladies in their jumble sale buys
Have established depots of buckets and bins
That the boys not there do not kick over
Along the corridors and the caretaker has reeled
Eels of flex out from the power points to the floor-polishers.
In my own classroom the portraits I have stood for
In felt-tipped pen and ink have been washed off
The wooden pages of desks towards the back:
Who was the Mary so many boys loved last term
And who wrote "I hate Sir" and "I love me"?
"They ought to have detention," one lady says,
"And clean up the muck they've made", wishing herself
Out of a job now she has everything
Spick as a sick room. But what are they doing now?
Reading comics in bare feet in front of the fire
And letting their sisters go the errands, I should think,
Covering the carpet with records of pop
Like overlapping lilies on a pond
And behaving in some way or other like little men.

Stanley Cook

how well did you understand the poem?

1. Why has the poet chosen to start with a long, rambling sentence that runs
   for seven lines? Explain why you feel it suits, or doesn't suit, this particular
   poem and its subject.
2. What does the poet mean when he talks of the cleaning ladies "in their jumble
   sale buys"? Is this a good way of describing them? Why?
3. The short phrase "reeled eels of flex —" contains two literary devices often
   used by poets to give a poem a pleasant sound or feel. The first one is repetition
   of a consonant sound ("l"), and the second one is repetition of a vowel sound
   ("ee").
   (a) What are the names of these literary devices?
   (b) Find another example of each from the poem and quote the lines in which
       they appear.

4. ''Eels of flex'' is a metaphor, picturing the electric cords connected to the floor-polishers as eels. Suggest at least *two* similarities between eels and electric cords.
5. (a) Does the teacher feel the behaviour of the boys in his class has been fairly bad during the past term?
   (b) Try to put into your words the way the teacher *does* feel about his class.
   (c) How are we made aware of the teacher's feelings about this class?
6. ''Spick as a sick room''. Somehow this simile seems both appropriate and inappropriate at the same time. Think why the teacher used it, and try writing down your explanation. What does it tell you about him?
7. The last line also seems a bit unexpected. Why is it the sort of finishing line you don't expect? How would you rate it as a finish — poor, good, very good, excellent? Explain your rating.